TORMENTED BY
INNER DEMONS . . .

Ever since the night of Conor McInnerney's death, Rowan had been experiencing a roil of emotions. It was more than just the death of the baby. Rowan felt a welter of conflict. He began to feel estranged from his colleagues. It seemed to Rowan that people blamed him for Turner's troubles. If he hadn't tried to save the baby to begin with . . . If he'd only done more to try to save the baby . . . If he'd been as medically objective and inured to death as he was supposed to be, like Turner . . . If he hadn't called Dr. Jackson . . . If he hadn't supported Laurie and Vicki in their feelings that something was wrong . . . If he hadn't told Stegbauer what had happened . . .

This was a familiar, indeed, never-ending mind cycle for Rowan. All of his life he'd been tormented by the twin demons of self-doubt and perfectionism. Indeed, his fears of failure in almost every sphere of his life drove him to excessive worry that could only be dispelled by driving himself harder and harder to be perfect; he was no good, he had to work harder. Each side of his view of himself fed the other, relentlessly.

His wife Deborah Lu Rowan was the pillar that Bruce clung to in time of stress—which, for him, was most of the time. But by late February of 1998, after eight years together, even Debbie was becoming a cause of stress for Bruce. And the consequences of that were about to become catastrophic. . . .

Dear Reader:

The book you are about to read is the latest bestseller from the St. Martin's True Crime Library, the imprint the *New York Times* calls "the leader in true crime!" Each month, we offer you a fascinating account of the latest, most sensational crime that has captured the national attention. St. Martin's is the publisher of perennial best-selling true crime author Jack Olsen whose SALT OF THE EARTH is the true story of one woman's triumph over life-shattering violence; Joseph Wambaugh called it "powerful and absorbing." Fannie Weinstein and Melinda Wilson tell the story of a beautiful honors student who was lured into the dark world of sex for hire in THE COED CALL GIRL MURDER. St. Martin's is also proud to publish critically acclaimed author Carlton Stowers, whose 1999 Edgar Award-winning TO THE LAST BREATH recounts a two-year-old girl's mysterious death and the dogged investigation that led loved ones to the most unlikely murderer: her own father. In the book you now hold, BITTER MEDICINE, veteran reporter and bestselling author Carlton Smith looks at the tragic death of a baby boy—and the shocking events that followed it.

St. Martin's True Crime Library gives you the stories *behind* the headlines. Our authors take you right to the scene of the crime and into the minds of the most notorious murderers to show you what really makes them tick. St. Martin's True Crime Library paperbacks are better than the most terrifying thriller, because it's all true! The next time you want a crackling good read, make sure it's got the St. Martin's True Crime Library logo on the spine—you'll be up all night!

Charles E. Spicer (signature)

Charles E. Spicer, Jr.
Senior Editor, St. Martin's True Crime Library

BITTER MEDICINE

TWO DOCTORS, TWO DEATHS, AND A SMALL TOWN'S SEARCH FOR JUSTICE

CARLTON SMITH

St. Martin's Paperbacks

ACKNOWLEDGMENTS

The word was *arrogant*; if there was any word to be heard in Port Angeles, Washington, in the early spring of 1999, that was it: *arrogant*.

Doctors were arrogant, because they played God and decided who should live and who should die; lawyers were arrogant, because they believed that they alone knew who was guilty; psychiatrists were arrogant, because they were the only ones who knew who was lying; hospital administrators were arrogant, because they knew what the public ought to be told; and police were arrogant, because they took it upon themselves to decide what was a crime, even if it was only mercy.

Everyone, it seemed, knew the right thing to do, and the only thing that prevented them from doing it was—yes, the *arrogance* of others, people whose sinful sort of pride said that, while *he himself* or *she herself* was pure, everyone else was venal, consumed by the arrogant blindness that came from the fruit of the tree of perfect knowledge.

But the world is not so simple; it is made of real people, every one of us with our own flaws, and none of us perfect; decisions are made and perhaps later regretted, based on quick limns of understanding, founded on our all-too-human perceptions. And there are other factors: hidden stresses that warp those understandings, things like chronic, well-hidden depression, and the inability to accept or understand its origin or its consequences.

And in the aftermath of action come the reassessments—*If I had but known . . .*

The events that transfigured a small town in Washington State during the year 1998—which eventually led to two prominent physicians being charged with two separate murders—and the town's struggle to understand and accept what seemed both monstrous and at the same time, understandable: these are the basis of this book.

This book tells the story of two doctors—one who believed there was mercy in death, and a second who believed that only death could deliver true mercy.

Constructed from interviews, court records, trial exhibits and transcripts, the combined story that eventually emerged was one of human frailty, of courage and cowardice, of the attempts by a small community to come to grips with things in their midst that many could not bring themselves to declare as real, or even evil . . .

In the end, this is a story about the boundaries of compassion—where it begins, and where it ends.

Special appreciation for assistance in the preparation of this book belongs to Detective Sergeant Terry Gallagher, and Detective Eric Kovatch of the Port Angeles Police Department; Chief Criminal Deputy Fred DeFrang and Sergeant Steven Snover of the Clallam County Sheriff's Department; Clallam County Prosecuting Attorney Christopher Shea; Seattle lawyers David Allen and Jeff Robinson, along with others from that city who wished not to be named; John Brewer of the *Peninsula Daily News*; Cyndi Nash and Richard Zahler of the *Seattle Times*; and a variety of helpers from Port Angeles, voluntary and involuntary, who freely shared their opinions of, and insights into, the actors and events with an itinerant journalist from San Francisco, who had no right to expect any such thing. My thanks to all of you.

As in previous books, I've tried to make a graphic distinction between words that were actually spoken, as reflected in interviews, depositions and transcripts, and those where the gist of the remark is agreed upon, but the actual words were not recorded. Thus, words that appear between quote marks are actual words reflected in the official records or interviews, while those rendered in paraphrase without quote marks represent witnesses' best recollections as to what was said at the time.

Carlton Smith
San Francisco, California
June, 1999

BITTER
MEDICINE

BABY
MCINNERNEY

1

THE STORM

The snow began in mid-morning. At first it fell in big, fat, wet flakes that disappeared almost as soon as they hit the ground; later in the afternoon, as temperatures fell, they became small and hard, and so began to stick.

The storm was from the northwest, made pregnant by the evaporation from the warm north Pacific current; its moisture-laden airstream rose over the masses of the Olympic Peninsula, where the colder air awaiting atop the peaks froze the evaporation into ice crystals, which hung in the air, growing heavier by the hour. The wind drove the crystals southeast across the southwest corner of the state of Washington, toward the Columbia River and then, in a carom shot off Oregon's share of the Coast Range, due east toward Portland. Heavy snow and rain shut down Portland International Airport that afternoon, and soon forced closures of the major highway arteries to the east.

Visibility was reduced to almost nothing on Interstate 5, the main north–south connector between Portland and Seattle. By dusk on Sunday, January 11, 1998, the snowstorm assaulted Centralia, Washington, eighty miles or so north of Portland, with almost a foot of whiteness, tying up all the local roads in the process.

Early the next morning, the winds shifted with increasing strength from the northwest to the west, and the snow and ice directed its attention to the Puget Sound area. By the afternoon of January 12, the white fallout had reached a depth of three inches in Seattle—a huge amount for a major urban area unaccustomed to significant snow. The accompanying cold led to a frozen fire hydrant near Tacoma, which in turn prevented a fire crew from extinguishing a blaze in a six-unit apartment building, which then burned to to the ground. Cars smashed into pile-ups from Olympia to south Seattle, and almost every road was decorated with the carcasses of stranded automobiles that had spun out on the ice before lurching into the parallel drainage ditches which accompanied almost every road in the region.

A man in Tukwila, a suburb south of Seattle, was killed when his pickup truck lost control and swerved in front of a tractor-trailer rig; a 12-year-old boy was seriously hurt when the sled he was riding lost control and slewed into oncoming traffic.

At the University of Washington, frat boys pelted each other with wet snowballs, and the police were called out to make sure that everyone kept as cool as the weather.

That same afternoon, the small town of Port Angeles, Washington—about 19,000 people, well-established on the south side of the massive strait of Juan de Fuca, some seventy miles west-northwest of Seattle and about eighteen miles across the water from Victoria, British Columbia—finally got its own taste of the snow that had tied up the rest of the region for the previous twenty-four hours.

Ordinarily, Port Angeles and the northern Olympic Peninsula of Clallam County missed most of the region's worst weather; the majestic Olympic Mountains usually acted as a barrier to the winter storms, and the warm current running into the strait from the Pacific helped keep temperatures north of the Olympic peaks above freezing for most of the year.

As a result, snow in Port Angeles was rare, far more rare than in inland locations like Seattle and Portland.

But based on the weatherpeople's predictions, authorities in Port Angeles knew they could expect to receive a substantial snowfall that afternoon; with plummeting temperatures and the Pacific storm hanging up on the crags of the mountains, more than a few inches of white could be expected to fall throughout the afternoon and evening. The Clallam County road crew started spreading sand along the roads that morning, in preparation for forecasts of unusually slick driving conditions.

By late afternoon, Port Angeles Police and Clallam County sheriff's deputies were overwhelmed with calls about minor fender-benders and incapacitated vehicles; one woman in a pickup was run over by a log truck as she tried to enter the main highway east of town, and had to be cut out of the squashed wreck.

By 4:45 p.m., the sun had finally set, even as obscured by clouds as it had been for several days, and the city of Port Angeles was plunged into its usual mid-winter darkness, while the snowfall grew ever stronger. After-school activities were cancelled, and many people rushed to the supermarkets to lay in supplies of food and other necessities in case the storm persisted.

From his own offices at the Peninsula Children's Clinic, across the street from Olympic Memorial Hospital, Dr. Eugene Turner watched the snow come down and tried to decide what to do.

That afternoon, he'd been scheduled to go ice-skating with a disadvantaged 14-year-old boy. That was the sort of thing Gene Turner did with his own time: getting involved with people who needed more than he did.

At 62, Dr. Turner was a legend; an Olympian, as it were, among the people of Clallam County. A pediatrician, the genial, sandy-haired doctor was said to have delivered as many as a third of the babies born on the Olympic Peninsula over the previous three decades.

Before that, he'd volunteered for the Peace Corps. In his off hours in Port Angeles, he cut wood for poor families, or volunteered for any number of good works. Turner had provided funds for Habitat for Humanity's first housing unit in Port Angeles, and had helped with its construction. His clinic even picked up the trash along a stretch of Highway 101, the main highway leading into town, and Gene Turner usually did it himself.

Around 5 p.m. Dr. Turner took a telephone call from his wife, Norma, a mover and shaker in her own right among the cognoscenti of Clallam County. Dr. Turner reminded Norma that he'd promised to take a boy ice-skating that afternoon.

But what about the weather? Norma asked. With all the snow, maybe Gene should postpone the outing, she suggested.

From his clinic window, across from Olympic Memorial Hospital, Turner glanced at the slate-gray sky, the darkening horizon and the increasing snow. He knew Norma was right. He cancelled the skating session and headed toward home, a few miles south into the foothills overlooking Port Angeles.

Even as Dr. Eugene Turner was making his way home, another family was settling in for the night of the storm. Martin and Michelle McInnerney had been married for less than a year; on the Friday before the storm Michelle had given birth to the couple's first child, Conor Shamus McInnerney. After spending Friday and Saturday at Olympic Memorial Hospital in Port Angeles, Michelle and Conor had been released to the couple's modest house on South Pine Street in the western portion of Port Angeles.

On the Monday following, at the height of the storm, they were visited by a close friend of Marty's, Byron Sifford.

The McInnerneys were young—she was 20, he was 22. Sifford was also young. They were representative of much of the population of Port Angeles: children of blue-collar workers who had labored for generations in the town's preeminent industries: lumber, paper and fish, the backbone of the town's economy—much of which had been decimated over the previous decade by dwindling timber resources and declining fish runs. Indeed, both Marty and Michelle had been marginally employed in the recent past, and their immediate economic future appeared bleak.

Sifford had worked with Marty when both were teenagers, and they had become friends. Later, he, Marty and Michelle had shared a house in Port Angeles. After spending some time in Oregon, Sifford had returned to Port Angeles and renewed his acquaintance with the couple. Married, with a child of his own, Sifford nevertheless spent a considerable amount of time with the McInnerneys.

On this Monday, in fact, Sifford dropped by the McInnerneys' house to show them a board game he had been given for a recent birthday. As the snows continued, the three set up the game and began to roll the dice to play.

Infant Conor was initially sitting in a child's swing. Sifford noticed that the baby seemed slightly agitated, but Michelle picked him up and walked him around to calm him, as Sifford later put it. A bit after that, Conor seemed hungry, so Michelle began to breast-feed him, even as all three continued the game. Michelle reclined on a couch while feeding the baby, and Marty and Byron rolled for her.

After a few minutes of this, Sifford noticed that Conor "started getting a little fussy."

Sifford asked Michelle what the trouble was, and Michelle told him that Conor wasn't yet quite proficient at breast-feeding. After a few minutes, Conor "quieted down," Sifford said later, and Sifford thought nothing more of it. The three kept playing the game, according to Sifford, with Michelle continuing to recline on the couch, tending the infant.

A few minutes after Conor had quieted, Michelle noticed that something was not right.

"Is he breathing?" she asked.

Sifford stopped focusing on the board game. He looked at Michelle and her baby and noticed that Conor wasn't moving. He knew something was dreadfully wrong.

2

HEARTSTOP

"Oh, my God," Marty said, taking Conor from Michelle. The baby's heart seemed still. Marty screamed at Sifford to call the paramedics. Michelle was panicking. Sifford remembered her milling around helplessly as Marty began performing CPR on the baby. It was just after 7:40 p.m.

The emergency operator told Sifford how to instruct Marty on CPR, but Marty already knew what to do. He opened his infant son's mouth and tried to breathe into the tiny lungs to get Conor to take a breath, while trying to massage the heart into resuming its beat.

The Port Angeles paramedics arrived less than four minutes later. They took Conor from Marty and tried to intubate him—that is, put a plastic tube down his throat—to make it easier to get air into his lungs. They also noticed that Conor's heart had ceased to beat. Time was running short. He was turning blue before their eyes.

Michelle continued to mill around the living room as the paramedics worked. Somehow she found her way to the couch and collapsed, moaning, "Don't take my baby." Marty stood by anxiously.

The paramedics were having difficulty with their intubation effort; Conor's throat was so small that it was difficult to seat the tube correctly. Strictly speaking, the tube wasn't vital; ordinarily it was helpful in anchoring a mask, which in turn was connected to a rubberized air bladder, over the face and mouth. Once in place, the tube would free a pair of EMT hands for other tasks by stabilizing the air bladder's input.

Somehow, the tube was inserted; one of the techs began squeezing the bladder to pump air into Conor's tiny lungs, while another attempted to get an interosseal line seated in Conor's lower leg; he was unable to do so.

The interosseal line, headed by a thin needle that was supposed to be inserted into the lower leg bone, ordinarily would have been used to administer life-saving drugs for a baby Conor's age.

Failing to achieve such an insertion put pressure on the EMTs to find another way to administer drugs. Usually a vein is the next best alternative. As it happened, the EMTs couldn't find a vein in so small a child, and were therefore unable to administer drugs intravenously to restart Conor's heart, which still refused to beat on its own. The EMTs then decided to administer the vital drugs through the throat tube. Epinephrine and atropine were given in an effort to jump-start the heart, with no apparent result.

With one of the paramedics continuing to "bag" the baby, and another attempting to massage his heart back into action, or at least force it to pump blood through his tiny system, the paramedics made ready to transport Conor to the Olympic Memorial Hospital emergency room, a bit over a mile away. Michelle climbed into the ambulance to accompany her new-born baby in the fight for his all-too-short life.

By the time the ambulance got rolling, it was just about 8 p.m.; by the official clock, baby Conor's heart hadn't had its own beat for more than twenty minutes.

To the people in the hospital, it seemed like it was taking far too long to receive the stricken infant.

The crew in the hospital emergency room got the call

about the distressed infant at just about the same time that the paramedics had. They began preparing to receive the baby, readying an infant "crash cart" with all the supplies and medications likely to be needed, finding a special hot-lighted bassinet known as a "baby warmer," all the while communicating with the paramedics, who were having so much trouble with the throat tube.

An emergency room team has much in common with other, far more mundane groups: like a basketball or base-ball team, every player has a part; the assemblage works best when everyone plays their own position, and does only what they are trained to do.

What makes an emergency room team different from an athletic ensemble is that it must deal with matters of life and death; and more, every decision has to be made within a matter of minutes, or sometimes even seconds. The pressure to be right as well as fast is tremendous.

The ER crew at OMH that night was headed by Dr. Bruce Rowan, a 33-year-old specialist in emergency care. Most people at the hospital thought of Rowan as a brilliant physician: bright, charming, caring—the sort of person any-one might want their daughter or sister to marry. He seemed down-to-earth, approachable.

A native of Idaho, he often signed his name with a sim-ple "Rowan," as if he had no need for the pretension im-plied by a full name accompanied by a medical degree; occasionally he referred to himself lightly as "Dr. Bruce," a touch that some thought indicated both his youth and his open nature.

Rowan was not a hospital employee, but an emergency room specialist in a partnership of doctors who had a con-tract with the hospital; each of the doctors in the partnership rotated twelve-hour shifts, around the clock, which meant that most worked about twenty-four highly paid hours a week, or about ten twelve-hour shifts a month. The spe-cialized work was lucrative; Rowan earned nearly $185,000 a year from the partnership.

As the emergency room physician on this evening, it was

Rowan's job to diagnose problems and direct the others on the team; in effect, Bruce was the ER's quarterback, calling signals to the other team members—"the code," as it was called.

And on this particular night, even as Conor McInnerney was being raced the mile and a half to the hospital, Rowan had his hands full with all manner of other medical emergencies.

No sooner had he dealt with the woman who had been run over by the log truck, than a man came in with a massive coronary. Rowan began calling for help, and soon, one of Rowan's emergency group partners was extending his own shift to take care of the heart attack victim.

The snow continued to pile up, and all the minor medical emergencies associated with the unusual weather continued to stream in.

In the midst of this, little Conor arrived at the emergency room about 8:05. His heart still wasn't beating, and his only breathing was being provided by the paramedics' "bagging" with the rubber bladder, which was forcing oxygen down the tube and into his lungs.

Ideally, this action might be performed by a respiration machine; as it happened, Olympic Memorial Hospital did not have a machine suitable for a three-day-old infant. So, in Room 2A of the emergency room, the staff continued the bagging and the heart massage, while Rowan began dealing with the most immediate problem: to get Conor's heart started.

If the heart can't beat, the blood can't circulate; if the blood can't circulate, it can't get to the brain. A brain without oxygenated blood quickly builds up an accumulation of carbon dioxide and other metabolic waste products, a condition leading to something called "cellular acidosis."

The acidosis in turn begins to kill the body's cells, including critical cells in the brain: first, the higher brain structures such as the cerebral cortex, then, as minutes unfold, ever more basic brain structures—the mechanisms that control breathing and heartbeat, mostly located in the midbrain and at the top of the spine, the brain-stem.

Generally, these systems begin shutting down after four to five minutes without respiration and circulation; when that happens, brain damage is almost always the result.

When Rowen first saw Conor, the baby's fingers, toes, arms and legs were cyanotic—that is, they were purplish-blue, the result of the lack of oxygen circulation in his bloodstream. Rowan knew, according to information from Marty and Michelle and the paramedics, that the baby hadn't registered a heartbeat for almost 25 minutes; there had probably been no oxygen circulated to the cells of Conor's brain for that entire time. In turn, that meant there was a strong likelihood that Conor had already suffered massive brain damage.

Still, very little is known about the development of an infant's brain in the first week after birth. It was remotely possible that a stabilized Conor might still somehow develop higher brain function if he survived. The only way to be sure that Conor's brain had stopped functioning was to test for electrical brain-wave patterns with an encephalograph. However, Olympic Memorial Hospital did not have such a machine.

Rowan kept working. An intravenous line was established in Conor's upper arm; a chest x-ray was taken and rushed off for processing. Epinephrine and atropine, already administered by the paramedics, was given again, without apparent results. Rowan gave Conor still more epinephrine, and ordered that the bagging be stopped to check for a response. It seemed that some sort of heart action was taking place, but the pulse remained flat.

Rowan now gave Conor a dose of lidocaine, useful to smooth out heart arrhythmias. The bagging was resumed, and this time the heart monitor indicated that some sort of disorganized heartbeat was finally starting. Rowan again called for the bagging to be discontinued briefly, and at that point, the heartbeat began at a fairly consistent number, 100 beats a minute, although the beat remained unstable. Almost thirty-nine minutes had elapsed since the original call to 911.

Now bicarbonate was put into the IV line. Conor's blood was tested; the results showed that the blood carried a high level of oxygen, but also a dangerous level of CO_2, an indication of acidosis.

This often occurred when poorly circulated blood was also forcibly oxygenated, as when artifical respiration from the bagging took place. The lack of heartbeat meant that the blood cells in the lungs were getting oxygen, but had no place to go—they weren't moving around swiftly enough to pass off oxygen and accept carbon dioxide for the return to the lungs and eventual exhalation.

Conor was thus loaded up with excessive oxygen, and, because the carbon dioxide wasn't being simultaneously removed, he became ever more acidotic as each molecule of oxygen was bladdered into his lungs.

In effect, Rowan was pumping Conor full of air, while the baby's lungs were unable to unload a sufficient exchange of gasses, freeing the cells for reuse by the incoming oxygen, which was necessary to achieve a proper balance between the chemicals carried by each blood cell.

Rowan gave Conor more bicarbonate to help decrease the acidosis accumulation. With Conor's heart now beating, the baby's blood was finally beginning to circulate; now Rowan needed to find out why Conor wasn't breathing.

At this point Rowan received the baby's chest x-ray. The picture showed that the plastic tube inserted by the paramedics was mis-seated down Conor's throat, according to Rowan's later account; in effect, only one of Conor's lungs was getting oxygen. Rowan repositioned it. Another x-ray showed that the tube was now okay, and the air was flowing into both lungs for the first time in more than 30 minutes.

Rowan next tested Conor's blood oxygen level and found that it was in the high 90s—a saturation level of 95 percent-plus, normal for every human being. But that was with the emergency crew manually forcing air into Conor's lungs with every squeeze of the rubber air bladder; once that was discontinued, no one knew what might happen.

Regional hospitals like Olympic Memorial routed their special cases to the major medical centers like Seattle Children's Hospital, which had equipment and expertise that the regionals often lacked. Early in "the code," Rowan had placed a telephone call to Dr. Craig Jackson at Children's. Jackson was a neonatologist, an expert in treating the medical problems of new-born infants. Jackson gave Rowan advice on how to proceed.

At that same time, Rowan asked that Jackson alert the western Washington air ambulance service, Airlift Northwest, to be ready to fly Conor to Children's Hospital, only to learn that the snowstorm made a flight impossible just then. After talking with Jackson, Rowan alerted Olympic Hospital's resident pediatrician, Dr. Kathryn Sprenkel, of Conor's condition; Sprenkel, in turn, called the on-call pediatrician to come in to take over the care of Conor McInnerney. Sprenkel called Gene Turner.

By all subsequent accounts, Dr. Turner arrived at the Olympic emergency room somewhere around 8:50 p.m., more than an hour after Michelle had first noticed that Conor had stopped breathing. At the point that he signed Conor's care over to his older, distinguished colleague, Rowan noted that Conor's heart rate was up to 150 to 160 beats per minute—fast for an adult, but normal for a newborn.

Conor's blood pressure was increasing; the main problem now was finding a way to get Conor to breathe on his own.

Turner had driven down from his house in the foothills; the snow had made everything a mess, and by the time he arrived, Rowan was up to his elbows in other immediate crises, including an ectopic pregnancy with a fallopian tube rupture. Still the snow kept falling.

By this time, Michelle's obstetrician, Dr. Palmer, was present in the outer emergency room, as were Marty, Michelle, Sifford, Marty's mother Diane Anderson, a family minister, and several other family members. They waited anxiously outside the emergency suite as the hospital staff worked desperately to save the life of Conor McInnerney. What no one in the emergency room knew at the time was the fact that, some years before, Michelle's mother had died in childbirth at Olympic Memorial Hospital; for her baby to face death in the same place was asking a lot, perhaps too much, for Michelle to bear.

3

TURNER

Afterward, almost everyone agreed that Gene Turner seemed a bit odd that night; or, if not odd, perhaps a bit off his usual game.

For one thing, they recalled, he made it clear from the outset that there was little point in trying to save Conor McInnerney.

"This guy's had it," one of the nurses later remembered him saying, almost as soon as he took over from Rowan. The implication was clear: if the chart showed that Conor hadn't had a heartbeat in at least twenty-five minutes, that had to mean he was either severely brain-damaged or possibly even brain-dead.

Still, Conor's Rowan-restored heartbeat continued, and the oxygen and carbon dioxide levels in his blood continued to improve. Turner and Palmer inspected Conor's pupils as Rowan had previously: dilated and fixed, unresponsive to stimuli, as noted by Rowan.

Later, controversy would develop as to whether this was because Conor was brain-damaged, or whether this was a result of the atropine, which has the side effect of dilating pupils.

When Conor was pricked with a sharp instrument, he

showed no physiological response, which was exactly what Turner expected from anyone who had gone without oxygen to the brain for at least twenty-five minutes.

In Turner's view, Conor McInnerney was so severely brain-damaged that the likelihood of his eventual survival was virtually nil.

Still, Turner and the rest of the emergency room crew soldiered on; much later, some speculated that the crew did so because they had been trained to fight for life to the last possible instant, and that Turner did so because, as the new code leader, he didn't want the others to think that he wasn't every bit as dedicated as they were.

At some point after 9:30 that night, it became clear to Turner that heroic efforts to save Conor McInnerney were doomed to fail. No matter what anyone did, Conor didn't seem to be able to breathe on his own.

While his blood oxygen level remained high, and the carbon dioxide in his system was falling back into normal limits, Conor was still alive only because someone kept squeezing the air bladder to force air into his lungs; without that, Turner concluded, Conor would die in minutes.

About 9:30 p.m., Turner "called" the code: Conor, he said, was, for all practical purposes, dead.

Now came the hardest job of the night for Dr. Turner—telling Marty and Michelle that their new baby was brain-dead. He and Palmer now approached the parents in the outer area of the emergency room. Turner explained that Conor's situation was dismal—he wasn't breathing, and, although his heart continued beating, it was certain that the long period without oxygen had caused severe brain damage. It was likely that if the bagging was stopped, Conor would soon pass away.

Marty and Michelle now agreed to allow the hospital staff to end the artificial respiration. The bagging ceased, and the endotracheal tube was removed from Conor's throat.

Marty and Michelle were brought into Room 2A to see

their child, now wrapped in a blanket. He was given to Marty to hold. He lay in Marty's arms, unmoving, with his eyes closed. Michelle wept and implored her baby to breathe; she stroked his feet, trying to get some sort of response. Marty passed Conor to Michelle and broke into tears. A nurse held him as he wept.

A hospital chaplain was called, and Conor was baptized. The nurses found two chairs for Marty and Michelle, dimmed the lights of Room 2A and left, allowing the young couple some last few private moments with Conor.

At 9:54 p.m., Dr. Turner pronounced Conor dead. He instructed the supervising nurse to begin filling out a death certificate, and then returned to Room 2A. He took Conor from Marty and Michelle and placed the baby back in the warming bassinet. One nurse collected Conor's clothing, while several others escorted the McInnerneys back to the emergency desk. The emergency staff hugged Marty and Michelle and tried to give solace to them. The McInnerneys and their families quickly left the hospital, overcome with grief.

Conor was left alone in the baby warmer.

4

BACK FROM DEATH?

Shortly after 10 p.m., Dr. Rowan had a spare moment. He decided to check on the progress of Conor McInnerney. He saw Turner and Sprenkel at the emergency room desk, "with very sad, sullen faces," as he put it later.

Rowan asked what had happened with the McInnerney baby. Turner and Sprenkel told him that the baby had died.

Rowan said later that he was "very surprised" to hear that; when he turned over the care to Dr. Turner, Conor "appeared to be stabilizing."

Said in retrospect by Rowan, this appears to have been a slight overstatement; after all, at the time he had turned the baby over to Turner, Conor still wasn't breathing on his own, even if his heart was going and his oxygen level was in the normal range. And Rowan certainly had to know that it was likely Conor had sustained serious if not severe brain damage from the long period without oxygen.

Marty and Michelle had left the hospital, along with Sifford and the rest of the families. Shortly after that, Dr. Jackson from Children's Hospital telephoned to say that the helicopter from Seattle could now be flown. Someone, either Dr. Sprenkel or the shift nursing supervisor, Ann

Duren, told him the aircraft was no longer needed, and that the baby had died.

Or had he?

The subsequent events of what would turn out to be one of the strangest nights in Port Angeles' history were made somewhat murky by the fact that only the most rough of contemporaneous notes were made, in pencil, and even those were subject to a discussion as to whether they should be thrown away.

As a result, most of the story later pieced together came from oral accounts of those present, and it was like the movie *Rashomon*, in which every participant's recollection contradicted the others.

One account came from an emergency room nurse, Laurie Boucher. Boucher had worked most of the day in the emergency room, and was scheduled to go back to work the following day at 10 a.m.

When the snow began falling, she decided not to try to drive home some twenty miles east of Port Angeles, but to sleep over at the hospital. She agreed to carry a beeper in case the storm prevented any of the night staff from getting to work and, as a result, she was needed to help out.

Shortly after settling into the hospital's short-stay accommodations at about 7:30 p.m., Laurie got a call from supervising nurse Duren, asking that she come to the emergency room to help with a days-old, cardiac-arrested infant expected to arrive in a few minutes.

When she got to the emergency room, Laurie set about preparing the pediatric crash cart and the medications that the baby would likely need. Also present were Duren; the usual night emergency nurse, Vicki Hallberg-Gross; a respiratory therapist, Dick Payne; and four others, all of them nurses. Conor arrived shortly after 8 p.m., and Rowan and the others went to work.

Laurie's job was to assist Vicki in preparing and administering the IV drugs. She stood at the head of the baby warmer, and so had a clear view of everyone as events unfolded. Gradually, as Conor's heart began to beat and his color returned, it looked like it was possible that he might actually make it.

Laurie wasn't paying much attention to the time; she recalled later that Dr. Turner arrived and took over from Dr. Rowan. At one point, a suggestion was made that more bicarbonate be given to the baby. Laurie recalled that Turner thought they should hold off.

As it became clear—at least to Turner—that Conor was not going to recover, Laurie recalled Turner informing Marty and Michelle that Conor had shown no neurological response, and that it was likely the baby was brain-dead. Turner told the emergency team that once oxygen was stopped, the baby would die quickly.

After Turner pronounced Conor dead, and the McInnerneys had left the hospital, Laurie returned to Room 2A and began clearing things up, and making an inventory of the crash cart. She had been planning to carry the baby's body down to the hospital morgue, but had to get clearance before she could do so. Laurie was in and out of the room, restocking the cart, while waiting for the authorization.

About ten minutes after ten, Laurie heard a gasp coming from Conor McInnerney.

Laurie went over to look. It wasn't just one gasp, there were several. Glancing at her watch, she noticed that the baby seemed to be gasping 4 to 8 times a minute—once every eight to fifteen seconds. Laurie touched the baby's chest, and could feel Conor's heart beating.

At that point Vicki Hallberg-Gross came into the room. Laurie asked her to look at Conor. Vicki thought Conor was now breathing perhaps ten times a minute.

"With each [breath]," Vicki said later, "I heard the infant making a soft, high-pitched noise. I noticed that his respiration increased in frequency as we watched him. At one point the infant was even able to grasp my finger."

Laurie left the room and went to look for Turner, who was with Rowan. Laurie told them what she had observed.

She asked them to come to see for themselves. Soon Turner and Rowan were back in the room, along with Ann Duren.

Turner picked up the baby and began vigorously rubbing his back. Laurie later recalled him saying something about the possibility of miracles. Laurie put the oximeter back on Conor's foot and noticed that Conor's oxygen level was at 95 percent—on room air without the bagging. His coloring was pink, although he remained neurologically unresponsive.

Turner checked the baby's eyes again. According to Laurie, Turner still believed that the baby was so severely brain-damaged that he would soon die. Because there was nothing else to be done, he said, he would go back to his clinic, across the street. According to Laurie, when asked if he wanted to be notified when the baby died, Turner said no.

It was now about 10:30 p.m. After Turner was gone, the others on the emergency teams began to discuss various options. The whole situation was highly unusual; no one, not Dr. Bruce or Ann or Vicki or Laurie, had ever seen anything like this before, not even anything remotely similar. What should they do?

Even as the four discussed options—preserve the baby's organs for donation; start working to save his life once more; fly him to Seattle for specialized treatment; or admit him to the hospital so that he might be allowed to die with Marty and Michelle by his side—Conor seemed to be getting even better; his oxygen saturation level rose to 97 percent. At that point Rowen asked Duren to call Turner back to the hospital.

When Turner returned to the emergency room, he'd forgotten his eyeglasses. The group discussed the various options, all of which required the emergency team to notify Marty and Michelle that little Conor hadn't quite died, after all. The hospital would need their permission to continue any further medical care.

"Dr. Turner told us," Laurie said later, "that he did not want the parents notified, to spare them further grief." Instead, Turner suggested they take things one step at a time.

"We continued to observe the baby, who continued to get pinker, but with no change in his neurological signs," Laurie recalled. "At one point I checked the baby and noticed that it had something like a grasp, with what looked like a clonus-type jerking of his arms when I let go of his grasp. His lower extremity remained flaccid. I also observed his respiratory rate picked up to approximately 16 to 20 a minute, although still sounding like gasps."

Was it possible that Conor McInnerney was returning from the dead? Against all expectations, *something* was going on in there.

Amidst these indicators, Dr. Turner now appeared to change his mind about Conor's chances. Or did he?

This was the first of several critical decisions made by Dr. Turner that night. He decided to reintubate the baby.

By this time, the respiratory therapist, Dick Payne, had left Room 2A and was busy elsewhere. When Turner was asked whether Payne should be summoned, Turner said they shouldn't bother, that he would do it himself.

Turner tried to put the endotracheal tube down Conor's throat at least fifteen times. Rowan offered to do it, but Turner waved him off, saying, "I need the practice." Conor's throat was soon a bloody mess. Rowan tried, and was also unsuccessful. Payne was called in, and was likewise unsuccessful. The tissues in Conor's throat were too bloody and swollen after all these efforts. Someone suggested that an anasthesiologist be called to help reduce the swelling, "but Dr. Turner said that we should not call for anaesthesia," Laurie recalled.

Those in Room 2A with Dr. Turner later confessed to some confusion over what he wanted to do in this unusual situation. Indeed, Dr. Turner had evidenced a curiously detached manner all evening—something no one expected from the leading pediatrician on the Olympic Peninsula. It was almost as if he had no enthusiasm for what he was doing, but nevertheless felt compelled to go through the motions, as long as everyone else expected him to do so.

It seemed that Turner's head, which told him that the baby was doomed to die, was at war with his heart, which told him to do everything possible to bring the baby back to life.

Several times over the next hour, Dr. Turner closed the baby's lips by pinching them lightly with his fingers; when he did so, the baby's oxygen level began to decline. But as soon as he released them, the oxygen levels returned to normal.

What was going on here? Was it possible the baby wasn't as brain-damaged as Turner believed? No one knew the answer, in part because Olympic Memorial Hospital didn't have the equipment used to measure brain function.

Without an electroencephalograph—called an EEG—to chart the brain's level of electrical activity, the only way of measuring Conor's brain viability was by looking at his fixed and dilated eyes, and prodding his skin with a sharp pin in hopes of eliciting some observable nerve response. But every time such tests were performed, Conor showed no reaction.

One horrible possibility haunted everyone in the emergency room that night: what if a severely brain-damaged Conor lived on for weeks, or months—or maybe even years—with no hope of ever regaining consciousness? The awfulness of such an outcome, for Marty and Michelle, for everyone involved, seemed impossible to accept.

The young couple had already been through one of the most emotionally traumatic events anyone can endure; now to call them back, to say that Conor had not only *not* died, but might go on as a living shell for an extended period— that would be monstrously cruel. Turner refused to let anyone notify the McInnerneys that events had not gone as he had previously predicted.

Turner continued to watch the baby breathe on his own; Rowan, Vicki Hallberg-Gross, Ann Duren and Laurie Boucher were in and out of the room at various times as midnight approached. At one point, Turner recalled a recent article he'd read in a medical journal that suggested that sharply cooling the body temperature was a possible method of jump-starting the body's nervous system—a "dive reflex," Turner called it.

Laurie and the others assumed this was an order from Dr. Turner, so they prepared ice-cold towels and wrapped the baby in them. Nothing happened; Conor exhibited no discernible neurological response.

Rowan, meanwhile, had developed some concerns about Turner's course of treatment. He went to his office and called Dr. Jackson in Seattle.

"This is kind of a political call," Rowan told Jackson. He explained that while he was no expert, the treatment with the cold towels seemed way off-base to him. Jackson thought the treatment was odd as well. Rowan asked: Would Dr. Jackson be willing to talk to Dr. Turner? Jackson said he would. Rowan said he'd get Turner to come to the telephone.

Back in Room 2A, Laurie, Vicki and Ann discussed how they should chart this unusual situation—that is, the work on a baby who had already been declared dead. After some discussion, they decided that Ann would keep notes in pencil until the situation was resolved, and they could figure out what to put on the chart later.

At that point, Turner "asked if he could just stand with the baby for a short period," Laurie later recalled.

All three nurses left Room 2A for a brief period. Shortly before midnight, Vicki returned to the room; she had heard an alarm going off. The lights had been dimmed.

"Even in that light," Vicki said later, "I could see the monitor and its reading from the doorway. I saw the [oxygen] saturation [rate] was at 45 percent."

This was less than half of what it had been only a few minutes before.

"As I approached the monitor, about two feet from Dr. Turner, I saw that he had the infant in his arms. I saw the infant's face and saw that Dr. Turner was pinching his nose. I was confused by what he was doing. I walked to the monitor and turned off the alarm. He said something like he could not stand to watch this go on much longer.

"I was upset by what I saw and left immediately and found my supervisor, Ann Duren . . . I immediately reported to her what I saw and I believed she would follow up with the proper steps. I saw her go into the room with Dr. Turner and the baby."

Vicki went on to see other patients, evidently assuming that Ann Duren would deal with Turner. In the meantime, Laurie Boucher also returned to Room 2A.

"Ann Duren . . . asked if there was anything he [Turner] would like, such as juice," Laurie recalled. "Dr. Turner indicated he would like juice. I volunteered to go get his juice, as I wanted to get myself a cup of coffee. I left the room for a couple of minutes and came back with some juice."

When she returned, Laurie saw Ann Duren at the doorway of Room 2A.

"She had her hand over her mouth and seemed upset. I went in and saw Dr. Turner with his hand over the baby's mouth, pinching his nose closed. I was quite surprised and I looked at the baby and noticed that he was cyanotic and the oximeter showed a heart beat of 50.

"Dr. Turner seemed surprised by my presence and appeared to let go of the baby's mouth and nose when he saw me. I was upset and confused by what I saw and I put the juice down on a chair next to him."

To Laurie, it appeared that Gene Turner was deliberately suffocating Conor McInnerney, as it also had, previously, to Vicki. At first, Laurie didn't know what to say—and then she did.

"Don't stop on my account," she snapped to Turner, sarcastically.

"After I said this," Laurie recalled later, "he put his hand back over the baby's mouth and nose, and I left the room crying."

Almost immediately Laurie ran into Vicki. Laurie pointed to Room 2A with her hand over her mouth and nose, but said nothing. Vicki could tell she was very upset; she went back into the room herself.

Meanwhile, Laurie went to tell Rowan what Turner was doing.

Rowan was just hanging up from his "political" conversation with Dr. Jackson. Laurie told Rowan he needed to go into Room 2A and see what was going on in there. She thought Rowan would know what to do to stop Turner.

Rowan went into the room just as Turner was leaving. Rowan told Turner that Jackson was waiting to speak to him over the telephone. Turner agreed to make the call. He left.

At that point Rowan and Laurie looked at the baby. Conor was "blue and cold and quite obviously dead," as Laurie put it later.

It seemed clear to Bruce Rowan and Laurie Boucher that Gene Turner had killed Conor.

5

THE ER CREW

Olympic Memorial Hospital is a modern, well-designed facility sited on a bluff overlooking the strait in north Port Angeles. It is a public hospital—that is, directed by an elected board of commissioners and partly financed with tax funds of about $700,000 a year. It is the second largest employer in Clallam County, after the county government itself, and holds enormous influence among the political elites of the county. And, like any other large institution, it has various ways of communicating with itself, both on paper and informally.

The circumstances of the death of Conor McInnerney could hardly have been kept a secret in such an institution. For one thing, the nurses who had observed Gene Turner's final treatment of Conor McInnerney were stricken; having been trained to save lives, they were horrified by Turner's act, which to them was inexplicable, perhaps even inhuman. They talked about what they had seen with Dick Payne and Dr. Rowan, who seemed just as upset as they were.

Eventually, Laurie did make the walk to the morgue with Conor's tiny body, accompanied by Dick Payne. Afterwards, she returned to the short-stay unit, where she tossed and turned for the rest of the night, unable to sleep, worrying over what she had seen, and what to do about it.

She finally got up at about 6 a.m. and took a shower. She decided that she would report what had happened to the hospital's director of nursing services, Joyce Cardinal.

As she was on her way to Cardinal's office, she encountered Sue Grisiatis, Ann Duren's relief as night nursing supervisor. Sue had learned of the events from Duren, and told Laurie that they needed to report to Cardinal right away. Laurie told Grisiatis that that was exactly where she was headed.

In Cardinal's office, the nursing director was joined by two assistant administrators of the hospital, Mike Glenn and Donna Davidson. Laurie filled them in on what had happened. Laurie told them that she was bothered about Turner's actions. Someone, she said, needed to tell the McInnerneys, as well as the authorities, like the Medical Quality Assurance Commission—the state's medical licensing board—or even the police what had happened. Cardinal assured Laurie that steps were being taken to make the appropriate notifications.

Still later, Laurie was asked to repeat her recollection of the events with the hospital's quality assurance officer, Raedell Warren, who took notes.

By this time, after repeating the events so many times, Laurie was feeling awful, and asked to be excused from work for the day. She went home; as soon as she arrived she typed up her own notes on the events and stored them in her computer. She had an idea that one day, under the circumstances, they might be needed.

Meanwhile, Vicki Hallberg-Gross had finally gone home, and she too was feeling very emotional about what she had seen. Karen Blore, the manager of the emergency department, had heard about Conor and Turner from Grisiatis; she decided to call Vicki to find out what happened.

Vicki told Blore substantially the same story that Laurie had already related to Cardinal, Glenn and Davidson. She recalled that while discussing the treatment options, Turner was adamant about not wanting to call the McInnerneys; it would be too upsetting for the young couple, Turner said, for them to be told that their baby was still alive, though without any real chance at life.

That in turn compounded the group's decision-making process, Vicki told Blore, because any further treatment options required the parents' consent, and under the circumstances Turner was unwilling to contact them. Turner had continued to insist that the baby would die if left on his own, Vicki told Blore.

"It felt awful to us," Vicki said, "like it was a done deal. I felt that he [Turner] was hurrying this along. I felt like it was taking a life."

After Turner had left the room and then later returned, he seemed to have changed his mind about the baby, that maybe some "interventionist" measures should be taken, Vicki said.

"Dr. Turner came back and said, 'Well, maybe we should bag the guy.' He got a[n air bladder], and then he said that maybe we should reintubate. He said to get this and that . . . he had no glasses and couldn't really see well, so he took Laurie's glasses and attempted the intubation. This was taking too long and I asked Dr. Rowan to help," Vicki told Blore.

"The baby was not getting good air during intubation. RT [respiratory therapist Dick Payne] came by and did blow-by [bagging]. Dr. Rowan attempted [intubation], then Dr. Rowan and Dr. Turner again. I was in and out during this time. When I came back in everyone had attempted [intubation] without success.

"It gets really gross at this point," Vicki continued. "It's hard to think of this."

The image of the tiny three-day-old infant, gasping for breath between attempts to thrust the plastic tube down his bloody, swollen throat, was recurrent in her mind.

That was when Turner mentioned the study he had read, Vicki said, about cooling the baby in an effort to jog the nervous system into action.

"He said to get some wet, cool towels," Vicki told Blore.

"We said, okay. It felt gross. We all said, yuck, this is not natural. We asked him again and he wasn't clear. I asked him, 'Why are we doing this?' and he still wasn't clear, only mumbled that this was something that he heard and you cooled them in order to revive them. We said okay. I believe that all of us in the room felt, yuck. I left the room again."

Then, Vicki told Blore, "I heard the alarm go off and thought, 'Oh, well, it is ending,' I went back in and saw only Dr. Turner in [the room] and the [oxygen] was only 45. I turned off the alarm. At that time Dr. Turner said, 'I can't stand it, I can't have this go on any more.' I felt that he was feeling great compassion for the infant, that he felt that death was inevitable, [and] . . . 'let's expedite it.' I saw him plugging off the infant's nose.

"We were shocked, numb. Laurie saw it too. I told Ann [Duren] and Ann asked if she should go in there. I was so surprised. Yes, we wanted her to go in there."

What Vicki and Laurie wanted was for someone to stop Dr. Turner from choking whatever life remained out of Conor McInnerney.

Now Blore wanted to know about the chart, the hospital's official—and legal—record of what had happened to Conor McInnerney. According to the official record, everything ended at 9:54 p.m., when Turner had pronounced Conor McInnerney dead, just after he had lain in his parents' arms. But it was clear to Blore from Vicki's account that a lot more happened after that, which never made it into the chart.

Vicki told Blore that she remembered sitting in Room 2A with Laurie, Ann and another nurse, when someone said, "This isn't going on the chart, is it?" As it turned out, Ann Duren had taken notes in pencil; if there was a "good" outcome, the notes would later be transferred to the chart in ink, it was decided.

"If there was not a good outcome," Blore's notes of her

conversation with Vicki later reflected, "then the notes would not go on the chart."

After discussing this unusual procedure with Ann and Laurie, Vicki told Blore, she'd concluded that "this didn't feel right, either."

What happened next? Blore wanted to know.

After talking with Laurie Boucher and Dick Payne that night about the baby's second death, Vicki decided to go home. But once on her way, she changed her mind and returned to the hospital to write an "incident report" about what had happened. She was concerned about the use of the cold towels, and most of all, about Turner's action to occlude Conor's breathing, neither of which was reflected on Conor's official chart—at least as it existed prior to Duren's pencil-written notes. She wanted to make sure that there was some official record of her concerns about Conor's unusual treatment.

At some point after returning to the hospital, Vicki contacted Dr. Sprenkel, the pediatric resident.

"She felt bad also," Vicki told Blore. "And she seemed nice. She said that she wished that she was there for the remainder of the code. She couldn't speak to any other issues as she wasn't there.

"I remember saying that the events weren't sitting well with the nurses and that Dr. Turner may hear more about this. Dr. Sprenkel said it was good to talk to Gene personally rather than have some committee talk to him. We stopped talking a little after that."

It sounded to Vicki as if Sprenkel had no desire to get caught up in the events surrounding Conor McInnerney's death—especially if it put her at odds with Turner; as a resident, Turner was her superior at the hospital. Next, Vicki contacted Bruce Rowan.

"I talked to Bruce [Rowan], saying how I felt; he agreed, and was surprised that the code was 'called' so early, especially with spontaneous breathing, good pulse, good oxygen, et cetera. He didn't understand the cooling measures [the wet towels] and [the] nose issue. He stated that some-

thing was wrong here and [he had] phoned the doc in Seattle."

It thus seemed to Blore that Vicki, over the course of
the early morning hours, had come to doubt Turner's actions and decisions more and more.

"Why didn't we question more?" Vicki told Blore. "God
only knows if there was a chance for a neuro-intact baby.
We saw it holding on to life. It's hard to see an elderly
patient taken off a ventilator, but this was a *baby*. I feel
partially responsible. I wish we had handled it differently."

At this point Vicki broke down and began to cry. Blore
tried to reassure her. It was obvious that the events had
traumatized Vicki; Blore arranged for her to receive coun-
seling for stress. Vicki said that sounded like a good idea.

Even as Blore was debriefing Vicki, another hospital official was on the phone to Rowan.

OMH administrator Tom Stegbauer was the hospital's
ramrod; it was his job to make sure that things ran smoothly
for the physicians on staff, hired employees like Rowan,
and most especially, for the political district which employed him. As such he was probably the hospital's most
visible public figure, the contact point with the politicians
and the movers and shakers of Port Angeles, as well as the
news media.

Something like the strange death of Conor McInnerney
was potentially a large problem for Stegbauer and his hospital, the sort of thing that it was Stegbauer's job to make
sure didn't spiral out of control.

The primary question was a matter of law: according to
the statutes in Washington State, any licensed medical professional who was aware of any form of child abuse was
required to report it to police, the district attorney or any
responsible law enforcement authority within forty-eight
hours. Failure to do so was a crime.

That meant that Turner, Rowan, the nurses and anyone
else who might have been aware of Turner's nose-closing
could be criminally liable for failure to report; moreover,

if the hospital facilitated this failure, it too might be held criminally liable.

For Stegbauer, this was a conundrum. Was hastening the death of an almost certainly brain-damaged, if not brain-dead, baby really child abuse? Or was it a mercy—for the baby, for the parents, for everyone? It wasn't as if there was any malevolence in Turner's act; indeed, it could be described as a kindness—just the sort of thing that one might expect of someone like Gene Turner, whose concern for humanity had been so well-documented throughout the years.

At this point, Stegbauer still wasn't clear on exactly what had happened, and what the likely ramifications were; or, for that matter, what the wisest decisions might be.

It was clear that the nurses—Laurie Boucher and Vicki Hallberg-Gross in particular—were terribly upset at what had happened; all of the morning staff agreed to that. But Stegbauer had other considerations.

If the story got out before anyone understood what was going on, it might be devastating for the hospital, he reasoned. Without enough information, without enough experience of the reality of the emergency room, people might not understand.

Accordingly, Stegbauer issued directives that information about the events leading to Conor McInnerney's death be kept strictly controlled within the institution; and after that, he placed a call to Dr. Bruce Rowan.

"Dr. Bruce" lived in a split-level house with his wife Debbie and adopted two-year-old daughter Annika some miles south and east of Port Angeles, along a rural road called Yellow Rock Lane, just off one of the conduits into Olympic National Park, Mount Pleasant Road.

Rowan was slightly over five-ten; he weighed just over 170 pounds. He had dark hair, blue eyes, and wore glasses. His calm and pleasant demeanor had charmed virtually everyone he came in contact with over the eighteen months that he'd worked as an emergency room doctor in Port Angeles.

As an emergency room specialist, Rowan was not part of the inner circle of Olympic Memorial, as Stegbauer and Dr. Turner were. Instead he was a hireling—one of a number of easily replaceable specialists who contracted with the hospital for specific tasks.

Indeed, Rowan's first love was travel; he and Debbie had agreed in the months before their marriage, some six years before, that emergency medicine was the key to a preferred exotic life—six months to two years earning a very handsome income at someone's emergency room in the United States, followed by six months or so as a doctor in third-world locales such as Africa, South America or Asia. That would give the Rowans the best of both worlds: money as well as adventure, comfort as well as easily changeable horizons. Or so Bruce thought, and, at least initially, Debbie had agreed.

The events of the previous night had disturbed Rowan in a visceral way. As a child growing up in the small town of Weiser, Idaho, Rowan had seen first-hand the effects of brain damage on a newborn: his own older sister had been born with brain damage—in Rowan's view, the result of an obstetrician's mistake at the time of delivery. It was an event which had affected the lives of Bruce and his entire family for years.

Now, the knowledge that Dr. Turner had snuffed the life from a baby precipitated a severe conflict in Bruce. On one hand, he intellectually understood Turner's reasoning—that the infant Conor was almost certain to die at some point because of the heavy brain damage that Turner believed existed. But at the same time, Rowan was aware of a deep, hidden resentment toward members of his own profession: the idea that doctors, like Gene Turner, somehow had the emotional distance and certitude—the *arrogance*—to decide who would live and who would die irritated Bruce as much as it frightened him.

To Bruce, people who claimed this sort of omniscience

about the mysteries of life and death dredged up his worst fear: that somehow he himself lacked the inner emotional steel to have the same fortitude, the same coldness to walk away from someone who was beyond saving. Such claims to perfection forced him into an untenable posture: either he doubted those who were his mentors and teachers, like Turner, or he doubted himself. Which in turn led to an inescapable conclusion—either the older, distancing doctors were fakers, or *he* was. It was a difficult problem for Dr. Bruce.

Indeed, Rowan had been conflicted for a number of years between his view of himself as a scientist—as an objective practitioner of medicine—and his desire to live as a human being, freed from the persona of "doctor" that he found so constricting, as well as so demanding.

At least twice while in medical school at the University of Washington in Seattle, Rowan had dropped out of his course of instruction while trying to grapple his way through the internal conflict between the austere demands of his chosen profession, and his wish to be an ordinary fellow, free of the responsibility for omniscience which he believed a doctor was required to maintain.

In these crises, Rowan had fled the university to work as a fisherman in Alaska; there, he would later say, was the only place he'd ever lived where people never posed or pretended, but stood as themselves—raw, straight-forward, vital in their personal truths and interactions with others, however flawed.

Rowan had long coped with his internal conflict by ignoring the weightier questions of his emotional suitability to perform the role of a physician. Instead he focused on his technical expertise; even as the horrific events in Port Angeles unfolded over the next few months, Rowan continued to describe himself to others in terms of his knowledge and skills, rather than in any emotional terms. It was as if he saw his work as an emergency doctor as a means to an end, something he was good at that paid quite well, but nevertheless something that had no claim on his true soul.

Rowan, it appeared, was willing to spend some portion of his life dealing with broken bodies and sick people, provided that it assured him of a comfortable income and the chance to go places that could only be imagined in a small town like Weiser or Port Angeles.

His lucrative emergency room work had the effect of making him a crisis hero, without requiring him to get too deeply involved in his patients' lives, or demanding a response to emotions that Rowan consistently tried to suppress.

On this morning of January 13, 1998, Stegbauer dialed the Rowan home. Rowan came to the telephone. It was just after 9:30 a.m., almost the same time that Blore was interviewing Vicki Hallberg-Gross.

What happened last night? Stegbauer wanted to know. Did Gene Turner really suffocate a baby? Were you there when it happened?

Rowan filled Stegbauer in on the events, at least as far as he knew them. He himself had not seen Turner suffocate anyone, he said. If Stegbauer needed to know exactly what had happened, he should talk to Laurie and Vickie, who'd been there when whatever happened actually took place.

Still, Rowan told Stegbauer, he'd had doubts about Turner's treatment of Conor McInnerney; that's why he'd called Dr. Jackson in Seattle around midnight—because of the ice-cold towels, and Turner's persistent insistence that Conor was brain-dead.

Jackson had told him, Rowan said, that it was difficult, perhaps impossible, to detect brain death in a less-than-one-week-old baby without readings from an EEG; in any event, even those readings were difficult to interpret in so young an infant, because no one really understood how the infant brain developed in the first week after birth. At the very least, according to Jackson, EEG readings over several days were needed to make any accurate determination of brain function, Rowan told Stegbauer.

Rowan next told Stegbauer that Jackson had been dubious of Turner's treatment of Conor, at least as Rowan had described it; Jackson was, after all, the expert in the field, at least as far as Rowan and Turner were concerned.

The whole situation was emotional for everyone involved, Rowan continued; the nurses were upset, and after the baby was observed to be dead the second time, he'd tried to comfort them.

With these words, Rowan had confirmed Stegbauer's worst-case scenario: that Turner *had* suffocated Conor McInnerney, and on top of that, had done so without a full range of medical evidence necessary to prove that the baby was legally brain-dead at the time.

Stegbauer asked Rowan to write a confidential memo on the events of the night in the emergency room.

Rowan now asked whether the matter would be reported to the authorities; at this point, according to Rowan's later statement, Stegbauer seemed to suggest that it would be kept within the walls of the hospital, despite Joyce Cardinal's promise to Laurie Boucher that all the appropriate people would be notified.

Sometime that same day Stegbauer contacted Dr. Turner at his clinic; the exact contents of their conversation will probably never be known to anyone other than themselves. However, it appears that Stegbauer tried to convince Turner to tell the McInnerneys the truth about what had happened.

Turner was reluctant to do this, perhaps because he wished not to appear fallible, as some later suggested, or because he wished to spare the young couple still further grief. Exactly why Stegbauer wanted Turner to do this is also open to multiple interpretations: some later thought Stegbauer wanted to use Gene Turner to head the McInnerneys off from any sort of litigation against the hospital, by attempting to mollify them, or more hopefully, win them over to the hospital's side in case a public relations nightmare was to erupt.

This, after all, was Stegbauer's primary responsibility,

to run the hospital efficiently. Preventing it from taking a major legal and political hit was vital to his continued employment.

On the other hand, there were those who felt that Stegbauer believed the parents deserved to know the truth about what had happened, and that was why he prevailed upon Turner to talk to the McInnerneys.

In any event, on January 15, Turner met with the young couple and told them what had actually happened after they left the hospital. Turner explained that sometimes the body might go on living even after the brain had died, although there was no hope of recovery; that was why he'd ended Conor's primitive physical existence before natural events had taken their course—to spare Marty and Michelle any further suffering. The McInnerneys told Turner that they understood.

6

THE COVER-UP?

That same evening, the executive committee of the hospital met to consider what to do about Conor McInnerney and Gene Turner. It had now been sixty-six hours since Turner had plugged the baby's nose and mouth and helped him die—eighteen hours past the statutory deadline requiring caregivers like doctors and nurses to notify law enforcement authorities if they had observed a case of child abuse.

The executive committee of the hospital was the institution's true brain trust; while the elected commissioners might oversee the budget, the real decision-making was done by the medical professionals, headed by chief of staff Dr. Paul Pederson. The thirteen-member group that night included the chief of surgery, Dr. Rex Averill; Joyce Cardinal; Tom Stegbauer; Dr. John Yergan—Rowan's boss; and Dr. Eric Schreiber, the immediate past chief of staff and, like Turner, a man married to one of the town's most serious political players.

The meeting began around 6:30 p.m. on January 15, 1998. The minutes don't reflect whether Turner attended, or if Stegbauer or someone else summarized his position; moreover, as written, they do not indicate who specifically said what, since all recorded remarks were unattributed.

"The meeting was convened to discuss ethical and legal ramifications of a case involving a three-day-old child, which occurred on Monday, January 12, 1998," the minutes read.

Whoever briefed the hospital's committee quickly ran through the salient facts of Conor McInnerney's brief life and death.

After noting that Conor had first attained a heartbeat 39 minutes after the call to 911, the briefer ran quickly through the measures employed to save Conor's life prior to 10 p.m. on January 12.

"The situation was regarded as dismal and the parents were consulted," the minute-taker noted. "It was decided to cease advance[d] life-support measures. It was the presumption that the infant would die, and it promptly stopped breathing and was pronounced dead in the parents' arms. The infant was then put back on the cart; the parents and medical staff left the room."

The briefer then described the strange events that followed.

"Subsequently," the minutes noted, omitting the crucial time element, "the nurse noted a few gasping respirations, which increased somewhat in frequency, and the infant started to pink up in color."

Duren was notified, the briefer continued, according to the minutes, and Turner returned to the emergency room. After efforts to intubate were unsuccessful, ". . . Dr. Turner declared the infant to be brain-dead."

This, of course, was inconsistent with the observations of nurses Laurie Boucher and Vicki Hallberg-Gross that night; at no time *after* Conor began breathing on his own did Turner declare Conor brain-dead, at least in their description of the events; instead, this had happened before, a bit after 9:30 p.m., when Turner declared the baby dead the first time.

If Turner still believed the baby was brain-dead once he started breathing on his own between 10:20 and midnight, why did he attempt to reintubate? The idea that Turner tried to put the tube down Conor's throat simply because he needed "the practice" was intolerable; indeed, to the bitter end, everyone in the emergency room except Turner seemed to believe that Conor McInnerney still had a chance, including Rowan, who was on the telephone with Dr. Jackson even as Turner was squashing the baby's nostrils shut and covering his mouth.

The inconsistency in the minutes seemed to reflect the conflicting loyalties of the executive committee: on one hand, the committee desperately desired to find "St. Gene" blameless; on the other, the idea that Turner used the McInnerney baby for intubation "practice" was unstomachable.

The solution, it appears, was for the committee—or the briefer—to simply assert that Turner had declared the baby "brain-dead" a second time when this never actually occurred, at least according to the recollections of Boucher, Hallberg-Gross and Rowan.

Now the committee was edging into the tricky part: when did death actually occur; or, more importantly, how was it defined? There seemed to be two disparate definitions: one, when heartbeat and breathing stopped; and second, when electrical activity in the brain could no longer be measured. Turner had done some rude tests to measure brain activity, and Conor had failed to respond; but did that really mean he was brain-dead?

Under the first definition he was actually alive: by breathing on his own and with a viable heartbeat, Conor met the definition of life under Washington State statutes. But if Turner was right about the lack of brain activity— the absence of response to being pricked, and the nonresponsiveness of his dilated eyes to light—that could mean he was brain-dead, exactly as Turner had said almost from the beginning. Under some case law in Washington State, that indeed might mean that Conor was legally dead.

But was Turner's crude neurological testing adequate to make this determination? Maybe yes, maybe no; no one could say with certainty, absent clear proof that Conor had actually been brain-dead when Turner suffocated him. The hospital didn't have such proof, only Turner's experience.

The briefer noted that Dr. Jackson had told Rowan, at least, that brain damage was almost impossible to verify with infants under a week old, especially without an EEG.

What was abundantly clear was that the hospital had a major problem on its hands, legally as well as in terms of public relations. For one, under these circumstances—in which the moment of death was in question—was the hospital still required to notify the law enforcement authorities, even assuming that what Turner had done was "abuse"? Secondly, once the story of Conor's last hours emerged into the community at large, would the hospital's reputation be damaged? Would it prevent people from trusting the primary caregiver in Clallam County? Could the McInnerneys sue the hospital for the wrongful death of their infant son at the hands of Dr. Turner? And finally, for Stegbauer and the elected board of hospital commissioners who had hired him, would there be political fallout?

The meeting of the hospital's executive board was to last until almost 10:30; as reflected by the minutes, there is little as ineffectual at deciding anything as a committee which prides itself on achieving consensus, but avoids hard issues in order to do so.

Couched in the flat, declarative, factual phrases of the minute-taker, the notes of the meeting of the Olympic Memorial Hospital executive committee can only hint at the drama that must have unfolded on the evening of January 15, 1998; in part that was because the way the minutes were rendered, it was impossible to discern who favored what course of action. Anonymity may breed candor, but it does considerably less for accountability.

Gradually the discussion turned away from the causes and the unanswerable questions toward the subject of what was to be done now that the awful event had occurred, and couldn't be taken back.

Some offered practical if fuzzy advice: "It was pointed

out that it has been a painful struggle to deal with this situation, and . . . it might be appropriate to provide a healing environment to understand and cope with the trauma and the event." Nothing in the minutes indicates, however, just what such a "healing environment" might include.

What about the McInnerneys themselves, now that they knew what had happened? "They behaved graciously during Dr. Turner's description of the entire episode," the minute-taker recorded. "Their response was that of listening, holding each other's hands, indicating that their general opinion was 'we understand,' that the baby had seemed very dead and the situation was hopeless. There was no response like 'Couldn't you have done something?' The tone of the meeting was one of mutual compassion."

What could explain the incomplete chart? "It was noted that a complete medical record will be produced."

Some members of the committee wanted to zero in on Turner's motivation in smothering the baby. "It is important to know why Dr. Turner stopped the baby's breathing. What was the intent? Why didn't he wait for nature to take its course? It was noted that Dr. Turner has not really given an explanation."

Some now asked whether Turner might have been, "in a sense, treating the parents more than the patient?"

And what about the legal questions? What was the act of stopping the breathing? Could it be defined under the law? "It was noted that in the ER that night there was an impression that life-supporting efforts were delivered, and there was a positive response to those efforts," the minute-taker noted. "Then care was transferred to the appropriate individual and the perception was that a different approach started, and that all of the efforts that seemed to be heading in a positive direction were essentially stopped. That seemed to create a great deal of concern, including the final, more poignant events. Was it a change? And if it was, was it appropriate?"

This was the crux of the matter: the committee thus learned that some members of the ER staff believed

Conor's life could have been saved, but that Turner, in taking over the care, had seemingly decreed otherwise.

But now it appeared that some members of the committee wanted to veer away from the legal implications of Turner's actions; a suggestion was made that [only] once the clinical treatment was understood, "the societal issues . . . could be dealt with."

This was a bit like saying that grappling with the legal question of Turner's actions would be fruitless until the issue of whether Conor was brain-dead could first be addressed. If Conor was legally dead when Turner stopped his breathing, there was no legal issue to consider; in that case, there could be no "child abuse," because Conor would not be a living person.

At this point, one of the hospital's attorneys, Donna Moniz, threw a clunker into the emerging consensus. She suggested that the critical issue was Turner's decision to block the baby's airway. What needed to be done immediately about this? Moniz asked.

Another member of the committee, Dr. Thomas McCormick, a medical ethicist from the University of Washington, then suggested that the words used to describe what had happened were "critical."

"The question of how active euthanasia is treated in the state of Washington is important," the minute-taker recorded. Apparently McCormick then suggested that the event should "probably be reported to the Washington State Medical Quality Assurance Commission, who could then investigate the events thoroughly.

"Stopping the airway is the most problematic, most ethically and legally troubling," the minute-taker recorded, apparently reflecting the substance of McCormick's remarks to the committee.

Besides notifying the medical commission, it was now suggested, the hospital needed to recognize the significant public relations issues that were looming just over the horizon.

"[O]bviously a number of people in this community are

aware of this case," someone observed. "Very early on, one person ought to be designated as the spokesperson for the hospital or the medical staff and be prepared in the event of a call from the public arena."

Now attorney Moniz pointed out that under the law, health professionals were required to report the injury or suspicion of injury of a child to "the criminal authorities" within 48 hours. The medical commission was not such a criminal authority under the statute.

At this point, someone observed that "the local community may not be able to cope with such a report" to the "criminal authorities."

Although it was never stated explicitly in the minutes, it appears that while Moniz was providing sound legal advice—that the hospital tell "the criminal authorities" as soon as possible what had happened, as it was required to do—others on the committee wanted to keep the information away from the police.

"The Medical Quality Assurance Commission may be an appropriate outside agency to receive a report," the minute-taker noted from the discussion.

It was now decided to report the event to the medical commission rather than the police "as soon as possible"; Moniz was directed to write a letter to the commission "with the assistance of Dr. Pederson," the chief of staff.

Moniz next raised the question of Turner's hospital privileges, particularly whether Turner should be suspended, at least temporarily, until matters were sorted out.

"Consensus was that the group did not want to in any way be perceived as punishing Dr. Turner," the minute-taker reported. "The issue was raised that this event will eventually become public, and the hospital needs to be prepared for questions about allowing a physician under this veil of suspicion to continue practicing at OMH. It was noted that this is a time to support one another and express collegial support to Dr. Turner to avoid emotional damage to all involved."

What to say to the public, then? "It was suggested that

a carefully crafted statement be prepared and [be held] at the ready."

This, then, was the consensus: the hospital would keep the event under its collective surgical bonnet for the time being, avoid telling the police what had happened, and prepare "a carefully crafted statement" to be used only when and if it was caught.

That, as it turned out, was only a matter of time, and a short time, at that.

7

THE WHISTLEBLOWER

In accordance with the committee's decisions, the word went forth throughout the hospital the following day: dummy up. An email was circulated instructing the hospital staff that under no circumstances were they to discuss the recent "quality management issue" in the emergency room with anyone.

If inquiries were made, they should be immediately reported up the chain of command.

As for the decision to notify the Medical Quality Assurance Commission—known colloquially by its acronym, MQAC (rather unfelicitously pronounced "Em-Quack")—it appears that the letter was written the following day, Friday, January 16, but not received by the commission until January 20.

What does seem clear is that the hospital's staff was already beginning to divide over the issue of Conor Mc-Innerney's treatment at the hands of Gene Turner: the doctors, almost down to their last scalpel, stood by Turner, apparently under the reasoning of "There, but for the grace of God, go I."

While they might not have approved of what Gene Turner did, few were willing to assert that under the same sort of pressure and in the same situation they might not make some mistake themselves. Standing with the doctors were the upper hospital management people, such as Stegbauer and other administrators.

Meanwhile, dissension over the committee's keep-it-quiet-stupid edicts began to spread among the lower ranks—particularly among the emergency room people such as Rowan, Hallberg-Gross, Boucher and others who had been there.

This dissent from the company line was exacerbated by the sense, at least among Rowan and the two nurses, that they were being blamed for bringing the issue to the administrators' attention in the first place.

Both Boucher and Hallberg-Gross had the idea that Turner and some of the other top dogs at the hospital felt the younger staff were being too emotional about the situation, that they should have had the stomach and the fortitude to accept that such things sometimes happened, and the loyalty to look the other way.

This was also Rowan's feeling; and indeed, it tapped into some very potent psychological cross-currents in Bruce's personality. At least twice this conflict had driven him out of medical school to go fishing in Alaska; now it was back, worse than ever.

Over the next three or four days, Rowan, Vicki and Laurie exchanged telephone calls and tried to reassure one another that they had done the right thing in reporting Turner's actions, no matter what others might suggest or imply. But more and more, they began to feel as if they were the pariahs of the hospital community, the real bad guys, even though it had been Turner who had smothered the baby.

This was the situation by the afternoon of January 19, when emergency medical technician Daniel Heassler reported to the emergency room. Apparently Heassler had been off for several days, because when he came to work, he had no idea of what had happened the previous week.

Heassler read the email warning people to keep quiet

about the "QMM" (quality management issue). When he asked what this was about, one of the nurses—reluctantly—filled him in on what had happened seven days before.

This story troubled Heassler enormously. A former fire department EMT, it appears that Heassler had some strong convictions about health care professionals and the taking of human life.

After his shift ended at 11 p.m., Heassler went home and immediately called his neighbor, Clallam County Deputy Sheriff Matt Dalton. Heassler related the facts about the last hours of Conor McInnerney's life, at least as he understood them, to Dalton.

Around 5:30 that morning, after Heassler had provided a formal, handwritten statement to the Clallam County Sheriff's Department, Dalton called an acquaintance on the Port Angeles Police Department, Detective Sergeant Terry Gallagher. Because the hospital was inside the city limits, the city police, not the sheriff's department, had jurisdiction over any investigation there.

"What do you think about physician-assisted suicide?" Dalton asked Gallagher. But after Dalton told Gallagher what Heassler had reported to him, Gallagher had another idea.

"That doesn't sound like physician-assisted suicide to me," Gallagher said. "That sounds like first-degree murder."

At 44, Gallagher was married and the father of three children. All of them had been cared for by Dr. Gene Turner. He'd known Turner for years, and liked him. But no matter what his personal feelings, Gallagher was above all a cop—some said, one of the toughest, straightest and most relentless cops that Port Angeles had ever seen.

There had been four generations of Gallaghers in Port Angeles. His grandfather had served as a deputy sheriff, and after that, as a member of the Port Angeles Police Department. His older brother was on the department before quitting to attend a Catholic seminary; afterward, he'd returned to law enforcement, joining the Olympia, Washington, Police Department as the only combination priest-cop in the state. An uncle had served as a cop in eastern Washington, and had been shot dead in the line of duty in 1949.

"So, Irish Catholics," Gallagher said later, "we can be priests or cops. Most of us are cops, and my brother got 'em both."

But Terry Gallagher almost missed out on the family tradition; after serving in the U.S. Army's military police in Germany in the 1970s, Gallagher had decided that the last thing he wanted to do in his future was enforce the law. He'd been assigned to a garrison town in southern Germany, and just about every weekend, there were fights—lots of fights.

For soldiers who were in a constant state of readiness to meet the Russian invader, there were weeks of boredom and loneliness; once off active status, it was time to party. Most were young, with a lot of steam to blow off. Partying led to drinking, and drinking led to fighting, and fighting led Gallagher and his fellow MPs into the bars and beerhalls with billyclubs swinging. There was no way, Gallagher swore to himself when he got out, that he'd ever spend his nights fighting with drunks again, and that meant there would be no badge in Gallagher's future civilian existence.

But circumstances alter perceptions; after returning to Port Angeles, Gallagher had gone into the boat-selling business; when the business sprang a leak and went bankrupt, Gallagher came to believe that, economic necessities being what they were, making a living as a cop wasn't so bad as all that.

At least he had some experience at it.

After taking the tests and being hired at the Clallam County Sheriff's Department, Gallagher prepared to go to work as a deputy sheriff. His first supervisor, a deputy named Fred DeFrang, warned Gallagher that he'd better not change his mind and go to work for the city's police department if he got a better job offer there. Gallagher assured DeFrang that he wouldn't.

Imagine Gallagher's surprise when he almost immediately learned that he'd also been hired as a Port Angeles policeman. The salary as a city officer was significantly higher than a deputy sheriff. He called DeFrang and told him he was quitting to join the city cops. DeFrang pointed out to Gallagher that he'd already promised he wouldn't do that.

"Hey, Fred, I lied," Gallagher said, laughing. But DeFrang understood the reasons for Gallagher's decision, and over the ensuing years they had remained good friends.

Gallagher had risen through the ranks of the city's police department, becoming strawboss of the city's detective division, while DeFrang eventually became the county's chief criminal deputy sheriff. Gallagher and DeFrang, therefore, were responsible for the most complex and difficult criminal cases each department had, up to and including murder.

Now Gallagher was faced with what promised to be the most difficult case of his career so far.

What Dalton was describing seemed scarcely credible to Gallagher, early on that morning of January 20; that Gene Turner would do such a thing seemed unreal.

Gallagher got on the telephone with his superior, Deputy Chief of Police Tom Riepe. Riepe couldn't believe it either. "Frankly," Gallagher said later, "we had trouble believing what we were told."

But both men knew Heassler when he'd been at the fire department, and he wasn't the sort of person to make something like this up.

By this point, almost seven days after Conor's death, portions of the story had become garbled as it had found its way through the he-said, she-said underground network of the hospital staff.

As the story came to Heassler, Conor McInnerney was four months, ten days old—a remarkable transformation from his actual age of three days. One effect of this was to

make Turner's actions seem even stranger—at least to the
law enforcement people who had no contradictory information at the time. .

Further, Heassler's statement indicated that he had been
told that "ER Doctor Bruce Rowan was not involved" probably a reflection of how the ER people were already feeling
disparaged by the hospital's higher-ups; the fact that Heassler was made to understand that Rowan had nothing to do
with Conor's death seemed to indicate how far the lines
had already been drawn between the emergency room team,
and Turner and his supporters.

There was a variety of other misstatements in Heassler's
hearsay accounting. "No attempt had been made to secure
a BP"—apparently "blood pressure"—Heassler asserted,
based on what he had been told; but the ER crew had taken
blood pressure measurements as soon as a heartbeat had
been established. Likewise, Heassler asserted that he'd been
told that Vicki and Laurie wanted to remove the tube from
Conor's throat, but that Turner had told them to wait until
Marty and Michelle had spent some time with their baby;
that was completely backward.

Of course, Heassler wasn't present when any of the actual events were going on; he was only reporting what
someone else had told him. The fact that much of what he
was told was only partially true, and in some important
respects untrue, wasn't his fault. It only shows how unin-
tended distortions of fact quickly occur when the truth is
deliberately suppressed.

Heassler, in his recitation to Dalton, went on to assert
that neither the charge nurse, presumably Duren, nor Dr.
Rowan, had been made aware by Turner of what was going
on, once Conor was noticed breathing on his own. That,
too, was completely wrong.

As for the cold pack, Heassler asserted that he was told
that Turner directed the nurses to "fill the sink with ice
water and soak blankets [sic] in the ice water, then wrap
the child from head to toe in the blankets—telling them it
would be easier to intubate the child this way." That wasn't

the case at all, as Vicki and Laurie, and even Rowan, later attested; Turner's idea was to stimulate Conor's nervous system, not make it easier for him to put the tube down the baby's throat.

Heassler's statement went on: "After 30 or 40 minutes of this the child is still breathing on its own. Still unable to intubate, the nurses said Dr. Turner then placed his hand over the child's nose and mouth until the child stopped breathing."

The following day, Heassler continued, an email was sent out to all the ER staffers "that a QMM occurred in the ER and that we were not to discuss it with anyone in the ER or outside the ER." After that, Heassler continued, a closed-door meeting was held among the charge nurses by the head of nursing for the emergency room, in which the situation was discussed.

Finally, Heassler related, he'd been told that Vicki wanted to go to the police, but was warned off by the hospital administration; further, the baby's chart was incomplete, and the facts of the event were being turned over to the state medical commission—or so the nurses had been led to believe.

Because Terry Gallagher was the lead investigator on a murder case that was then in trial, and Riepe decided to assign one of Gallagher's detectives, Steve Coyle, to ask around at the hospital to find out whether any of what Heassler said he had heard was true.

Later that morning, Coyle contacted Matt Dalton and obtained a copy of Heassler's statement.

Coyle next met with Riepe, and showed him the statement. Riepe called Dalton, who confirmed that he'd taken it from Heassler. Riepe asked Coyle to call Vicki Hallberg-Gross, to whom Riepe happened to be related by marriage, and whom Coyle knew personally as well; Coyle's wife, in fact, had an affiliation with the hospital, and was well-acquainted with Vicki.

Coyle called Vicki shortly after 9 a.m. and asked: What

was all this about a baby being smothered to death in the emergency room?

Vicki told Coyle that she'd been instructed to say nothing, and to refer any calls to her supervisor.

With that, as Gallagher put it later, the police knew that *something* had happened, that there might be some truth to Heassler's story, however unlikely it had first seemed on the surface.

Shortly after this, Coyle learned that a baby had in fact died in the hospital emergency room around January 12; he so informed Riepe and Gallagher.

Riepe then called Port Angeles Police Chief Steve Ilk to let him know what was going on. As he was filling Ilk in, the telephone on Ilk's desk rang.

It was Stegbauer.

8

THE COPS

Having been alerted by Vicki's supervisor that the police were on to the story, Stegbauer did what he might have done five days earlier: he called Chief Ilk to report the death of Conor McInnerney.

At 3 p.m. on the same afternoon, Tuesday, January 20, Stegbauer, accompanied by two lawyers, finally briefed Riepe, Ilk and Coyle on the events of the night of January 12.

According to Riepe's subsequent account of the discussion, no mention was made of the hospital's failure to notify the "criminal authorities" within the forty-eight hours as was legally required; still, it had to have been an issue that everyone was thinking about at the time.

After all, anyone who knew about the smothering, who was a health care professional, and who had failed to report it, was at risk of potential criminal prosecution, to say nothing of the prospect of losing their license to practice medicine.

Indeed, these risks were one reason why Heassler had told Dalton the story of Conor McInnerney almost as soon as he heard about it, because his own certification as an EMT was potentially in danger.

And for Gene Turner, now that the information had come into the hands of the "criminal authorities," the risks were even greater: depending on how the event was interpreted, Turner might even be liable for prosecution as a murderer . . .

About the same time that he called Chief Ilk, Stegbauer had also placed a call to Clallam County Prosecuting Attorney David Bruneau, who, along with Gallagher, was tied up in the unrelated murder case; as a result, Bruneau wasn't immediately able to return Stegbauer's call.

Ironically, Bruneau's sworn enemy in Clallam County politics was none other than Norma Turner, Dr. Gene Turner's wife. Later, Norma Turner was to claim that Bruneau's antipathy toward her had led the prosecutor to charge her husband with the crime of murder—but that was yet to come.

To fulfill his obligation under the law, Stegbauer now finally told the police about the events of January 12. He told them that he'd conducted his own inquiry into the events surrounding Conor McInnerney's death, that the whole problem was a hospital matter, the hospital knew how to handle it, and there was no need for the police to get involved, since the hospital had everything under control.

Stegbauer next provided a description of the affair that differed from Heassler's third-hand version, but which mostly conformed to the accounts of Laurie Boucher, Vicki Hallberg-Gross, and Bruce Rowan, none of whom the police had yet heard from.

The hospital's executive committee had met, Stegbauer added, and collectively decided that the best course of action was to report "the event" to Em-Quack—the state's Medical Quality Assurance Commission—especially given the uncertain circumstances about Conor's actual condition at the time Turner had suffocated him.

From the facts, it wasn't clear that any abuse had actually occurred, Stegbauer next suggested, because it was almost certain that the baby was legally dead at the time Turner had acted. Stegbauer said that everyone agreed that Conor was "brain-dead" at the time of Turner's act; and under the law, being brain-dead was the same as being statutorily dead.

If Conor was therefore legally dead, Stegbauer added, he couldn't be abused; if there was no abuse, obviously, there was no need to report to the police, which was why no one had called the authorities; but because the circumstances of Conor's actual medical condition at the time he died remained murky, the hospital's executive committee had therefore decided to ask the experts, MQAC, to investigate.

This was certainly putting the best face on the "event," as Stegbauer insisted on terming it. Certainly the three police officers got the impression that Stegbauer was suggesting that the police were meddling in matters they had no expertise in, since, by Stegbauer's standard, they were medically ignorant.

But while all of Stegbauer's statements might be perfectly accurate, Ilk, Riepe and Coyle knew it would be wrong to simply accept the administrator's solo verbal report as the best evidence: after all, Stegbauer personally wasn't anywhere near the emergency room when all this occurred, so how could he know anything for sure?

As a result, Riepe now indicated that the Port Angeles Police would need to inspect the hospital's records regarding Conor's death, and interview the various nurses and doctors who had been present at the times in question. Stegbauer assured Riepe, Ilk and Coyle that the records would of course be provided for the police department's perusal; further, Stegbauer said, the hospital staff would be told to cooperate with the police.

That wasn't what happened, however—at least not right away.

*   *   *

Even before Stegbauer began his spin in Ilk's office on the afternoon of January 20, Heassler had called the emergency room intending to say that he felt too sick to come to work that night; as he put it later, hearing about Conor Mc-Innerney's death had seriously upset him.

But when Heassler's call was put through to nursing supervisor Karen Blore, she informed him that he'd been suspended from his job indefinitely. Heassler now formed the impression that he was being punished because of his report to Matt Dalton.

As it happened, Coyle's calls to Vicki Hallberg-Gross, passed through the chain of command, had alerted the hospital higher-ups like Stegbauer that the police were now aware of the problem posed by Conor McInnerney's death; in turn, that led to Stegbauer's attempted damage-limiting calls to Police Chief Ilk and Prosecutor Bruneau earlier that day.

It soon became clear to Heassler that he was in bad odor among the hospital muckety-mucks, and that management was all too willing to deliver the message.

Heassler now called an attorney.

The following day, Detectives Coyle interviewed Marty and Michelle McInnerney, who told him that, in the conversation they'd had with Turner on January 15, Turner had admitted smothering Conor, even as he explained that their baby was essentially brain-dead, and that hope for recovery was nil.

The day after that, January 22, Sergeant Gallagher reinterviewed Heassler, who said that it was now official: he'd been told by Joyce Cardinal that he'd been suspended—with pay—for providing "misinformation" to the police. Cardinal told him, Heassler said, that he wouldn't be allowed to return to work until he agreed to provide the hospital with copies of any statements he had made to the authorities about the McInnerney case.

Heassler also told Gallagher he'd heard that the upper management of the hospital was deliberately hiding important records, and was preparing to engage in a full-scale cover-up. Paranoia, anger and fear were rampant at the hospital, he added. Heassler then informed Gallagher that he had hired a lawyer; so, too, he said, had almost everyone else at OMH.

On Friday, January 23, 1998, Port Angeles Police obtained a search warrant for the hospital, seeking "all records and documents . . . relating to the admission and treatment of the infant Conor McInnerney occurring at Olympic Memorial Hospital on January 12, 1998."

As a courtesy, Gallagher had told the hospital that a warrant would be served; this took place at a meeting on Monday, January 26, in the law library of the Clallam County courthouse. Present were Riepe, Prosecutor Bruneau, Stegbauer, and hospital attorney Greg Miller. The group again went over the events of January 12.

This time the subject of why the hospital hadn't met its legal obligation to report Conor's smothering to law enforcement was raised.

"It seemed like common sense you should involve the authorities," Gallagher said later. "Arguably, a murder had occurred."

At the meeting in the law library, Miller disputed that.

"Frankly, we didn't report it because we were afraid you'd embark on a frenzied investigation," he told Gallagher.

"The reason we're having a 'frenzied investigation' is because you *didn't* report it," Gallagher shot back. After some additional "animated" conversation, as he later described it, Gallagher said that the police department had to insist on going forward, wherever the trail led. "We have an obligation to investigate this," Gallagher told Stegbauer and Miller, "and the bottom line is, if we *don't* investigate it, or if I didn't investigate it, I'd probably be unemployed three months from now, as would my boss."

So, too, Gallagher added, would be anyone at the hospital who tried to prevent the facts from coming out.

The following day, Stegbauer came to the police department with a black three-ring binder containing records and statements relating to Conor McInnerney's death in the emergency room two weeks before. Included was the hospital's "event log," a fairly sketchy list of different activities that had taken place on the night of the 12th; a truncated portion of the minutes of the executive committee meeting that had taken place on January 15; and the notes of Karen Blore, relating the substance of her telephone conversation with Vicki Hallberg-Gross on the morning after Conor McInnerney was pronounced dead. Gallagher read the binder and was not happy.

The hospital, he concluded, was still not cooperating; or at least the pooh-bahs weren't. Indeed, it appeared that they'd circled the gurneys around the embattled Dr. Turner.

9

THE PARIAHS

It turned out that Heassler was right: virtually everyone at the hospital who knew anything about what happened to Conor McInnerney, especially the executive committee, was soon lawyered-up. The hospital paid for all the legal talent—more than $360,000 by the time the whole thing was over a year later.

"The difficulty we were in, here," Gallagher later recalled, "was that everybody at the hospital got an attorney. There were more attorneys involved in this case than any case I've ever seen. People that we had no intention of prosecuting . . . wouldn't talk to us without an attorney. At one interview I asked if I could record it and the attorney wouldn't let me.

"So, first we had to get over the hurdle of everybody getting their attorneys, and then we had to get [those] attorneys to tell us [that] we could talk to them [the witnesses]."

It was a logistical mess, Gallagher said; the most obvious witnesses—Laurie, Vicky, Rowan and others, including Stegbauer, and the members of the committee, and other administrators—had to be concerned about their own legal liability, not only in possible criminal terms for the failure to report, but also for their professional licenses.

Eventually, after the hospital-hired lawyers had provided the medical board with formal written statements from the principal players, permission was granted for the police to begin interviewing a variety of individuals as witnesses.

Gallagher assigned this task to Port Angeles Police Detective Eric Kovatch. Kovatch was 39 years old, married, and the father of three children—each of whom had been cared for by Gene Turner. In earlier years, when his children were sick, Kovatch had demanded that only Gene Turner should treat his kids. Now he was assigned to investigate him, mostly because Steve Coyle, his counterpart under Gallagher, was married to a nurse who worked at the hospital. Eventually, Kovatch was to conduct nearly 100 interviews of hospital personnel as he attempted to find out what really happened to Conor McInnerney on the night he died.

Three days after Stegbauer brought the black three-ring binder into the police station, Kovatch conducted an interview with Vicki Hallberg-Gross in the detectives' interview room at the police station.

Vicki's written statement to her hospital-hired lawyer was essentially consistent with what she'd told Karen Blore the morning after Conor died, with one exception: where she'd told Blore that Conor's first breathing was "apneic—heavy breath, little sighs with soft sounds," in her lawyer-written statement Vicki asserted that the baby's breathing was "anginal."

Questioned by Kovatch, Vicki said that what she'd really meant was "agonal"—conveying the idea that Conor's breathing was indicative of a person who was dying.

As for Laurie, she continued to insist that Conor appeared to be improving as the hours passed.

In addition to obtaining Laurie's account of the events in the ER, Kovatch wanted to develop any evidence that anyone at the hospital had taken steps to conceal what had happened. He asked Laurie if failing to maintain the chart was out of the ordinary.

"Well," Laurie said, "first of all, this whole evening was out of the ordinary. And when Dr. Turner was called back . . . well, he came in when I found the baby's heart rate was still going and the baby was breathing. I went and got him and brought him in.

"And then he assessed the situation and thought the baby would die soon because of lack of oxygen and the gasping that the baby was doing.

"It was a different kind of breathing," Laurie continued, "almost a swelling in the throat type of breathing. It was a high-pitched gasping . . . and he [Turner, when Laurie called him back] was very relaxed and . . . saying that he felt the baby would die soon. And then he went back to his clinic." Laurie said she thought that Turner was right, "that the baby would stop breathing soon.

"And the baby did just the opposite," she continued, "started breathing more and more regular and pinked up more, and the heart rate was still real stable, and this was without added oxygen. So that surprised us."

She wasn't surprised that Turner had left to go back to his clinic, given his prediction that the baby would soon die. Still, Laurie was bothered by the decision not to call Marty and Michelle McInnerney back to the hospital under the circumstances.

"I . . . wished that the family would be called back to be at the baby's side," she said, "even though I know it would be terribly upsetting. [If] I try to put myself in their position . . . I feel like I would have wanted to have been called back, even if the baby did die just another ten minutes later."

That was when "we started talking about options," Laurie told Kovatch.

"We said, well, it's Dr. Turner's feeling that this baby is definitely brain-dead, and that's the way it is. We still have a real viable body here, that would be perfect for organ donation."

As Laurie, Vicky and Rowan discussed their possible courses of action, Conor's blood gasses continued to improve, with the acidosis declining. "It was almost close to normal," Laurie told Kovatch. Other vital blood chemistry indicators were likewise improving. "And this whole thing was very, very odd because we—I—had never been in a position like this."

No one knew what to do about the chart, she added. "How do you chart a baby that's already been declared dead? How do you chart that you're just observing this baby and you're not doing anything because nothing had been ordered or all options that were brought to the doctor were turned down?"

This indeed appeared to be part of the whole situation: that the ER people, trained to respond to life-threatening crises, were helpless and frustrated in the light of the absent Turner's reluctance to do anything further. Then, after Turner returned and attempted to reintubate the baby, and failed—after Laurie saw him cover Conor's mouth and nose—Laurie became upset. She talked with Vicki, Rowan and Dick Payne; all agreed that the whole scene was wrong.

She went back to the short-stay unit, Laurie told Kovatch, and "cried and thought, cried and thought the whole night." She'd concluded that her supervisor, Joyce Cardinal, needed to know what she'd seen.

The following morning, and on each of the next few days, Laurie had asked Cardinal whether all the appropriate people had been notified of Turner's actions.

"In my heart I felt like it was not right," Laurie told Kovatch. "And that . . . the proper people needed to know about what really happened that night."

"The proper people being . . . ?" Kovatch prompted.

"The family and the police and the medical board and . . ."

"Okay," Kovatch said.

"And she said, 'Yes, Laurie, trust me that the appropriate people are going to be told about this.' "

The next day, January 31, Kovatch interviewed Rowan, also at the police station.

Before the interview, Rowan gave Kovatch a copy of the four-page confidential report that Rowan had dictated at Stegbauer's request the morning after Conor's death. He told Kovatch that he'd given the statement to Dr. Pederson that day, or perhaps the day after.

"Okay," Kovatch said. "Have you had conversations with Tom Stegbauer regarding this incident?"

"Yes," Rowan said.

Rowan explained that he was unsure how to dictate the memo in such a way that it would remain confidential; Stegbauer told him that he could do it with "a very limited dissemination, essentially to me, make it to me, and not go anyplace else."

"Did you talk to Tom Stegbauer over the next couple of days?" Kovatch asked.

"Yes," Rowan said. "Well, my conversation with him was probably the following day, most likely the fourteenth . . . My concern was how this case was going to be managed. I felt that it was extremely important that appropriate channels be notified, particularly, the state board of medicine . . . and making sure that this was something that would be followed up on and not be . . ."

"Did Tom Stegbauer have any comment about that?" Kovatch asked.

"His feeling was that it would most likely stay within the walls of the hospital," Rowan said, "and within the organization itself, and be dealt with appropriately in that fashion."

He himself hadn't actually seen Turner smother the baby, Rowan said, but he had been told about it by Laurie.

"I went to the room and found the child which appeared to be clearly dead," Rowan told Kovatch. "Laurie Boucher was in the room and she was quite tearful at that point. She . . . was concerned about what had happened and I said, 'What happened?' she said, 'I'm not sure you want to know.'

"I said, 'I think I should know.' She told me that she had witnessed Dr. Turner covering the child's nose and mouth and making . . . Dr. Turner making some statement to Laurie . . . 'Come on in, don't be afraid of this situation.' "

"Did you make any comment to her?"

"I was . . . very surprised. I don't recall if I made an exclamation type of comment or not, but I'm sure I expressed true surprise," Rowan said.

Afterward, when Vicki Hallberg-Gross returned to the emergency room to fill out her incident report on the smothering, Rowan said, he'd told her she was doing the right thing.

"What incident report are you talking about?" Kovatch demanded.

It was a standard in-house form, Rowan said. And as Kovatch knew, it was not among the documents of the three-ring binder previously turned over by the hospital.

10

THE THIN WHITE LINE

Almost as soon as he'd leafed through the black binder delivered by Stegbauer, Gallagher had realized there were references in the file to documents that had not been provided.

For one thing, the notes of Raedell Warren, the hospital's quality assurance officer, were missing; so were written reports filed by the ER nurses Laurie Boucher and Ann Duren; any reports by Rowan; not to mention Conor's complete medical record; to say nothing of Vicki's so-called "incident report."

All of this, combined with Heassler's assertion that he'd been suspended and the fact that the various players from the hospital had all hired lawyers, stoked Gallagher's suspicions.

He began to believe that he had *two* possible criminal cases: first, the murder of Conor McInnerney by Dr. Turner—only the most eminent pediatrician on the Olympic Peninsula—and second, a case against the hospital and its employees for attempting to conceal Turner's possible fatal abuse of Conor McInnerney. As a result, two separate investigation files were opened by the Port Angeles Police Department: one on Turner, and a second on the hospital and its staff.

"From a police standpoint," Gallagher recalled, "we're trying to think critically and somewhat suspiciously. And what it appears to me, is, first off, the report [of Conor's death] wasn't made in a timely manner; secondly, the employee who chooses to report it appears to face some sort of discipline; it also appears that the records have not been made available in full.

"After Heassler had alleged there was a cover-up taking place, we began to think that perhaps the hospital wasn't being as cooperative as they wanted us to believe."

Later, Gallagher came to understand that at least part of the difficulty lay in the clash of cultures—the hospital culture versus the police culture; each side had its own way of seeing reality, which blinded it to the perceptions of the other.

"My impression is that hospitals are accustomed to handling things in-house," Gallagher said later. "Hospitals don't believe that other people could possibly understand the issues that they face within the hospital, issues that sometimes are matters of life and death.

"They have a system that's evolved, it seems to me . . . that allows the people involved in that community to rationalize their behavior in such a way that they could say, we don't need to report this, child abuse is a medical diagnosis, so we simply decide there's been no child abuse, [and therefore] we don't have to report it.

"I think medical arrogance had a lot to do with how this case played out. I think that the hospital could have been more forthcoming, not just with the police, but with the press. I think they would have had a far easier ride than they did throughout this affair."

Afterward, Gallagher saw parallels between his own profession and that of the doctors.

"I've heard of the thin blue line," Gallagher said, referring to police officers' well-known tendency to close ranks against outside critics. For many cops, it is a given that outsiders—"civilians," in the officers' parlance—have no idea of what's truly involved in a police officer's job. This buttresses many officers' commitment to keep quiet, even when they've observed a fellow officer abusing his badge, or worse, breaking the law. "I've never seen it in my career, although I understand that it exists. But, I've *seen* the thin white line," the medical professionals' similar attitude.

"I think the rationale is the same—that, 'We as physicians have a terribly difficult job, that the public can't possibly understand.' It's no different than the rationale that a dirty cop might use, when he says, we as the police have a difficult job, and you of the public who are not the police can't possibly understand it.

"And so, you can use that rationale to justify all sorts of behavior, and it's not appropriate."

But this wasn't a matter of simple misconduct, police or medical; Gallagher was suspicious that real crimes had been committed, possibly even murder. He didn't care a whit how doctors saw themselves, however they believed that their lives could never be understood by ordinary, non-medical people.

"In our opinion, we're involved in a murder investigation," he said later. "Time is critical in any murder . . . I think any experienced investigator will tell you that you want to get on it *right now*.

"And we had already started this case behind the eight-ball, to where we had to be concerned about people's memories, what might be happening to people's memories."

Gallagher redrafted his search warrant. This time there would be no warning.

"I told my detectives to go over there and get the material requested in that second warrant, and to make damn sure that the hospital understood what we wanted and that we wanted it *now*. And that we were not above coming over there with whoever was necessary and searching that hospital to insure that we received the records that we thought were necessary to advance the investigation."

As anyone who has witnessed a thorough police search can attest, the prospect of a platoon of uniformed police scouring every nook and cranny of the hospital on a paper chase was daunting indeed to administrators.

"As it turned out," Gallagher said, "I think the hospital realized that they were better off to try and do what we were asking for. My impression is that initially they thought we would go away."

But the cops weren't going away; and worse than that, for the hospital, the secrets about the death of Conor McInnerney were about to become very public.

11

BREWER

As the end of January approached, all the snow that had fallen on the afternoon and evening of Conor McInnerney's death had melted; the temperature had risen to an almost balmy 51 degrees. The city of Port Angeles lay beneath its towering mountains, facing its strait, for the most part unaware that it was about to embark on one of the most tumultuous years in its 136-year existence.

Even as Laurie Boucher was giving her emotional interview to Detective Kovatch, Port Angeles gained a new resident. This was John Brewer, the newly named editor and publisher of the local newspaper, the *Peninsula Daily News*. Brewer was a veteran newspaperman who had previously headed the Associated Press bureaus in Seattle and Los Angeles, and had also worked for the AP in New York City. Later, he had headed *The New York Times'* news service, which provided stories to newspapers across the country.

When *The Times* decided to reorganize its news service, Brewer, a resident of Peekskill, New York, found himself remaindered—in other words, laid off.

Over the years, Brewer had maintained a casual friendship with the editor and publisher of the *Peninsula Daily*

News, Frank Ducheschi; they'd gotten to know one another years before when Brewer ran the AP's Seattle bureau.

In those times, Brewer had come to the Olympic Peninsula and Port Angeles on various stories. "This town always had news," Brewer was to say later. "Always had news. When I was in Seattle, I used to remark that Port Angeles had the wildest stories in the world." He could still remember when FBI agents had arrested the fugitive spy, Christopher Boyce of *The Falcon and the Snowman* fame, in a Port Angeles fast-food drive-in.

"Drop that hamburger!" the G-men commanded, in what was to become an immortal line.

In Brewer's mind, the mix of population, the proximity to one of the world's most beautiful natural settings, the relative isolation, and finally the nearness of Canada across the strait made Port Angeles unique.

On the event of his departure from *The New York Times*, Ducheschi had a proposition for Brewer: since Ducheschi was about to retire, would Brewer be interested in taking over his paper, the *Peninsula Daily News* in Port Angeles?

Thus was a veteran newspaperman—and more importantly, an outsider—chosen to take over the area's principal organ of public communication just as events were about to convulse Port Angeles. Even a year later, a lot of people in town were still complaining, however inaccurately, that if it hadn't been for Brewer, with his out-of-towner, New York edge, none of the turmoil that was to happen would have ever taken place.

Port Angeles was a town that was founded under unusual circumstances to begin with. In the 1860s, while Lincoln was still in the White House, a man who had the ear of the President proposed that a federal district not unlike the District of Columbia be established on the Pacific Coast. In a tour of the Pacific Northwest, the man noticed that some miles west of Washington Territory's most important town, the shipping center of Port Townsend, lay a fine natural harbor, formed by a gigantic sand spit that extended into the strait.

Ediz Hook, as it came to be called, was said to be the largest naturally formed sand spit in the world; as such it enclosed a huge anchorage.

The idea of making the area into a federal district came to nought, but a small town began to take shape on the harbor. Over the last part of the 19th century, the town changed its name twice—to Cherbourg, then Angeles City—before finally settling on Port Angeles.

Shortly after the turn of the century, the sharp ridge just south of the harbor was sluiced down, creating additional flat building areas along the harbor front and above the city. Just before the First World War, an impressive array of brick and stone structures appeared in the downtown area, replacing the clapboard buildings that had dominated Front Street along the harborside for nearly half a century. The town began to take on its present character.

"Most of what you see downtown was built about 1914," Brewer said, a year after he'd first arrived. "They sluiced down the hill, just like they did in Seattle. They brought back all the stuff they'd learned up in the Klondike ... [Before that] this was a town where you'd get off the boat and have to hack down a tree to get into town.

"They hosed down all these cliffs, just like they did in Seattle, and now they have a downtown, about 1914. They called it sluicing the hogback, because the hogback was the big cliff, and in 1914, they built most of what you see downtown."

There was one major road into the growing city, arriving from the east; later it was designated U.S. 101. As it entered Port Angeles, it became First Street; as a result, most of the east–west streets in town became numbered, with Front Street at the filled-in harbor's edge. Meanwhile, the downtown north–south streets were named after trees, like Laurel, Oak, Cherry, Pine, Cedar, and the like.

Some of these streets ran over the old Hogback and headed into the hills, and then toward the majestic, snow-capped mountains to the south that so dwarfed the town.

The U.S. Navy arrived in the 1930s, and was soon followed by the Coast Guard. The little town prospered on the timber and fish resources that surrounded it, and as the century unfolded, generations of families worked in its lumber and paper mills, raised children, and generally considered themselves to be among the most fortunate of Americans, blessed with steady jobs, a salubrious climate, and one of the most spectacular natural settings in North America.

A brisk cross-strait trade developed with Vancouver Island, and on weekends the small town filled up with a swell of Canadians and Americans lining up to take the ferry across Juan de Fuca strait. This, at least, was the Port Angeles Brewer remembered from his earlier time in Seattle.

But by the time he arrived in Port Angeles to take his new job, the town's biggest paper pulp mill was about to close, the Canadians couldn't afford to visit anymore, and the town was desperately trying to transform itself into something that didn't need to depend on the dwindling timber or fish resources that had sustained it for more than a century.

The 1997 announcement of the coming closure of the ITT Rayonier pulp mill, which had been the area's biggest employer before the county and the hospital district, was devastating. The fact was, the mill was old and the supplies of timber were becoming increasingly pricey as the supply of timber in the Olympics diminished with all the cutting.

"It had a great psychological effect on the town," Brewer said later. "It really was a turning point, I think, for a lot of people here—from what they tell me."

Faced with an increasingly hard-to-come-by supply of logs, the forthcoming shutdown of the mill and the soon-to-ensue depression in the pulp industry marked a sea-change in people's expectations in Port Angeles.

"The era when you could drop out of school in the tenth grade, marry your pregnant girlfriend, get an $18.50-an-hour job in the mill, support a family and be a good, contributing citizen—those days were over with," Brewer said.

As a result, when he arrived in Port Angeles on Friday, January 30—the same day that Laurie Boucher was being interviewed at the police station by Eric Kovatch—Brewer was confronted by a town in transition, a small city facing an uncertain future.

For his first few days in town—he was scheduled to take over the paper on Monday, February 2—Brewer stayed with Frank Ducheschi and his wife. Almost as soon as he arrived, Brewer learned from Frank that the *News* was working on what promised to be a huge story: the smothering of an infant at Olympic Memorial Hospital.

"This is a small town," Brewer said later, "and we have people here [at the paper] who are married to people who work at the hospital, or their neighbors work there. [And] at the hospital, there was [talk] something was going on, that something bad had happened.

"And later we found out that the administration had gone around telling everybody to erase email messages, and was saying, 'Don't tell anybody about this, keep it hush-hush!'

"And meanwhile, two nurses were being treated for trauma."

In the midst of all this, the paper's police reporter, Mike Dawson, had heard rumors about Gallagher's investigation into the smothering of Conor McInnerney. So, as Brewer prepared to take over for Ducheschi, the talk was rampant that something was about to blow.

"Anyway, Sunday night I was at home, with the Ducheschis," Brewer recalled. "I'd only been here a couple of days, I'm staying with them at their home. They [the Ducheschis] had told me [about] the story, and that they hoped to have something for the Monday paper. So I called in, and the editor filled me in on what they had, and he said, yeah, they'd got it."

What the paper had, to back up the rumors heard earlier in the week by Dawson, was a press release from Police Chief Ilk. It seemed clear that the statement had only been issued in response to Dawson's questions.

"The Port Angeles Police Department," the press release

read, "is investigating the circumstances surrounding the death of an infant that occurred on January 12, 1998 . . . "The infant was treated by a physician who is not a hospital employee."

This was later seen as a concession by Ilk to the public relations concerns raised previously by Stegbauer; while Turner was "not a hospital employee," he was certainly affiliated with it in terms of staff privileges, as well as the fact that the hospital's resident, Sprenkel, had called him in to take over the case.

But Ilk's statement did not identify anyone as the physician.

After briefly describing the events of Conor's treatment, Ilk went on to report that a hospital employee had later "lawfully" reported to the authorities that circumstances surrounding the baby's death were questionable.

Ilk's statement went on to confirm that the Medical Quality Assurance Commission had simultaneously initiated an investigation into the events.

"Specific details of the investigation and the identities of all individuals are remaining confidential at this time to protect the privacy of the family and [to] maintain the integrity of the investigation . . ."

But if Ilk was choosing not to name the doctor, that wasn't the case with MQAC. A reporter's call to a spokesman for that agency produced the name of Gene Turner. The editor on duty at the paper told Brewer who it was. Brewer turned to Ducheschi.

"Have you ever heard of Gene Turner?" Brewer asked.

The Ducheschis were flabbergasted. It was as if someone had just said that Marcus Welby was a closet baby-strangler. To the Ducheschis, along with thousands of others in Clallam County, it was simply inconceivable. Frank Ducheschi called Turner and spoke to his wife, Norma.

Was this true? Ducheschi asked. Had Gene really smothered a baby at the hospital? Norma wouldn't say, and Gene had no comment.

Gene Turner had nothing to say, Ducheschi now reported to Brewer; Norma said he had yet to be interviewed by the police. For his part, Eric Kovatch was later to say that the failure to interview Turner before the story became public was the Port Angeles Police Department's biggest mistake.

12

SCOOP

The following day's issue of the *Peninsula Daily News* was
the year's biggest seller, as Brewer recalled later.

Baby's death investigated, the paper headlined. **PA
doctor allegedly obstructed airway**.

"Eugene Turner, a prominent physician who has prac-
ticed medicine for 37 years, is under investigation by police
and a state medical quality board for allegedly facilitating
the death of an infant," the paper's Christina Kelly reported.
Kelly recounted that both the spokesperson for MQAC,
Maryella Jansen, as well as the Port Angeles Police, had
said that an investigation was underway. "Ilk said police
are using search warrants, which are sealed, to obtain information from the hospital," Kelly reported, "such as documents surrounding the infant's death."

Ilk told Kelly that no one from the police department
had yet spoken to the physician. The paper called Stegbauer, but the hospital administrator declined comment.

Chief Ilk refused to say whether "hospital officials
would be investigated for not reporting the incident to authorities."

Almost from the time this edition hit the streets of Port
Angeles on Monday, February 2, it was controversial.

Brewer later recalled that the paper almost immediately began receiving calls from parents who had Turner as a pediatrician; the substance of the telephone calls was, initially, that the paper had to be *wrong*—there was no way that someone like Gene Turner would do such a thing.

"We immediately started getting complaints from people," Brewer said later. "They couldn't believe it. We had obviously made this up, or something."

The fact that the other two regular news outlets in town—a radio station which happened to be next door to the newspaper, and a local cable television channel—both ignored the story left the newspaper hanging out there all by itself. This suggested that the newspaper had made a gross error.

"I listened to the radio that morning, and there was nothing on this," Brewer said. "And they have a television station in town, nothing on that either. It was sort of peculiar. Then they actually did use some stuff, but they said they would not identify the doctor because no criminal charges had been filed. That was sort of a moralistic hoopah.

"But now we started having people calling us saying, 'How come you *named* him? He hasn't been charged.' "And we said, wait a minute, the state authorities are investigating him, they gave us his name and told us about it. Didn't do any good, though."

People were furious with the newspaper for having fingered Turner, Brewer realized.

The following day, Christina Kelly tried for an interview with the embattled doctor. Turner, it appeared, had hired a lawyer the same day that the *News* had broken the story. The police called him to request an interview, Turner told Kelly, but he hadn't yet responded.

Still, Turner was well aware of what was about to happen to him; he knew as well as anyone in Port Angeles that his actions on January 12 were certain to concentrate an enormous amount of public attention on him.

"I am participating fully in this investigation," Turner

said, "and have been instructed by my lawyer not to make any comments."

Turner said he and Norma had received many calls of support from former patients and their families.

"I know I did the right thing under the circumstances," Turner told Kelly. "There were mitigating circumstances."

As it happened, Turner had spent part of that day on jury duty; before that, he'd gone out to Highway 101 to pick up trash as part of his volunteer work.

Kelly next contacted Diane Anderson, Marty's mother. Anderson said that Turner had told her, "from his lips to my ears, he told me the baby was brain-dead."

But Anderson, a licensed practical nurse, wanted to know how Turner was so sure, since the hospital had no EEG.

She'd been in the ER when Turner had first said that Conor was brain-dead, Anderson said, and she'd assumed that they'd run an EEG brain wave test on the baby before declaring him brain-dead. No one at the time had mentioned that the hospital didn't actually have an EEG. The fact that the hospital had no EEG equipment bothered her, Anderson said.

Anderson was likewise upset that no one had told Marty and Michelle that Conor appeared to be coming back to life after having been declared dead. "What bothers me is that we didn't get a chance to decide. Without the proper equipment to determine that this baby was brain-dead, how can such an absolute decision be made? He [Turner] should have called us and let *us* decide.

"I don't want to see any doctor guessing," she added. "I don't wish the Turners any ill, but I want the truth to come out."

The *News*' Kelly had also tracked down Stegbauer, and apparently asked him why the hospital hadn't reported the situation to the police.

"On the advice of legal counsel, the report was made to MQAC, rather than to local authorities, primarily because of the sensitive nature of the incident, and the amount of fact-finding required," Stegbauer said.

Stegbauer's assertion that "legal counsel" had advised the committee to notify the medical board instead of the police was a rather significant stretch of the truth, given attorney Moniz' insistence at the executive committee meeting that the "criminal authorities" be called.

But at that point, only the police knew that Stegbauer was fudging to the *PDN*'s Kelly, since they had collected the board's minutes under their warrant; the minutes clearly showed that Moniz had in fact urged notification of the police, not MQAC.

Still, after Diane Anderson's interview, a couple of new issues emerged.

How come the hospital—with a $40 million reserve surplus in its bank accounts—had no EEG? And why didn't it have a mechanical respirator suitable for an infant?

Representatives for the hospital admitted that the institution didn't have either of these pieces of equipment, but said that, as a regional care facility, it wasn't necessary. Usually, the hospital said, patients needing such specialized equipment would be transported to larger, better-equipped facilities in Seattle. It was only the snowstorm of January 12 that had prevented that from happening in Conor McInnerney's case.

Even while Kelly was gathering this information, *PDN* reporter Mike Dawson was on the trail of Heassler's suspension. The fact that the person who finally reported the death to the "criminal authorities" had been suspended made the hospital look bad.

Heassler's lawyer, Lane Wolfley, went on the attack. "Essentially," Wolfley said, "he was disciplined for telling the police." Wolfley claimed that the hospital had suspended Heassler without pay until it learned that Heassler had hired a lawyer, at which point the institution had restored Heassler's pay, while maintaining the suspension.

The hospital disputed Wolfley's claim, at least partially. Although admitting that Heassler had been suspended, a

personnel director said that Heassler had actually been suspended for refusing to report to work on January 20, and
for spreading gossip that violated the McInnerney family's
right to privacy.

13

OUTRAGE

The town quickly divided into those who blamed the newspaper for making the matter public, and those who believed that no matter how wonderful a man Turner was, his act couldn't be excused. The debate even took place inside the newspaper.

Five days after breaking the story, the *News* assigned Mike Dawson to write a profile of Turner.

"The man at the center of the investigation may be one of the most beloved people in the community," Dawson reported. Dawson ticked through Turner's good deeds: donating property for Habitat for Humanity, serving as a youth soccer referee, donating home-grown garden produce and beef, chaperoning youth activities, hosting an annual picnic for disabled children—complete with pony rides—as well as volunteering to teach health classes for kids and parents alike.

"On his way to his lawyer's office Wednesday, Turner took two hours to pick up litter on his clinic's portion of the Adopt-A-Highway program," Dawson reported. Dawson went on to provide opinions of Turner from his numerous patients.

A 22-year-old woman, herself one of Turner's patients

as a child, said she trusted Turner with her life, as well as the lives of her children. "He just goes out of his way to make children feel safe around him, and he does the same for the parents," Holly Wickersham told Dawson.

Her sister-in-law, Kim Wickersham, felt much the same. "He's the kindest, gentlest person I know," she said.

At first, Brewer had no idea that the Gene Turner story would be so controversial in his new home town. But based on the immediate and vociferous reaction to the first stories, Brewer realized that he had a huge tiger by the tail.

"This is a guy—and now we're doing stories about him," Brewer said. "I'm reading for the first time about him. You know, the fact that [while] he's on his way to his attorney's office, he stops for two hours to pick up litter, because this is his day to pick up litter on the mile he sponsors on [Highway] 101. Incredible stuff.

"I'm reading these stories about the guy chopping wood for the mentally retarded, which he still does, by the way. Taking kids kayaking . . . an amazing individual, and a guy who also delivered half the babies on the peninsula. And who was virtually—I can't include any exceptions here—the women we have in the office here, who have children, he was their *doctor*.

"And so they were all upset, too. Everybody was confused and upset, and going on about this."

As the next few weeks unfolded, the controversy only increased, while the newspaper continued to draw criticism from the public for continuing to print Turner's name.

"It was the naming of him," Brewer said. "That's all we heard about. It was naming, naming, *naming!*"

If the paper had only not printed Turner's name, Brewer was told again and again, it would have been much better.

As additional bits of the story began to come out—Heassler's identity as the tipster, and his subsequent suspension, the warrant that the police had gone to the hospital with in order to search for records, and the fact that the affidavits in support of the warrants had been sealed—battle lines began to form in town, between those who supported Turner, and those who supported the newspaper's right to report the information.

All the criticism, however, didn't faze Brewer and his staff.

After learning about the search warrants, the newspaper went to court to get the documents unsealed. When Prosecutor Bruneau had no objection, the documents were made public, including the minutes from the hospital's executive committee meeting of January 15—where someone had suggested that the public would never be able to deal with the truth of what had really happened in the emergency room that night.

"Anyway," Brewer recalled, "we got the documents, and of course, the most interesting thing was the smoking gun stuff, where they talked about this at the [executive board]. And even despite an attorney saying, you really should tell the authorities about this, they decided, no no, we'll only talk to the state people [MQAC], *they* have law enforcement authority.

"You know, you can see all this rationalization that they are going through.

"And then, of course, this famous quote, about how the community couldn't take this, if we let it out. It was like something out of Watergate, a Nixonian-type thinking, of how we can do it." By this, Brewer meant that the minutes seemed to show that the hospital's excutive committee hoped to hide any misdeeds, and manipulate the system to get away with it.

The report on the committee's minutes only stoked the flames of debate. Now there were new arguments around town about the "arrogance" of the hospital's executive committee's deciding just what the public could stand to know, or whether the hospital should have gone to the police directly, rather than the state's medical bureaucracy.

"A lot of people felt very strongly that this [reporting to MQAC] was the right thing to do," Brewer said, "that the authorities from the state would [take care of] it, and no one outside the hospital should ever have been told.

"We wrote that story and *that* caused a great upset within the community, too."

Still, as far as Brewer could discern, "everybody still seemed solidly on Turner's side.

"I went back to advertising, three weeks later, and there was a press release in the fax machine," Brewer recalled. "It was saying, 'We're going to demonstrate at the *Peninsula Daily News*. They've unfairly done this, and that.' "I can't remember exactly what they said. Then somebody here, one of the mothers here, was faxing it off to her friends from inside our own building! We had people, even in here, who were obviously feeling we weren't doing the right thing."

The flyer began with a question. "Are you outraged at the *Peninsula Daily News*' coverage of Dr. Turner? We are! Join us in a 'display of hearts' for Dr. Eugene Turner . . . [in] front of the *Daily News* office. *PDN* needs to explain their biased reporting."

Brewer now received a letter from the demonstration's organizers, asking for a meeting—at the same time the demonstration was to take place.

"We have attempted to contact you about our concerns regarding recent coverage in the *PDN* via email," they wrote, "but have received no reply. We therefore request you meet with members of the community Tuesday, February 17 at 4:30 p.m.

"It is our understanding Mr. Brewer is new to Port Angeles. We look forward to meeting you. Welcome to Clallam County. Please call . . . to confirm the time and day."

Brewer called the organizers back: what did they want? The answer, to Brewer, seemed a bit confused.

"All they know is, they want to shelter him [Turner]," Brewer said afterward, "and protect him. They said, 'We want you to come out and answer some questions from us.'

"I said, 'Do you want to come into the office to talk about this? Why don't you come into the office and we'll just talk about this?'

" 'No,' they said. 'We want to see you outside.' And I said, 'Okay, that's fine.' "

Thus, on the afternoon of February 17, 1998, just as the sun was about to go down, Brewer looked out his office window and saw a large crowd gathered in the newspaper's parking lot—along with several television cameras, including every station from Seattle.

Until this day, the Seattle media had largely ignored the allegations against Turner; but once some people in Port Angeles decided to demonstrate against the newspaper to protest its coverage of Turner and the hospital, the whole thing suddenly became a news story. At least, that's the way it seemed to Brewer, who thought the real news was what happened on January 12.

Brewer decided to greet the protestors with his best foot forward. "So I ordered coffee and cookies for the demonstrators," Brewer said. "Set it up all nice. I'm looking out and car after car arrives, and we have a big bunch of people out in our parking lot, and they're all in front of the radio station [next door]. And they have little heart-shaped balloons, saying 'We love you, Gene,' and [picket] signs . . .

"So," Brewer continued, "I go out and wade into the group."

No one booed him, Brewer recalled later. "They didn't say anything, they just watched me. I just walked out [into the parking lot] and they were very quiet. And all the television stations were there, from Seattle, along with our local cable company. "Which I thought was funny. I mean, they're [the cable station] still doing this farce of not identifying the physician, which was funny because they're showing all these pictures of people with signs—'We love you, Dr. Turner,' and, of course, the little heart-shaped balloons.

"And then they [the television station] go into this moralistic thing, 'Oh, we cannot identify the doctor because he's not been charged. We have, you know, high standards of . . .' What bullshit! They just didn't want to take the heat over it. And they saw what happened to us, and they weren't about to do it themselves." Clearly, Brewer's ideas of community journalism were different from what the community expected.

"So I went out [into the parking lot] and they asked me questions.

" 'Why did you identify him?' "

"I explained that, that the medical people had provided his name, and given the circumstances, the newspaper was obligated to report it." With that, Brewer said, the demonstrators appeared to back off.

"The demonstrators said to me, you know, 'We're not here to complain about the *newspaper*. We're here to show support for Dr. Turner.' And then [one of the organizers] turned to the crowd: 'Isn't that true?' "And everybody goes, 'Yeah! Yeah! Yeah!' " Brewer recalled.

"Then all these cameras are looking at me . . . [which] is a funny feeling. I'd never really gone through that before."

Suddenly, it was Brewer who was on the spot, answering questions instead of asking them. The way the cameras were pointing at him, Brewer abruptly had the feeling that *he* was the bad guy.

Which was very disconcerting; and which gave Brewer the sudden realization that, whatever his ideas of Port Angeles had been when he was still back in New York, the town had definitely changed.

14

THE EXPERT

Even as Brewer was trying to steer his newly inherited newspaper through the complexities of reporting a highly emotional and technically difficult story, the Port Angeles Police were continuing their investigation of Dr. Turner.

Principally, Detective Kovatch was interested in talking to Dr. Craig Jackson of Seattle's Children's Hospital.

By now, Kovatch had learned that Rowan had been in conversation with Jackson at almost the same time that Conor McInnerney was dying; that Rowan had expressed concerns to Jackson about Turner's treatment of the baby; and that Jackson had been in contact with the helicopter service several times that fateful evening. It was necessary, therefore, to interview Jackson to see what he had been told by the players at Olympic Memorial Hospital.

On February 9, almost a week before the demonstration supporting Turner in the *PDN* parking lot, Kovatch went to Seattle to interview Jackson.

Jackson's version of the events at OMH generally corresponded with the recollections of Rowan, with the exception of the times. He thought the baby had died the first time around midnight.

"I thought this event was over," Jackson told Kovatch,

"until I received a call at approximately 2 or 2:30 from Dr. Rowan, who indicated that he was very uncomfortable with circumstances that were going on at that time. He had turned over care of the patient to Dr. Turner, but had been apprised of the circumstances, and felt they were inappropriate.

"As he described them to me, they were confused," Jackson said, "and it didn't make sense to me."

The cold towels sounded weird, Jackson said; and he agreed with Rowan that it might be best for Jackson to talk directly to Turner. Rowan said that Turner would call him back, Jackson said, but "no such call ever occurred."

Kovatch asked Jackson if he was sure about the times, and Jackson admitted he could be off by a couple of hours.

Now Kovatch wanted to get Jackson on the record about Turner's smothering of the baby.

"What is dead, the legal definition of dead?" Kovatch asked.

"In Washington State, death is defined in either of two ways," Jackson told Kovatch. "First is, complete cessation of all cardiac and respiratory activity. Alternatively, patients who are brain-dead are also dead, if there is complete cessation of all brain and brain-stem activity."

What about the cooling with the wet towels? Would that be useful in preparing a body for organ donation? Kovatch asked.

"I'm not aware of why one would try to cool a patient down prior to organ donation," Jackson said. "It doesn't sound likely."

There was, Jackson added, some recent evidence in neonatal resuscitation in the emergency room that cooling of the brain might lead to reduced injury to the brain if resuscitation was successful—Turner's "dive reflex"—although it wasn't as yet a widely accepted procedure.

This seemed to indicate that even as late as the time the cold wet towels had been applied, Turner might have had doubts about Conor's supposed brain-death, which he had formally declared at least an hour earlier.

How long should an ER crew work on an infant who had the symptoms of Conor McInnerney? Kovatch asked.

There was no average time, Jackson said. Generally, he said, medical assistance would continue for as long as the patient was breathing and had a heartbeat—at least until it became apparent that intact survival wasn't a possibility.

In that case, it would be appropriate to call off the efforts, Jackson said.

What were agonal breaths? Kovatch asked.

"Agonal breaths are usually deep and infrequent respiratory activity that occurs shortly before complete cessation of respirations and death," Jackson said.

"If somebody were actually having agonal breaths," Kovatch asked, "would occluding their airway be an accepted medical practice?"

"No," Jackson said. "I can't conceive of circumstances where it would be appropriate. Patients who have agonal respirations or any respirations are, by definition, not brain-dead, nor . . . do they [have] cardio-pulmonary death. So, intervention to interrupt someone's airway would be a form of active euthanasia."

Active euthanasia, Jackson added, was illegal in the United States. Unlike where a doctor pulls the plug on a respiration machine and a patient thus dies, active euthanasia was a conscious decision to proactively end the life of a patient.

Nor was there any way to accurately measure the amount of brain damage in an infant of less than seven days of age; without EEG tests, most appropriately taken over several days, it would be impossible to know for sure, Jackson indicated, whether Conor McInnerney had viable brain function after being revived.

There was more, but at this point Kovatch had what he needed: according to a reputable expert in the field of neonatology, baby Conor wasn't legally brain-dead when Turner had smothered him; moreover, that such an act was "active euthanasia," that euthanasia was a crime, and finally, there was no way that Turner could definitely have known that Conor was brain-dead without an EEG.

Moreover, Jackson told Kovatch, with infants under the age of seven days, it was extraordinarily difficult to gauge the actual level of neurological activity, since the development of babies' brains in the first week was very poorly understood.

What a physician should do under the circumstances faced by Turner, Jackson went on to suggest, was to stop all aggressive efforts to revive the child, and simply monitor the situation. If the brain damage was extensive, the child would eventually die.

At the very least, other tests might be run to determine whether the baby had suffered brain damage, and if so, how much.

That, of course, was exactly what Turner had first proposed to do—at least until Conor seemingly began to improve by breathing on his own, "pinking up," and improving his oxygen/carbon-dioxide ratio.

Just why Turner reversed his field and attempted to save the baby the second time around, and then re-reversed himself by smothering him, was a mystery known only to Turner. But based on Jackson's expert opinion, Kovatch returned to Port Angeles with the evidence needed to charge Gene Turner with murder.

15

VENDETTA?

By February 17, even as the demonstrators were picketing the newspaper's parking lot, Port Angeles Police had compiled a gigantic file on the death of Conor McInnerney; by this point it comprised two large three-ring binders, 791 pages in all—and this was only the beginning.

Turner's criminal lawyer, Jeff Robinson of the prestigious Seattle firm of Schroeter, Goldmark and Bender, had already been in contact with Clallam County Prosecutor David Bruneau as a result of Turner's awareness of the police investigation—as reported by the newspaper—and from the earlier police request to interview him. Bruneau had promised to send copies of the police file to Robinson as soon as it was assembled and delivered to the prosecutor's office.

Already the case was shaping up as a political hot potato—if not for the police, the hospital and the Turners, then certainly for Bruneau.

Norma Turner had long been at odds with Bruneau over a variety of issues. She was one of a number of people in Port Angeles who believed that Bruneau's office failed to take domestic violence cases seriously. Norma, in fact, had been the campaign manager for Bruneau's last election opponent, Alan Merson, in 1994. Her well-known opposition to Bruneau's continued incumbency had quickly led to some dark suspicions about the investigation of Gene Turner.

At the demonstration at the paper that afternoon, one of the speakers had claimed that the police probe of the doctor was obviously Bruneau's effort to get even with Norma Turner for her prior opposition to Bruneau's continued tenure as prosecutor.

Reached by the newspaper later that night, Bruneau said that that idea was patently ridiculous. The case had been initiated by the Port Angeles Police Department, not his office, Bruneau said. He had no control over what the police did or didn't do. If and when they brought him any charges against Turner, he would consider the matter fairly and impartially, as his duty required him to do.

Duty was a very big thing for Bruneau. He'd been in office since first being elected in 1982—sixteen years in the county's top law enforcement post. At 51, Bruneau was a conservative Republican in a county that was growing both older, and increasingly attractive to retirees—especially former military pensioners, who generally were just as conservative as Bruneau, if not more so.

A U.S. Marine Corps veteran, Bruneau had served in Vietnam between 1965 and 1969—in many ways, the hardest years of the war. In keeping with his conservative philosophy, he was a hard-nosed prosecutor. His stand on drug courts—venues where people accused of possession of drugs were often tracked into diversion programs—was controversial in the county, mostly because Bruneau refused to let anyone over 18 appear there. Instead, the adults involved with drugs should go to prison, under Bruneau's view of his responsibility as a prosecutor.

That in turn made a lot of people in Clallam County angry.

"Bruneau insisted he's not going to have any adults in this program," the newspaper's Brewer recalled, "only children, only juveniles, and that as long as he was prosecuting attorney, no adult would ever have a date in drug court. And that pissed off a lot of people in this community."

Brewer was once again struck by how the area had changed from the days when the FBI had nabbed Christopher Boyce and his hamburger. The fact was, all the retirees who had moved to the community had changed the political dynamic, made it more conservative. That, coupled with the demise of the mills and the resulting economic disconnection, had rendered the more liberal blue-collar families less politically potent, as the affluent, non-native retirees gained ever-more-increasing influence.

"You've got all the out-of-state people pulling the levers here, but you've got the blue-collar people, who've lived here a long time," Brewer observed. "And here's little Billy, who's been arrested for methamphetamine, because he's out of a job and had no place to go, but Bruneau sends him away for five years. There was a tremendous backlash against Bruneau, because he wouldn't let those young people go into drug court for diversion."

A feeling began building that Bruneau was too tough, too rigid—and too much in the pocket of the wealthy interlopers who had moved into the county over the previous twenty years.

When people thought of Bruneau, they thought of Teddy Roosevelt. It appeared to be an image that he deliberately cultivated, right down to the handlebar mustache and the round spectacles. On his office wall was a poster of TR; his general approach to most matters of controversy was head down, bulling straight ahead, big stick at the ready.

Police Detective Sergeant Terry Gallagher, who'd known Bruneau for years and liked him immensely, was well aware that the political currents were running against Bruneau as 1998 unfolded. It would have been the easiest thing for Bruneau to do to let Turner slide on the possible charge of murder, given the circumstances of Conor McInnerney's death; to Gallagher, it was to Bruneau's everlasting credit that he agreed to examine the evidence against the husband of one of his biggest political enemies, without fear of the consequences. That was, Gallagher later declared, an example of the sort of integrity that David Bruneau had always possessed.

The police file was delivered to Bruneau on February 19, 1998—all 791 pages of it, including the interviews with the nurses, Rowan and Jackson. Now Bruneau had to decide whether criminal charges against Turner were justified, and if so, what charges, against a backdrop of rising criticism of the police, the newspaper, his office and himself personally—the essence of which was, that the powers of self-righteousness were conspiring to crucify the kindest, gentlest, most giving man then living on the Olympic Peninsula, Dr. Eugene Turner.

"I'm not going to be run off by people who are trying to politicize this thing," Bruneau told the *Peninsula Daily News'* Dawson on the day he got the file from the police. Nor would he ask for a special prosecutor to be appointed, as some had already suggested, given his well-known enmity with Norma Turner.

"I will continue to conduct my duties of this office consistent with my oath, as I always have," Bruneau said, sounding as TR-esque as ever.

Port Angeles Police Chief Ilk rushed to Bruneau's defense.

"Any suggestion," Ilk said, "that he initiated or directed this investigation is complete nonsense and extremely insulting to the police department." Once Heassler had reported what he'd been told, for the police to ignore the matter would have been unprofessional, and "nonfeasance," Ilk added.

Even Gallagher weighed in.

The whole question, Gallagher told the newspaper, was well beyond local politics. To believe that, he said, would be "greatly trivializing the death of an infant."

A few days later, the state Medical Quality Assurance Commission weighed in with its own initial offering on the Turner–McInerney case. At an emergency meeting, Gene

Turner was charged with unprofessional conduct for "abuse of a vulnerable patient," and "gross lack of judgment" in pinching Conor's nose and mouth closed. Turner was ordered to refrain from practicing any further resuscitative efforts, and to contact another physician immediately if such efforts were required, pending the completion of an investigation by MQAC into Turner's competence to work as a physician.

Turner's lawyers shot back almost immediately.

"Dr. Turner is still in practice," said Seattle lawyer Katherine Brindley, who was hired to represent Gene before the medical board. The restriction imposed by the board was only temporary, she observed, until the full facts were developed, and Turner was ultimately exonerated.

Meanwhile, Turner's criminal lawyer, Jeff Robinson, fired some salvos of his own. "As a result of these leaks," Robinson told the *PDN*'s Kelly, "there [has been] numerous information that is unfounded and inaccurate. We would love the opportunity to talk about this, but now is not the time or place." Exactly which "leaks" Robinson was referring to wasn't immediately clear; all the information that had so far been published had come from the court file, or from the statements of Heassler's lawyer. Apparently, the unsealing of the search warrant affidavits describing the hospital committee's deliberations, and emergency room supervisor Karen Blore's notes were, in Robinson's view, "leaks," although at that point all were public documents.

But Robinson's first goal was to cast his client, Dr. Turner, as the helpless victim of unfair attacks by the police and the prosecutor, channeled through the newspaper; at least that way, the now-growing battle for public opinion could be somewhat neutralized.

The next day, civil attorney Brindley struck once more. In a press conference in her Seattle office, she complained about both the police investigation and the reporting of it in the news media.

"The erroneous charges of misconduct against my client, a well-respected pediatrician, who has maintained his private practice in Port Angeles for three decades, are completely without merit," she said. "This baby suffered massive and irreversible brain injury—one incompatible with life—well before Dr. Turner was involved in attempts to revive the infant."

Having opened a line of inquiry with this statement, Brindley now loaded it with innuendo by omission; when asked how such a brain injury occurred, Brindley declined to say.

"I don't know the answer yet," she said, "That is the question we all need to be asking."

This oblique suggestion was instantly translated into a hint that perhaps the McInnerneys themselves were responsible for their baby's "irreversible brain injury."

The Associated Press quickly put this issue to Marty, whose guileless response told volumes.

"We don't know what happened, really," Marty told the AP. "The coroner agreed there was no trauma. They found nothing that was out of the ordinary at all."

So much for Brindley's subliminal hint that somehow, Marty and Michelle were responsible for the death of their three-day old baby—conveniently buttressed by attorney Brindley's inaccurate assertion that the baby was dead on arrival.

Still, the trouble that Brindley, and eventually Robinson, would have to cope with was the fact that Turner's actions had already been described as "active euthanasia, which is illegal" by a highly qualified expert, Dr. Jackson, who had put the matter quite simply: if there was breathing and a heartbeat, there was "by definition" no brain-death.

If Conor wasn't brain-dead, he therefore must have been murdered; and if he'd been murdered, the killer had to be the lovable doctor who'd put his kindly hand over Conor's nose and mouth.

DR. BRUCE

16

ROWAN'S SECRET

If matters were getting dicier for Dr. Turner—in the legal sense, at least—as the end of February neared, they weren't getting much better for another Port Angeles doctor: Bruce Rowan.

Ever since the night of Conor McInnerney's death, Rowan had been experiencing a roil of emotions. It was more than just the death of the baby. Rowan felt a welter of conflict. He began to feel estranged from his colleagues. It seemed to Rowan that people blamed him for Turner's troubles. If he hadn't tried to save the baby to begin with . . . If he'd only done more to try to save the baby . . . If he'd been as medically objective and inured to death as he was supposed to be, like Turner . . . If he hadn't called Dr. Jackson . . . If he hadn't supported Laurie and Vicki in their feelings that something was wrong . . . If he hadn't told Stegbauer what had happened . . .

This was a familiar, indeed, never-ending mind cycle for Rowan. All of his life he'd been tormented by the twin demons of self-doubt and perfectionism; indeed, his fears of failure in almost every sphere of his life drove him to excessive worry that could only be dispelled by driving himself harder and harder to be perfect; he was no good, he had to work harder. Each side of his view of himself fed the other, relentlessly.

His wife Deborah Lu Rowan was the pillar that Bruce clung to in time of stress—which, for him, was most of the time. But by late February of 1998, after eight years together, even Debbie was becoming a cause of stress for Bruce. And the consequences of that were about to become catastrophic.

Bruce and Debbie both came from the small Idaho town of Weiser, located not far from the Oregon border, on the Snake River. The site of a famous annual Fiddle Festival— "I Fiddled Around in Weiser" t-shirts were sold there every year to the crowds who came from all over the country to hear the fiddlers and their bands—Weiser was a bucolic community of about 4600 people, where everyone knew everyone else.

Bruce was the youngest of six children born to Craig and Hortense "Tensie" Rowan. The oldest children were all dynamic students, good athletes and popular in school. Bruce's older brother, Barry, was to graduate from Harvard and go on to become a very successful businessman in Washington State. His sister, Peggy, born about a year and a half before Bruce, suffered from a developmental disability, possibly caused by complications at birth; she would never attain a mental age greater than that of a four-year-old.

Bruce, as the youngest, was doted on by his parents and his older brothers and sisters. But almost from the start it seemed that he felt overshadowed by his older siblings, and terrified that he would never be able to measure up to them.

Most thought of him as a vulnerable, sensitive boy, someone prone to intense self-criticism. Later, Bruce would tell with shame how humiliated he felt in the company of his slightly older, brain-damaged sister. He knew it was wrong to feel embarrassment, Bruce would say, but he couldn't help it; this in turn made him feel bad for *not* being able to help it.

Bruce was gifted—or cursed—with enormous reserves of empathy. He was never able to balance his deep feelings for the pain and suffering of others with the acceptance of the fact that he alone would never be able to eliminate it from the world; for some reason, relieving others' suffering was to become Bruce's special, impossible task.

As the weight of this sunk in as he grew up, Bruce became depressed. He couldn't show this to anyone, however; instead, he told himself to buckle down, work harder, push away the bad thoughts. Still, by the age of 12, Bruce would later recount, he even considered committing suicide with a shotgun. It would end his own torment of wanting to fix everything, and his fear of never measuring up to the task. He planned how to make it look like an accident: he didn't want his family to be embarrassed, and suffer humiliation because of him.

Bruce was thus a person who put a tremendous amount of pressure on himself to succeed; it was the one way he could drive off his demons, at least temporarily. He also developed an act to hide his depressions, so much so that most believed him to be bright, caring, generally happy and well-adjusted.

When people asked him what he wanted to do with his life, Bruce said that he wanted to be a commercial airline pilot—foreshadowing a psychic theme of escape that was to run throughout the rest of his life. Eventually, Bruce would earn a private pilot's license; he also became an accomplished scuba diver. Both skills demanded high technical proficiency—but also reflected his innate desire to remove himself from his immediate situation.

In high school, Bruce played on the football team and was active in student government; in fact, he was elected student body president. His grades put him in the top ten percent of his class. He was popular, genial and widely regarded as tremendously successful. People in Weiser were predicting a great future for him.

Few could have guessed that the thought of suicide kept recurring. Bruce never told anyone about it because he was too embarrassed. After all, he had everything going for him. Why should he, of all people, feel suicidal? It was irrational, unnatural . . . it was *ungrateful* . . .

In 1982, Bruce enrolled at College of Idaho in nearby Caldwell, where he took the chemistry and biology courses necessary to prepare him for medical school. His first year was miserable, because he was so lonely. By the third year, he had developed difficulty in concentrating; on one occasion, he stayed in bed for two days because he simply couldn't summon the energy to function. "That was very disturbing to me," Bruce said later, "because function was always the most important thing to me, to be able to function."

Bruce saw a college counselor. The counselor gave him pamphlets about study habits and time management; Bruce knew that wasn't the problem, but he didn't know what the problem actually was. All he knew was that he was terribly unhappy, and, because of his privileged background, had no justification to be. This made him ashamed of himself.

Somehow, Bruce managed to pull himself together, majoring in zoology, and graduate with high grades in 1986. That was when the University of Washington Medical School in Seattle accepted him as a student. But even at this point, Bruce's life-long ambivalence about being a doctor showed itself.

"I wanted to take a year off," he said later. "I got a lot of material about doing work in various parts of the country, Appalachia and southwestern migrant workers, that sort of thing, but the University of Washington refused deferring my going in."

Because he was from Idaho, the first year of Bruce's medical education, 1986–1987, was taken at the University of Idaho in Moscow. The school work was arduous, and as the year progressed he again began to have difficulty concentrating. He occasionally suffered extended crying jags. To prevent anyone from seeing him, he found private places to study in case the tears erupted unexpectedly. But Bruce didn't seek professional help for his troubles, and tried to keep his depressive feelings to himself.

During the second year of medical school—by now in Seattle, in 1987–1988—Bruce's concentration problems worsened. Seeking to escape himself and his school work, Bruce found himself dressing in dirty old clothes, and going down to the city's Skid Row to hang out with homeless people, where he'd just try to "blend in," as he put it.

"Why did you do that?" Bruce was asked, much later.

"I knew there was a good chance I'd end up there some day," Bruce said. "I thought I probably would."

For some reason, Bruce felt more relaxed posing as one of the homeless. Again, Bruce's empathy for the less fortunate drew him in, and his observations of how the better off treated the homeless—"they were cruel," he would say later—was evidence for his growing perception that the real world was filled with pain and suffering, validated his grandiosity: that he could do something about this, if only he measured up and succeeded in his attempt to become a doctor.

But at some deep level of his mind, Bruce knew the task of helping everyone who needed help was too big, too gargantuan. It wearied him, when he thought of the enormous responsibility. It was better to merge into the non-responsible, those who didn't have the burden. That was why he felt comfortable playing at being a Skid Row bum.

"People there . . . didn't have to function, didn't have to think, especially as far as academics and doing a lot of reading, and I felt normal," he said. It was a relief to pretend, to let go of the demands—but Bruce also felt ashamed. Here he was, with every advantage, a loving family, an opportunity to become fabulously successful, feeling sorry for himself and trying to imagine a life without the pressure to shoulder the burden of taking care of others. It was, he thought, slothful if not sinful.

By the end of his second year in medical school, Bruce was studying for a final exam in psychiatry. He read for the first time about symptoms of chronic depression, and realized that these applied to him.

This was disturbing, Bruce said later. It couldn't be *him*; he had no reason to be depressed. He reacted by going back on the streets; at some point he lost contact with reality, and wound up in the county hospital's emergency room. A psychiatric resident discovered that Bruce was a med student at the University of Washington. The resident placed a call to a psychiatrist at the medical school. Since officially, a psychiatric episode could have been damaging to his future career as a doctor, arrangements were made for Bruce to see the university psychiatrist without a permanent record of his visit to the ER. The psychiatrist attributed Bruce's depression to the stress of being a medical student, and prescribed a regimen of Prozac, at that time considered the most effective chemical anti-depressant available.

Somehow, despite the mental turmoil, Bruce managed to pass all of his classes at the university; that summer, as he had during most of his college years, Bruce returned to Alaska to work on a commercial fishing boat.

Almost immediately, Bruce began to feel better.

"It was a big relief to get up there and back to some place where I could just work," Bruce said. "I could just work and not have to think about or worry about anything."

Bruce was dreading having to return to medical school in the fall, when all the third-year students were scheduled to begin medical "clerkships," working with actual doctors and real patients; he wrote the medical school, asking for a leave of absence, and saying that he had suffered "a major depressive episode" the previous semester.

"Last spring," Bruce wrote the school, "I made a commitment to myself to do well academically at any cost to my personal growth. I found this approach leads to depression, and the diminution of one's person. In a way, medical school and post-graduate training do the same thing over a large period of time. Students and physicians spend such a large portion of their lives thinking in medical terms and paradigms that part of their humanity dies. They become less spontaneous in thought and conversation as their minds 'forget' how to grow in their own non-medical direction. I realize that these changes are subtle and take place over long periods of time.

"I particularly noticed these changes in other people after I returned from commercial fishing in Alaska this summer. The fishermen in general are much less 'appropriate' in their conversation. They tend to speak their minds without hiding behind over-educated verbiage. Their feelings tend to come out unedited, raw, and *genuine*. Many medical students and doctors lose site [sic] of their gut feelings and emotions by over-intellectualizing them to traditional, appropriate paradigms.

"I would like to expand so that I can get closer in thought to the people I will eventually be treating. I want to become a doctor while nurturing my understanding of life from their point of view, not sacrificing it to become more intellectual and distant.

"This fall I plan on going king crab fishing in the Bering Sea, returning in late October, finishing all outstanding work before *enthusiastically* starting clerkships in winter."

Eventually, the leave was approved. Bruce stayed in Alaska throughout the fall of 1988, and was re-admitted to medical school in the spring of 1989.

But the problems didn't go away.

17

DEPENDING ON DEBBIE

By the winter of 1990, Bruce was back in medical school, doing his clerkships. In January, he began a clerkship in pediatrics—Turner's specialty—in Spokane. While there, he had contact with an old high school friend, Deborah Lu Fields, who was about three months younger than he was.

He'd known Debbie, a recent Santa Clara University graduate, since they were in high school together, in Weiser. Debbie was naturally ebullient, if a bit feisty; in many ways she was the opposite of Bruce's lugubrious inner self. The upside of Debbie attracted Bruce; the downside of Bruce attracted Debbie, although for vastly different reasons.

Debbie was born in April of 1964, the daughter of Richard Fields, a lawyer, and his wife Shirley; the Fieldses, in addition to Debbie, had two other daughters and a son. In a small town like Weiser, the Rowans and the Fieldses had of course known one another for years.

As his January pediatric rotation in Spokane commenced, Bruce had considerable opportunity to get together with Debbie, who had just returned from a year in Japan. Apart from the attraction of opposite personality types, Bruce and Debbie had other things in common besides

Weiser: they both wanted to travel and see the world. Bruce had the idea that after he finished medical school and his residency, he and Debbie might go to third-world countries as medical professionals; Bruce's abiding concern for helping people had not abated, especially for the underdog.

In early February of 1990, Bruce asked Debbie to move in with him when he returned to Seattle. This she did on February 10. At first there were a few difficulties: because she was the same age, and had known him a long time, Debbie wasn't averse to confronting Bruce; Bruce was fairly rigid about doing things his way. They put their differences down to the normal adjustment period for any newly joined couple.

About five weeks after moving in, just before St. Patrick's Day, Debbie went to California for three days to attend a friend's wedding; it appears that Bruce wasn't happy about Debbie's decision to go somewhere without him, but he was in the middle of his psychiatric rotation.

As usual with Bruce, the topic of mental illness made him feel extremely uncomfortable; he preferred the sort of certainty that came with the harder sciences. Bruce felt he was botching the rotation, and began to feel depressed; Debbie's leaving to be with her California friends only exacerbated his bad mood. He'd already become dependent to some degree on Debbie to buck him up when he felt down.

"I felt like I was doing horribly," he said later. "I felt like I was failing miserably . . . I obviously didn't know anything about psychiatry, and with the patients I could see them very well and see how they could end up there, because the majority of them were normal people from everyday life."

Bruce later said he was surprised to discover that even professional people "like lawyers and engineers and secretaries" could have psychiatric problems. He had thought it was only people like the homeless who suffered from mental illness.

Bruce approached his resident supervisor for the rotation

and apologized for being inept. The resident said he was amazed. As far as he could see, Bruce had been doing just fine; in fact, Bruce was one of the better students in the rotation.

This only made Bruce feel as though psychiatry was a lot of mumbo-jumbo, where the ability to spout complicated words passed for treatment while the real problems lay unaddressed.

If the resident couldn't see that Bruce was faking it, would there ever be any way to deal with the black demon inside of himself who kept telling him life wasn't worth living?

After Debbie left for California, Bruce went to University Hospital and completed all his work, updating his patients' charts for the weekend. His thinking grew increasingly disordered.

As Debbie was flying south, Bruce went to a supermarket and bought "many, many boxes" of Unisom, an over-the-counter sleep inducer. Then he drove his car to an isolated spot under a bridge near the university and began taking the pills. He wanted to make sure to commit suicide on the weekend so he would have time to get back to work on Monday.

"It seems so silly now," Bruce recalled. "I wanted to do it on a weekend so I wouldn't miss work. And Debbie was going to California for a three-day weekend."

On the surface, the idea of committing suicide on a three-day weekend so he wouldn't miss work on Monday can be seen as indicative of the confused thinking of a depressive; taken another way, it could indicate that Bruce wasn't lethally serious about killing himself, that he only wanted attention—attention he wasn't getting, from Debbie, flying off to join her old college friends, or from the psychiatric resident, who'd said he was doing just fine, even though he was miserable.

Bruce reclined his car seat and let the Unisom take over. "But things started happening that were very odd," he said. "I started feeling very strange and seeing things that I wasn't sure existed."

Bruce was asked what he saw.

"Just bizarre things, like my fingers getting real long, and all my skin coming off." The hallucinations panicked Bruce. "I was terrified. I made my way back up to [student health services] . . . it seemed like the place to go."

Why, Bruce was asked, if he wanted to kill himself, had he driven for help?

"I was scared," he said. "I didn't want to have major brain damage. I didn't want to mess up a suicide, jump off something, or do something else and survive it, then be really overdosed and brain-damaged, and physically damaged as well."

At the health center, doctors pumped his stomach, and sent him to the county hospital, where he was placed in restraints on a floor where he wouldn't be seen by any of his fellow medical students. The following day he agreed to commit himself for observation for five days, and was transferred to a private Seattle hospital.

At the private hospital, asked why he had tried to kill himself, Bruce said he had no idea. At one point during his five-day stay, Bruce was put in a group therapy session.

"I remember one time we were having a group session," he said, "and everyone was talking about what was wrong, what their plans were, and I got a little bit angry, because they had completely missed the point. They had just completely, from my point of view, the whole system, missed the point."

And what was the point? Bruce was asked.

"I didn't want to live, so . . . what was the point of talking about anything else, when you don't want to live?"

Why did Bruce not want to live?

"I don't know. Everything was going well. I was, surprisingly, doing well in psychiatry rotation, and the outlook for the future was excellent, especially with Debbie. We had gotten together and I had given her a hard time. We gave each other a hard time a bit, just testing a lot of times, and I told her that over the 10 years I'd known her before that I always thought there was a good chance to get married some day, and she said she wasn't so sure."

Now, after Bruce's suicide attempt, Debbie returned from California to find him in the psychiatric ward.

How did Debbie react to the news that he'd tried to kill himself?

"She was extremely supportive," Bruce said.

Did he still want to kill himself?

"At that point in time it was tough," Bruce said, "but Debbie made it very clear to me how hard it would have been for her if I had died. How devastating it would have been."

Now Bruce had proof of Debbie's commitment to him, as well as an interlocking dependency mechanism: if he couldn't kill himself without devastating Debbie, then Debbie couldn't leave him without the possibility that Bruce would thereafter succeed in killing himself, which would devastate Debbie. It was a neat, deadly little package.

18

SEEING THE WORLD

Following his suicide attempt, Bruce again withdrew from medical school, and after a few months in Seattle, returned to Alaska to go fishing. Debbie came with him—part companion, part keeper, part wife-in-waiting.

With his experience, Bruce got a job on a fishing boat quite easily, but there was no work for Debbie. In six weeks, Bruce's share of the take from the sea was about $32,000; Debbie drove a taxi.

After the fishing was over, Bruce and Debbie began a trip around the world.

"How did you and Debbie get along on that trip?" Bruce was asked, much later.

"Well, it was hard," he said. "It was hard. It was the first couple of months we . . . there's a lot of things to work out in a relationship when you're literally not more than ten feet from each other for literally every day. And we had some disagreements about how to do things. I remember one time specifically in Moscow, in the Soviet Union then, it was very expensive to be there, so we couldn't spend very much time there, and it was my idea to get up at six in the morning and go and do everything we can and go to bed at 11 at night.

"And after about one day of that she knew that wasn't what she wanted to do, and we always joked after that that we had our own cold war in Moscow. So we looked back on it fondly, because that was a turning point in our relationship . . . when she said, 'I think I want to go home . . . I think I want to go home. And I think I want to leave you here.' "

Here it was again: the abandonment–suicide padlock.

"I don't know why we worked it out," Bruce said later, using rather curious language, "why" instead of "how." "But we worked it out, and after a couple of more months we were just doing very well."

The trip took Bruce and Debbie from Finland to the Soviet Union, Poland, Yugoslavia, Bosnia, Greece, Turkey, Egypt, Kenya, Uganda and Pakistan; India, Nepal, southeast Asia, Indonesia, Singapore, Hong Kong, China, Korea and Japan. Somewhere along the road, Debbie contracted dysentery. By the time they got back to the United States she'd lost about fifty pounds, and weighed a fairly svelte 145. She was also sick of being sick.

For Bruce, though, the trip was a sort of Cook's Tour of all the third-world locales he imagined himself working in as a heroic, self-sacrificing physician on the order of Dr. Schweitzer, or Tom Dooley.

Before he could become a have-doctor-bag, will-travel saint, though, Bruce had to finish the rest of medical school.

Rather surprisingly, given his psychological history, the university agreed to re-admit him for the last big push. Later, questions would be raised as to whether this was the wisest decision, for the school or, certainly, for Bruce. But as even Bruce admitted later, it's almost impossible to flunk out of medical school, in part because of the expensive training and education that have so far been invested in the student.

Indeed, the emphasis on training would-be doctors has little to do with their psychological fitness for the job, and everything to do with their capacity to measure (accurately) such technical yardsticks as body temperature, blood chemistry, reaction to a variety of traumas and the like; all hard, objective science, testable and quantifiable; none of which has very much to do with whether a person is emotionally prepared to deal with matters of life and death; science is one thing, living and dying, another matter altogether.

Debbie and Bruce married in November, 1991, in Boise, Idaho; somehow, with Debbie's support and the help of the anti-depressants, Bruce managed to make it to the end of medical school without further psychological mishap. In the spring of the next year, 1992, Bruce accepted an internship-residency position in family practice medicine in Pennsylvania.

In some ways, the four years that Bruce and Debbie spent in Pennsylvania were the best years of their lives together. The academic grind was over, and no one was demanding that Bruce prove his intellect; instead the issue was Bruce's ability to discern his patients' real-life problems. In this, Bruce's unchallenged technical skills, coupled with his empathic talent—or curse—made him one of the best physicians-in-training ever to have come to Pennsylvania.

"Moving to Pennsylvania, when I became an intern, I gained a lot of confidence," Bruce said, "and found that medicine was just a lot of things. It was a lot of fun, and it was a lot of hardship, and it became a passion. It became a passion."

Debbie initially had a hard time finding work; eventually she enrolled in a master's degree program in social work at the University of Pennsylvania.

Despite the reward of actually working as a doctor, instead of being told how to be one, Bruce continued to have depression; he changed his anti-depressant drug, and began prescribing for himself, a practice he continued to follow for years afterward.

One side effect of chronic depression is a low sperm count, and Bruce's was low. As a result, he and Debbie tried to adopt a child. After three failures, Bruce and Debbie were granted custody of an infant girl in November of 1995. They named her Annika.

After completing his residency in 1995, Bruce elected to stay on at the Pennsylvania hospital as an emergency room physician while Debbie completed her course work at the university. Bruce found the emergency room environment well-suited to his personality, because of its varied challenges and its often-hectic pace. There was little time for brooding.

Besides, Bruce realized that, as a qualified emergency room specialist, he would have no difficulty in finding a job. That meant, without having to be responsible for regular, long-term patients, Bruce and Debbie would have the opportunity to travel the world, as he had long desired.

Somehow, Bruce came to believe that Debbie shared his vision of a life as a nomadic medical missionary.

But it doesn't appear that Debbie was as entirely onboard with this plan as Bruce had presumed.

In early 1996, as Debbie neared the end of her university program, she and Bruce decided to return to the west coast with their baby daughter. He contacted a Seattle-area employment agency that specialized in placing medical personnel, and was put in touch with a partnership providing ER physicians to hospitals on the Olympic Peninsula—a partnership that included a physician who had served as dean of the University of Washington's medical school when Rowan was a student there.

Bruce moved to Port Angeles in mid-1996, Debbie and Annika following a few months later. At first, they rented a house on Port Angeles' west side, but soon began looking for a house to buy.

Before the first of the year, they had found one: a fairly modern split-level on Yellow Rock Lane, in the foothills above Port Angeles. From the front, the house looked as if it had one story. A wooden deck ran around the side to the rear. A second, lower level containing a guest bedroom and other rooms extended to the rear as the slope of the land ran downhill. The dwelling was surrounded by approximately five acres of pasture. Bruce and Debbie paid $125,000 down, and took a mortgage of $100,000; they also began extensive renovations. As a pet for Annika, they adopted a lamb named Wooly, who played in the pasture.

By the middle of 1997, the Rowans were settling into their new existence. Bruce was earning a substantial sum as an emergency room doctor at Olympic Memorial Hospital and another facility in Port Townsend. He worked ten twelve-hour shifts a month in the ER, mostly at night. The hours required sleeping during the day, and to cope with the abnormal conditions, Bruce began taking a sleep-inducing drug.

The management of the household was largely left to Debbie, who was responsible for the cooking and cleaning as Bruce slept off his nocturnal hours. Debbie began making friends in the Port Angeles community; she helped found a nursery co-op involving other young parents, with the assistance of the area's community college.

So far, so good. But as 1997 turned into 1998, cracks began to form in the facade of Bruce and Debbie's relationship. First, Debbie wanted to buy a house that was far more expensive than Bruce had in mind, or so police came later to believe; next, Debbie wanted to turn their home into a foster care facility for troubled youth, because she had had experience in that field when they were in Pennsylvania.

Bruce refused to consider the foster care idea; it would, he told Debbie, only make him a target for some teenager who might bring false accusations of molestation, or other such problems. Debbie was disappointed. Eventually she convinced Bruce to agree to a second adoption. She filled out the papers required by the adoption agency in the fall of 1997, but Bruce was reluctant to sign them.

Later, psychiatrists and others were to point to these facts as evidence of a conflict between Bruce and Debbie that was slowly gathering strength. While Debbie was doing what mothers do—nesting, putting down roots, preparing to raise a family—Bruce was feeling increasingly tied down. For Bruce the point of life was to travel, to heroically do for others in less fortunate circumstances; these steady accretions of property, friends, children and community connections threatened to preclude escape.

Even more significantly, some thought, where before Debbie had done for Bruce—taking care of him, bucking him up, making him the center of her existence—now Debbie's major focus was on Annika. That, some later said, became a threat to Bruce. It was, in a way, as if Debbie was no longer willing to place Bruce first in her life, to give him the primacy that had allowed him to cope with his chronic depression for so many years.

Then came the death of Conor McInnerney, and all of the attendant, roiling emotions that assaulted Bruce in the aftermath.

Brain damage—flash on his older sister, and the pain his family endured. Self-doubt—was he too emotionally mushy to be a physician? Disapproval—did others in the hospital disapprove of his actions in trying to save the baby? Did they think less of him because he'd reported what had happened? Should he have done more?

In the week or so after Conor McInnerney's death, the Rowans applied for a $500,000 life insurance policy on Debbie. Bruce later said the idea about the insurance had been in the works for some time, in part because of the adoption plan he and Debbie had agreed to for Annika; if something happened to Debbie—Bruce had his own $1.25 million policy—then the baby would be adequately cared for. In the event of their deaths, the adoption plan called for Debbie's sister and brother-in-law in Colorado to take over the raising of Annika.

Then an event occurred which would ultimately have the effect of upsetting the delicate balance between Bruce and Debbie.

19

BREAK A LEG

-

On January 22 or 23, even as Gallagher and Kovatch of the Port Angeles Police were starting their investigation of the Turner–McInnerney controversy, the lamb, Wooly, wandered away from the Rowan property. Debbie gave chase.

Jumping over a fence, Debbie landed awkwardly, injuring her ankle. Later it was discovered that she had torn her left Achilles tendon.

It appears, however, that the severity of the injury wasn't clear to either Bruce or Debbie immediately after it occurred. A few days after the accident, the family went to a ski resort east of Seattle. While it's doubtful that Debbie skied, Bruce took Annika on his shoulders and schussed down the mountain.

By Friday, February 20—the day Gallagher and the Port Angeles Police had delivered their report on Dr. Turner's role in the death of Conor McInnerney to prosecutor David Bruneau—it was clear that Debbie's injury was no sprained ankle. Bruce took her to an OMH doctor, who guessed that Debbie had a torn Achilles tendon. If the tendon was completely torn, Debbie might need a graft; in that case, the doctor said, he'd have to remove a tendon from her hamstring area, and transplant it to the Achilles. It wouldn't be possible to know until he operated, the doctor added.

Surgery on Debbie's Achilles was scheduled for the following Monday, February 23—Bruce's birthday. As it happened, Bruce was off-shift for the better part of a week; that would allow him to take care of Debbie while she recovered from the operation.

Bruce took Debbie to the hospital on February 23. The doctor had explained to Bruce exactly what he was going to do and Bruce indicated that he understood. Late that afternoon, Debbie underwent surgery, while Bruce waited at the hospital; he kissed Debbie before she went in, and then went to the records section of the hospital.

"I went to medical records and tried to catch up on my charts," Bruce said later, "but I had a hard time."

"So, you weren't the doctor anymore, you were her husband?" Bruce was asked.

"Right," he said, "I was a nervous wreck . . . I was a lot more nervous than I thought I would be."

Bruce said he was concerned that something might go wrong during the anaesthesia process of the operation—that somehow, Debbie might die.

"All kinds of bad things happen," he said later.

But Debbie survived the operation, and was wheeled into the recovery room. While she was still coming out of the anaesthesia, Bruce left the hospital and went home.

Later, Bruce was hazy on what he did, after learning that Debbie had come through the surgery with no ill effects; he recalled phoning various members of the Rowan and Fields families to let them know that Debbie was all right; he remembered taking Annika to see Debbie, either that night or the following day. But much of the rest of what happened in the immediate aftermath of Debbie's surgery was to become lost in the mists of Bruce's mind.

What was clear was that Debbie would be incapable of walking for some time. The surgeon fitted her with a cast that required her to keep weight off her foot; on the way home from the hospital the following day, Bruce stopped at a medical supply emporium and procured a pair of crutches for Debbie.

This inability to walk, in turn, put pressure on Bruce: instead of Debbie doing the shopping, the cooking, the cleaning, now it would all be up to him. Instead of Debbie taking care of Bruce, Bruce would have to take care of Debbie.

By Sunday, March 1, 1998, Debbie was still recovering from her surgery. Bruce took Annika shopping. They bought a number of plastic garbage bags, a miniature wooden baseball bat, an outdoor vacuum cleaner, and some junk food. That evening, he and Debbie had planned to see the movie *Titanic* at a nearby mall. Bruce arranged for a babysitter to stay with Annika, and around 4:30 or so, he drove Debbie, with her crutches, to the theater some 10 minutes away.

Bruce thought the movie was awful, filled with all sorts of posturing and shallow silliness; Debbie liked it, especially the romantic sentiments expressed by the main characters. For all its technical panache, there was only one scene in the movie that stood out in Bruce's brain: when the *Titanic*'s deck officer, overwhelmed by a rush for the lifeboats, pulled out a pistol and shot a man who was panicking to board one of the boats; then as Bruce watched, fascinated, the deck officer shot himself.

"What went through your head when you saw that scene?" Bruce was asked, later.

"Just the relief," Bruce said. "The tremendous relief of being dead before . . . just before he even hit the ground. It was like a pheasant. You shoot and it just crumples and it's dead instantly. That was graphic for me."

The thought of the deck officer killing himself and ending all of the pain and distress dwelled in Bruce's mind for the rest of the evening, he said later. It haunted his thoughts, kept recurring in the internal cinema of his mind.

After the movie, Bruce and Debbie returned to their home, chatted for a while with the babysitter and her sister, made and took a few phone calls—one from Debbie's sister in Lacey, Washington—and turned in about 10 or 10:30 p.m.

Neither could get to sleep, in part because of all the junk food both had eaten at the theater—they'd had no dinner—and because Annika was up and wanted attention. At some point Annika was in Bruce and Debbie's bed, and Debbie turned on a television movie. At another point, Annika was in her crib and Debbie was dozing. Or perhaps not; maybe she was going to the store. Bruce would never be clear about what really happened. But even he would admit, later, that it was horrific.

MINDSNAP

20

YELLOW ROCK LANE

About half past midnight on Monday, March 2, a young man named Jefferson Davis—the son of a Clallam County deputy sheriff—was heading south on the ridge-line hill of Mount Pleasant Road toward the Olympics. About 15 minutes in, surrounded by the small, pastured estates that abound in the neighborhood, Davis saw a late-model Subaru Legacy station wagon sprawled sideways across the roadside drainage ditch, lights on and engine running. It appeared to Davis that the car had somehow run off the road and crashed.

Davis stopped his own car to see what the trouble was. Inside he saw a woman lying across the front seat. In the back he saw a child's safety seat that had been turned over. His first thought was that a baby might still be in the seat.

Davis opened the rear door of the Legacy and removed the baby carrier; it was empty. He looked back at the woman sprawled across the front, and saw two ugly, bloody gashes in her forehead. Blood was visible on the driver's headrest. It seemed to Davis that the woman was dead. He got back into his car and called in what looked to be a fatal accident.

Clallam County Deputy Stacey Sampson picked up the

call. She drove to the scene on Mount Pleasant Road. The Subaru was athwart the drainage ditch; it had apparently piled into a heavy fence post after its right front wheel had run off the road into the ditch, causing it to flip violently to the right.

When Sampson looked into the car, she saw what Davis had seen: the apparently dead body of a young woman lying sprawled across the seats, with blood across the headrest; the car's airbag had deployed. The woman had a cast on her leg. Sampson called in, and was soon joined by another patrol deputy, Derrell Spidell.

According to the department's protocol, Spidell and Sampson now called the department's traffic investigator; whenever a vehicular fatality occurred in the sheriff's territory, that was standard operating procedure. But even as they waited for traffic investigator Dave Ellefson to arrive, both Spidell and Sampson knew that they weren't looking at an ordinary traffic accident—for while the windshield of the car was intact, there were the two large cuts on the forehead of the dead woman. On the floor of the car was a wallet containing the identification of Bruce Rowan, along with an initially unrecognizable metallic object and a plastic child's watering pail.

Spidell and Sampson weren't pathologists, but it wasn't difficult for them to discern that there was something way off about this car wreck. The two grievous cuts in the victim's forehead were bad enough to reveal two open flaps of skin in slight arcs in two different places; in addition, a number of teeth appeared to be broken. Blood was everywhere. But none of the wounds made sense.

If the windshield wasn't broken in the wreck, where had the cuts come from? These wounds had no resemblance to any accidental violence that either Spidell or Sampson had ever seen before. Instead, they looked as if they'd been intentionally inflicted. It was the only way to account for them, given the relatively undamaged condition of the Legend.

But this would have to be Ellefson's call, not theirs.

Both waited for almost half an hour for Ellefson's arrival. When he got there, he agreed with Sampson and Spidell that it was impossible for the woman to have died in such a comparatively inconsequential wreck; for one thing, Ellefson had noticed that there was blood inside the car's door jamb, which seemed to indicate that the woman had been injured *before* the wreck.

A bit after 2 a.m., Ellefson put a call into the dispatcher. It looked, he said, as though they had a case of homicide on Mount Pleasant Road. Would the dispatcher please notify the on-call homicide detective to come to the scene? The dispatcher put a call out for Detective Chuck Fuchser. Soon Fuchser was on his way to the wreck to see for himself.

Meanwhile, Spidell and Sampson had run the Legend's license plate through the state's vehicle licensing computer. They discovered that the car was registered to Bruce Rowan, whom they both knew from many prior interactions in the ER, at 241 Yellow Rock Lane—a residence less than 200 yards away from the scene of the crash. Spidell and Sampson drove there following Ellefson's inspection.

Sampson saw something in the driveway in front of the garage. It was a pair of crutches. Sampson retrieved a camera from the patrol car and snapped a photograph. The two deputies then approached the front door of the house, and knocked.

Dr. Bruce appeared to have been waiting for them.

The whole situation seemed a little squirrely to Spidell and Sampson both; they had a woman apparently dead from severe, bloody head injuries less than 200 yards from home, in a car that showed no evidence of broken windshield glass; a pair of crutches apparently abandoned in the driveway; and a husband who seemed preternaturally calm about the whereabouts of his wife, even though it was now nearly 2:15 a.m.

Did Bruce know where Deborah was? Spidell asked.

Bruce said he wasn't sure, but that around midnight

she'd left to go to the supermarket to pick up some things.

Now Spidell told Rowan that it appeared there had been a car wreck, and that Deborah was dead. Bruce fell to his knees, as if staggered by this news. Spidell helped him into a chair. But then it appeared that Bruce took himself in hand and grew composed. Spidell explained that Debbie had crashed only a short distance away from the house. They'd found Bruce's wallet in the car, Spidell added.

We just have a few questions right now, Spidell told Bruce. Did he have any idea of what had happened?

Bruce covered his forehead with his hand again, and sighed. He guessed that she might have lost control of the car. He explained that since her Achilles operation in late February, Debbie had been unable to drive, because of the cast. She'd decided to try to do it for the first time that night, he said, because they were running low on food supplies and other staples. Perhaps the cast had interfered with her control of the car; or, since sometimes one of the neighborhood dogs liked to drop rocks onto the driver's-side floor of the car, maybe a stone had gotten wedged under the pedals, and had thus interfered with Debbie's driving.

To Spidell and Sampson, this seemed almost surreal— Rowan giving these explanations for what might have befallen his wife, almost as if he were offering a medical diagnosis. And the story about the dog? It was, on its face, unbelievable.

Spidell asked Rowan about the crutches. Rowan shrugged and said nothing.

Whoa! Spidell thought. This was getting really strange. A barely ambulatory woman decides at midnight to drive to the supermarket, but somehow leaves her crutches, without which she can't walk, then crashes her car less than 200 yards from home, and sustains injuries that can't be accounted for by the accident? It wasn't a very likely story.

Spidell was instantly suspicious of Bruce, and so was Sampson, although neither gave voice to their thoughts in front of him.

Instead, Spidell decided to go back to the car wreck to

report his contact with Bruce to the homicide detective when he arrived. He and Sampson left, telling Rowan that someone would be back to talk to him very soon.

At about 2:45 Fuchser made it to the scene of the crash and inspected the wreck, while hearing Spidell and Sampson tell of their encounter with Bruce. Just before 3 a.m., Fuchser called his superior, Detective Sergeant Steve Snover—Gallagher's equivalent as the head of the county's detective bureau—and told him that he had a probable case of murder on Mount Pleasant Road.

Snover in turn notified DeFrang, who lived not far from the Rowan house. By 3:30 in the morning, both Snover and DeFrang had arrived at the scene, and it was decided that Fuchser would go up to the Rowan house and talk to Bruce, accompanied by Spidell.

This time, Spidell and Fuchser noticed that the crutches had been removed from the driveway.

Bruce greeted both deputies at the front door, and invited them in. After a few minutes' discussion, Fuchser produced a tape recorder and began an interview. Bruce was very calm and cooperative. He seemed absolutely flat, emotionally.

After running through some preliminaries, such as the address of the house and who lived in it, Fuchser began to take Bruce through the previous night's events.

"Now you say there were no injuries to your wife, except for her leg?" Fuchser asked. "What happened to her leg?"

"She injured it about six weeks ago," Bruce said, "when she jumped over a fence."

"And that was here on the property?"

"Yeah."

"What kind of an injury was it?"

"She ended up having surgery a week ago," Bruce added.

"Okay, what was the surgery to repair?"

"Achilles tendon rupture."

"Okay, and what were her limitations due to the injury and the surgery?"

"Well," Bruce said, "she was on crutches, and I think that's pretty much her main limitation. She has a real hard time driving around. Was the first time she had driven, tonight."

"I see."

"She was real nervous about driving."

"She's been on crutches for how long?" Fuchser asked.

"For a week."

Fuchser was leading Rowan carefully, trying to give him the idea that the police believed the wreck really was an accident; if Bruce was involved in the apparent murder, he might grow careless and offer false embroidering details to try and lead the police to believe that it was a simple wreck.

Was Debbie taking any medication?

No, said Bruce.

Did she drink?

Some, socially, but not in the last few days, Bruce said. "Only lots of soda pop at the movies tonight."

"Okay," Fuchser said. "You went to the movies tonight. What movie was that?"

"It was *Titanic*."

After some additional discussion about Bruce and Debbie's movements and arrangements for babysitters for Annika, Fuchser began trying to focus in on the critical questions.

"Okay, was there any kind of conflict between you and your wife, or anything like that?"

"Not at all, not at all."

"Okay."

"Any conflict at all," Bruce said.

After leaving the theater about 8:30, he and Debbie had spent about an hour with the babysitters, Bruce said.

"Okay. And how was your wife . . . during that hour you spent with them after the movie?"

"She was fine," Bruce said. "She seemed fine. No problems, just that we had both eaten a lot of . . . actually felt kind of ill. We'd eaten a lot of popcorn and candy. We didn't eat any dinner. We drank a lot of soda pop and it kind of made us real nauseated. She wasn't throwing up or anything."

Again, it was as if Bruce was diagnosing a medical problem in the ER, listing symptoms.

After the sitters left, Bruce continued, both he and Debbie were tired and decided to go to bed.

"We lay in bed for a while," Bruce went on, "and then our daughter wanted to get up . . . so she [Debbie] got up and tried to watch a movie for a little while and [so did] our daughter, Annika, for a little while."

"Okay."

"And then Debbie said she was having a hard time sleeping, [that] she drank too much soda pop."

"How much soda pop would you say she drank?"

"Oh, she drank one of those great big, like, huge things," Bruce said.

"Okay, continue on then. What else happened after that?"

"About midnight or so she came in and said that she couldn't sleep and she was going to get up for a while, she might even go to the store."

"Okay, so you had gone to bed, then?"

"Well, we had gone to bed."

"What time did you go to bed?"

"Oh, I don't know, ten o'clock or so, ten thirty, it was kind of a long process . . . with the girl. She was up watching a movie for a little while, and then she went back to bed and . . ."

"Did she ever fall asleep?"

"Maybe she did briefly."

"Okay."

"Briefly, and I was just kind of up and down, too, because I had a lot of soda pop as well."

"Okay, so your wife got up then about midnight?"

"Roughly."

"Okay."

"About midnight, she's said that she was there for a while and might even consider going to the grocery store, 'cause our refrigerator was pretty bare. I've been doing the cooking for the last week and . . . the cooking hasn't been, hasn't been very good. I went to the store a couple of days ago and I didn't stock very well, so—"

"I see," Fuchser said.

"—she wanted to go to the store at some point and . . ." Fuchser changed gears.

"Now, you work at the hospital, is that—"

"Right, right, yeah, yeah."

"What does your work amount to?" Fuchser asked, although he and Spidell well knew.

"It's in the ER," Bruce said. "I've seen you down there, I've met you there before."

Fuchser returned to Debbie's midnight rising.

"At midnight, when your wife got up?"

"Yeah."

"Did she say anything about how she felt?"

"Just that she was anxious and couldn't sleep and was jittery from all the caffeine," Bruce said. "And she wanted to go to the store, she hadn't driven yet. She was real nervous about driving with her cast on, but I'll be working on Wednesday, so she wanted to make sure she could do it at some point. And so she thought this would be a good opportunity for her to take some time and Safeway being open 24 hours, and she thought they had those scooter things that you can ride around on better than using her crutches."

This was significant. Where early in the interview Bruce had said Debbie "might even go to the [grocery] store," by this point it was becoming increasingly specific—down to Debbie's desire to test her driving, to go to the Safeway, and even to use the motorized cart to go shopping. This was how an interrogator worked: getting the subject to elaborate, to provide more and more detail until the improbabilities or lies began to come out. All of this was material that could be checked later.

"So what did you do when she got out of bed?" Fuchser asked.

"I don't know," Bruce said. "I kind of dozed and I don't know if she left right away, or she might have done a few things around the house. Try to clean up a bit even though it's hard for her to get around, you know, on crutches, so . . ."

"So you stayed in bed, then?"

"Yeah."

"Now, were you sound asleep at that point, or were you awake, or were you . . ."

"No, I was kind of up and down, up and down," Bruce said.

21

NO IDEA

"Tell me whatever you can remember from the point that she got up," Fuchser now prompted.

"Boy," said Bruce, "she left shortly thereafter, I think she probably left around twelve, or some time shortly thereafter. I don't know exactly what time she might have left. But then, I don't know, I woke up, maybe one or so, and I figured she ought to be back, but I wasn't sure what time she left, so . . .

"Then I started getting more worried and with her driving . . . considered calling the emergency department and making sure they hadn't seen her down there or something, and . . . then I just sort of sat and waited for a while longer. And then your officer came and told me she was deceased."

Deceased? Bruce's use of this word set all of Fuchser's alarms ringing. What sort of man would use such a formal, distancing word when talking about the death of his wife?

To Fuchser, this was subtle evidence that Bruce had to know much more about Debbie's "accident" than he was admitting.

"Can I help you any more?" Bruce asked.

Fuchser was so taken aback by Bruce's demeanor that he began to stutter.

"Betw . . . Betw . . . Between the time that she got out of bed and the time that the officer came to the door, how much time would you say, during that time where, you know, you [were] in a conscious state?"

"Oh, I don't know," Bruce said. "I was just kind of in and out of bed, maybe, and slept half the time, or something like that."

"Did you hear any noises?"

"No, no, no."

"Nothing that would make you think you had an intruder here or anything like that?"

"No, not that I'm aware of. I was just kind of in and out, up and down, but we have a lot of noise with dogs, and they bark and jump, or they jump on the deck."

"Did you hear the dogs barking during that time, at all?"

"I heard a couple of barks but nothing, nothing . . ."

"Nothing that would make you think anything was drastically wrong?"

"No, not anything, not anything unusual."

"Okay. Have you ever had any problems around here with prowlers or anything like that?"

Not really, Bruce said.

"Is there anybody that might , . . come to the house here at night that . . . would particularly alarm your wife or the dogs?" Fuchser asked.

"Oh, boy," Bruce said, "probably not. The dogs don't really alarm, they don't necessarily bark when people come up. They're just, they're kind of mellow dogs that way. I think I wouldn't expect to see anybody that late. I mean, we've had people . . . friends, come up from Seattle and sort of camp out on our lawn in the middle of the night. I'm sure our dogs wouldn't even lift a paw."

"Did your dogs bark when I came and rang the doorbell?"

"I don't recall, probably not."

Spidell now asked whether the doorbell had woken Bruce on his first visit earlier that morning, about 2:20 a.m.

"I was awake when you came," Bruce said.

"Does your wife have any enemies?" Fuchser asked.

Bruce mumbled something that was inaudible. Then— "[Did] somebody kill her, or something like that?"

"All that we're able to see out there on the road right now, we think that's a possibility," Fuchser told Bruce.

"No," Bruce said, "she's very well-liked and, you know, with her Pre-Three [school co-op] she's got a lot of friends that way and . . ."

"Nobody that there's ever been serious problems with?"

"Not that I'm aware of," Bruce said. "I know she had done this . . . youth thing, youth court thing, where they go and get kind of a second chance for first offender youth."

"Did she ever mention any problems between herself and anybody that she worked with then?"

"No," Bruce said. "She just went once and observed, but she said it was kind of odd how they could just put the person's last name in the paper. She felt it was kind of odd they would give those folks [news media] that much access . . ."

Fuchser was nearly done.

"Now," he said, "we're going to have to go through a documentation process, an evidence-gathering process that, until we can find out what happened for sure with this thing, [there's] a great deal of stuff that we need to do. And I hope that you understand that, that's just that we're going to try our best to find out what happened to your wife. During that process, do you have any problems if we look through the house, or around the yard, or anything like that?"

Fuchser wanted Bruce to sign a document giving the Sheriff's Department permission to search the house and property.

"Oh," Bruce said.

"In the event," Fuchser added, "that there was an intruder or something like that, that maybe you slept through or . . ."

"Huh," Bruce said, "I don't know, I felt kind of, umm, odd . . . uh, no, it's fine with me, as far as I'm concerned."

"Okay," Fuchser said.

Spidell was already considering what to do with the child in case evidence was found that pointed to Bruce's involvement in Debbie's murder. Or—had something happened to the baby as well as Debbie? He asked Bruce if Annika was asleep in the house.

"Yes," Bruce said, indicating that Annika was asleep.

"Is [she] upstairs?" Spidell asked.

"Upstairs," Bruce confirmed.

"If there was somebody who meant to do your wife harm," Fuchser asked, "do you have any idea who that might be?"

"No," Bruce said, "no, I don't."

After a brief discussion about the keys to the Legacy— the deputies wanted to make sure that no one but Bruce and Debbie were likely to have had access to the car keys— Fuchser gingerly tried to explain the problem the deputies had with Debbie's death scene.

"This is an unusual situation," he said, "and there isn't a one of us who has seen a car accident leave the type of injuries . . . anyway, that's why we're concerned and we're going to do what we'll do to try to resolve this and figure it out."

"Uh huh," Bruce said.

Fuchser said he'd bring in the permission-to-search form for Bruce to sign.

"We've just got the concern that perhaps there was an intruder . . . perhaps somebody meant to do your wife some harm."

"Oh, boy," Bruce said, "I really can't imagine. I really can't imagine."

"Okay."

"I really can't imagine," Bruce repeated.

Fuchser's primary objective was to get Bruce to agree to the police search of the house, or better, to induce him to deny the permission.

Given the proximity of the wrecked Legacy to the house,

that would be a telltale clue to Fuchser that Bruce had something to hide.

Spidell now slid into the bad cop role, in part to increase the pressure on Bruce.

"What was your explanation to me, Doctor," he said, "as to why your wallet was in the car?"

"Well, I assume she just took it to have money."

"To pay for groceries?" Spidell asked.

"Yeah, I assume," Bruce said. "She takes my wallet every once in a while."

Spidell wanted to know how much money might have been in the wallet. Bruce thought it might have been $150 to $180.

Fuchser asked Bruce if Debbie usually carried a checkbook, and whether Bruce knew if she had one with her when she left to go to the supermarket. Bruce said he had no way of knowing, but "if she didn't have her wallet, she'd take my wallet, she didn't have her checkbook."

With this equivocal answer, Fuchser prepared to shut the tape off. He'd been paged by DeFrang. Fuchser was convinced, by the evidence at the scene, and the answers he'd just received, that the killer of Debbie Rowan was sitting right in front of him—none other than the good Doctor Bruce Rowan.

Now he wanted to brief DeFrang, get Rowan's formal permission to search and find the evidence that would put Dr. Bruce away.

A view of Port Angeles, Washington, dominated by the rugged peaks of the Olympic Mountains, once thought to be impassable by human beings.
(PHOTO BY CARLTON SMITH)

Dr. Eugene Turner and his wife, Norma. Turner would be charged with murder after a nurse observed him suffocating a three-day-old infant who had sustained severe brain damage. (PHOTO BY KEITH THORPE, *PENINSULA DAILY NEWS*)

Dr. Eugene Turner ponders his future, shortly before being indicted for murder in the death of three-day-old Conor McInnerney. (PHOTO BY KEITH THORPE, *PENINSULA DAILY NEWS*)

The rear of the Rowans' house outside Port Angeles, Washington. Clallam County Sheriff's investigators believed that Dr. Bruce Rowan killed Deborah with an axe while she slept, loaded her body into a lawn cart, then moved it from the bedroom around the second-floor deck. Then, out to the garage and Deborah's car as part of a plan to make her death look like a fatal traffic accident. (PHOTO BY CLALLAM COUNTY SHERIFF'S DEPUTY RANDY PIEPER, EXHIBIT AT THE TRIAL OF DR. BRUCE ROWAN)

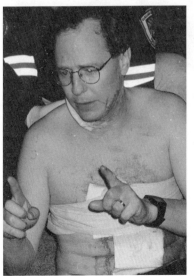

Dr. Rowan indicating the size of the knife that he used to stab himself in an apparent suicide attempt in the early morning hours of March 3, 1998. "I couldn't find the aorta," Rowan told investigators. Police were preparing to search the Rowan house for evidence of Deborah's murder when Rowan stabbed himself. (PHOTO BY CLALLAM COUNTY SHERIFF'S DEPUTY DARRELL SPIDELL, EXHIBIT AT THE TRIAL OF DR. BRUCE ROWAN)

Deborah Rowan's crutches, found on the Rowan driveway. The crutches, which had blood on them, were further evidence that Deborah Rowan did not die in a car wreck. (PHOTO BY CLALLAM COUNTY SHERIFF'S DEPUTY STACEY SAMPSON, EXHIBIT AT THE TRIAL OF DR. BRUCE ROWAN)

The utility shed in the rear of the Rowan house, where sheriff's deputies discovered blood-stained clothing and plastic bags, and the axe and bat used to kill Deborah Rowan. (CLALLAM COUNTY SHERIFF'S DEPARTMENT PHOTO, EXHIBIT AT THE TRIAL OF DR. BRUCE ROWAN)

Deborah Rowan's Subaru Legacy station wagon, after it crashed into the side of the road about 100 yards from the Rowan house. Clallam County police and prosecutors believed that Bruce Rowan put his wife's body in the car, then sent it driverless down the road to make the murder look like an accident. Annika's child car seat is on the road to the right, removed by the passerby who discovered the accident and checked whether a baby was in it. (CLALLAM COUNTY SHERIFF'S DEPARTMENT PHOTO, EXHIBIT AT THE TRIAL OF DR. BRUCE ROWAN)

Dr. Bruce Rowan after being booked in the Clallam County Jail. (CLALLAM COUNTY SHERIFF'S DEPARTMENT PHOTO)

Family and friends of Deborah Rowan gather in a Port Angeles park on the eve of Dr. Rowan's murder trial. In the foreground, from the left, Debbie's father Richard Fields, her mother Shirley, and her sisters Stephanie Bentley and Diana Fields. In the rear, Debbie's friends from the Pre-Three Parent Toddler Class, of which Debbie was one of the founding members. (PHOTO BY KEITH THORPE, *PENINSULA DAILY NEWS*)

Rowan defense lawyer David Allen argues that his client was a loving husband and father who suffered a psychotic episode brought on, in part, by the death of three-day-old Conor McInnerney six weeks before. Allen displays Rowan family photographs to illustrate his argument. (PHOTO BY TOM THOMPSON, *PENINSULA DAILY NEWS*)

Dr. Bruce Rowan stands at his murder trial in Port Angeles. His attorney sits at his left. (PHOTO BY KEITH THORPE, *PENINSULA DAILY NEWS*)

Dr. Rowan, with David Allen, listens as the verdict is read in his murder trial. (PHOTO BY KEITH THORPE, *PENINSULA DAILY NEWS*)

Craig Rowan, Bruce Rowan's father, is hugged by two of his son's friends at the reading of the verdict. (PHOTO BY KEITH THORPE, *PENINSULA DAILY NEWS*)

Clallam County Prosecutor David Bruneau (left) and challenger Chris Shea (right). Shea decisively defeated Bruneau in the 1998 election, in part because of Bruneau's handling of the Turner and Rowan cases. (PHOTOS BY KEITH THORPE, *PENINSULA DAILY NEWS*)

Michelle and Marty McInnerney shown together several months after their baby died at Olympic Memorial Hospital. (PHOTO BY KEITH THORPE, *PENINSULA DAILY NEWS*)

A view of Port Angeles, Washington, dominated by the rugged peaks of the Olympic Mountains, once thought to be impassable by human beings. (PHOTO BY CARLTON SMITH)

Dr. Eugene Turner and his wife, Norma. Turner would be charged with murder after a nurse observed him suffocating a three-day-old infant who had sustained severe brain damage. (PHOTO BY KEITH THORPE, *PENINSULA DAILY NEWS*)

Dr. Eugene Turner ponders his future, shortly before being indicted for murder in the death of three-day-old Conor McInnerney. (PHOTO BY KEITH THORPE, *PENINSULA DAILY NEWS*)

The rear of the Rowans' house outside Port Angeles, Washington. Clallam County Sheriff's investigators believed that Dr. Bruce Rowan killed Deborah with an axe while she slept, loaded her body into a lawn cart, then moved it from the bedroom around the second-floor deck. Then, out to the garage and Deborah's car as part of a plan to make her death look like a fatal traffic accident. (PHOTO BY CLALLAM COUNTY SHERIFF'S DEPUTY RANDY PIEPER, EXHIBIT AT THE TRIAL OF DR. BRUCE ROWAN)

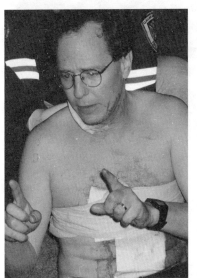

Dr. Rowan indicating the size of the knife that he used to stab himself in an apparent suicide attempt in the early morning hours of March 3, 1998. "I couldn't find the aorta," Rowan told investigators. Police were preparing to search the Rowan house for evidence of Deborah's murder when Rowan stabbed himself. (PHOTO BY CLALLAM COUNTY SHERIFF'S DEPUTY DARRELL SPIDELL, EXHIBIT AT THE TRIAL OF DR. BRUCE ROWAN)

Deborah Rowan's crutches, found on the Rowan driveway. The crutches, which had blood on them, were further evidence that Deborah Rowan did not die in a car wreck. (PHOTO BY CLALLAM COUNTY SHERIFF'S DEPUTY STACEY SAMPSON, EXHIBIT AT THE TRIAL OF DR. BRUCE ROWAN)

The utility shed in the rear of the Rowan house, where sheriff's deputies discovered blood-stained clothing and plastic bags, and the axe and bat used to kill Deborah Rowan. (CLALLAM COUNTY SHERIFF'S DEPARTMENT PHOTO, EXHIBIT AT THE TRIAL OF DR. BRUCE ROWAN)

Deborah Rowan's Subaru Legacy station wagon, after it crashed into the side of the road about 100 yards from the Rowan house. Clallam County police and prosecutors believed that Bruce Rowan put his wife's body in the car, then sent it driverless down the road to make the murder look like an accident. Annika's child car seat is on the road to the right, removed by the passerby who discovered the accident and checked whether a baby was in it. (CLALLAM COUNTY SHERIFF'S DEPARTMENT PHOTO, EXHIBIT AT THE TRIAL OF DR. BRUCE ROWAN)

Dr. Bruce Rowan after being booked in the Clallam County Jail. (CLALLAM COUNTY SHERIFF'S DEPARTMENT PHOTO)

Family and friends of Deborah Rowan gather in a Port Angeles park on the eve of Dr. Rowan's murder trial. In the foreground, from the left, Debbie's father Richard Fields, her mother Shirley, and her sisters Stephanie Bentley and Diana Fields. In the rear, Debbie's friends from the Pre-Three Parent Toddler Class, of which Debbie was one of the founding members. (PHOTO BY KEITH THORPE, *PENINSULA DAILY NEWS*)

Rowan defense lawyer David Allen argues that his client was a loving husband and father who suffered a psychotic episode brought on, in part, by the death of three-day-old Conor McInnerney six weeks before. Allen displays Rowan family photographs to illustrate his argument. (PHOTO BY TOM THOMPSON, *PENINSULA DAILY NEWS*)

Dr. Bruce Rowan stands at his murder trial in Port Angeles. His attorney sits at his left. (PHOTO BY KEITH THORPE, *PENINSULA DAILY NEWS*)

Dr. Rowan, with David Allen, listens as the verdict is read in his murder trial. (PHOTO BY KEITH THORPE, *PENINSULA DAILY NEWS*)

Craig Rowan, Bruce Rowan's father, is hugged by two of his son's friends at the reading of the verdict. (PHOTO BY KEITH THORPE, *PENINSULA DAILY NEWS*)

Clallam County Prosecutor David Bruneau (left) and challenger Chris Shea (right). Shea decisively defeated Bruneau in the 1998 election, in part because of Bruneau's handling of the Turner and Rowan cases. (PHOTOS BY KEITH THORPE, *PENINSULA DAILY NEWS*)

Michelle and Marty McInnerney shown together several months after their baby died at Olympic Memorial Hospital. (PHOTO BY KEITH THORPE, *PENINSULA DAILY NEWS*)

2 2

I HATE TO SAY IT

Fuchser went outside the Rowan house and got in his car
fo get the permission-to-search form, and call in to Snover
and DeFrang to brief them. Bruce had voluntarily consented
to a search of the residence and property, Fuchser told
them. Fuchser said that he was convinced that Dr. Rowan
had killed his wife—how and why would have to be developed.

After briefing DeFrang, Fuchser returned to the Rowan
house at 4:30 a.m. So far, no deputy had been farther into
the house than the living room.

The detective turned the tape recorder back on.

"Okay," he said, "the time right now is 0430 hours. As
I say, Bruce, there's still every indication that your wife
may have met with some kind of foul play. What I'd like
for you to do, would be to think and tell me whatever you
can think of that might help us solve this. Anybody that
might intend to do her harm."

Often, after a homicide—particularly in domestic disputes—as time goes by, guilt and remorse build up inside
the perpetrator. Early in an interrogation, the lies may come
easily, but as the event looms larger—even as it recedes in
time—a compulsion to clear the conscience may become

overwhelming. This is particularly true of otherwise law-abiding people who have simply lost control of themselves for a brief, if fatal, instant. Every ounce of Fuchser's instinct told him that Bruce Rowan had killed his wife; if Bruce was going to admit it, now was the time.

"Not that I can think of," Bruce answered.

"Okay," Fuchser said.

"And," Bruce added, "uh, you've done well."

What did this mean? Bruce was patting the deputies on the back? Taken one way, it might mean that Bruce was anxious for them to leave. Or taken another: was some part of Bruce conceding that the deputies were on the right track?

"Okay," Fuchser said. "What was the marital situation with you and your wife? Was it pretty good?"

"It was good," Bruce said, "it was good, it was good and getting better, really, as the years go on."

Fuchser now asked about Bruce and Debbie's friends; he wanted to find people who might be able to provide a window into their recent married life. Bruce provided names of people Debbie had known although he was unable to remember the last name of Debbie's best friend.

After some additional discussion involving the mechanical condition of the Rowan Subaru, Fuchser returned to the issue of who might have wanted to harm Debbie; this insistence on inducing a prime suspect to name others was classic homicide interrogation technique, again designed to entice an interview subject into extended discussion.

"What reason, what possible reason is there that somebody would mean to hurt your wife?" Fuchser asked.

"I don't know, I don't know why anybody would," Bruce said.

"What kind of disposition did she have?"

"Gregarious and gentle, real gregarious, lots of fun, friends and that sort of thing," Bruce said.

Spidell raised the stakes slightly.

"Remember," he said, "I explained to you that I saw a large aluminum object, a chrome-colored object [in Debbie's car]? I now know what that object is. It's your trailer hitch."

"Oh," Bruce said.

"Now was that inside the vehicle?"

"Yeah, it was, it was . . ." Bruce's voice trailed off.

"Whereabouts would it have been?"

"Boy, it would have been between the two front seats . . . uh, it's more kind of moving, [I] tend to move things around a lot. I've been trying to keep things picked up, I don't do a very good job of keeping things picked up. I don't know exactly where it would have been today."

Fuchser returned to the crutches. He'd noticed them when he first entered, and concluded that Bruce had brought them inside the house after Spidell's first visit.

"Is there any reason why your wife wouldn't have taken the crutches with her?" Fuchser asked.

"Boy," said Bruce, "I can't imagine. She'd mentioned she wanted to use the motor scooter thing at Safeway to ride around on."

"Was it easy enough for her to walk [without the crutches]?"

"No," Bruce said, "she'd definitely need her crutches. I think she forgot them, probably."

"I see," Fuchser said.

"Actually," Bruce added, "that was where she parked. That would be the place where she would get in the car and she just laid them right there. First time, that was her first time driving with her cast . . . she's not very well organized."

At that point in the interview, DeFrang pulled into the yard. Spidell went out to brief him.

"I think I should go check on my daughter," Bruce said suddenly.

Bruce got up and headed for the rear of the house, Fuchser trailing him, while still recording.

"How big's your house here?" Fuchser asked as they were walking.

"It's 2,000 square feet," Bruce said.

"Oh," Fuchser said. "Now you say your daughter is three years old?" He was wondering whether the little girl had seen anything happen between Bruce and Debbie.

"Yeah," Bruce said.

"She was watching a movie tonight? Is that what you were saying?"

"Mostly kind of uppity," Bruce said. "She'd been in bed, up and down . . ." His voice trailed off again.

They came to the sleeping Annika.

"Uh, Bruce," Fuchser said, "you know, I hate to say it, but I do think somebody killed your wife and put her in the car, and we're going to have to figure out who did it."

In his first non-sequitur of the evening, Bruce seemed not to respond to Fuchser's remark.

"I guess she's sleeping good tonight," he said, referring to Annika. Or was it Debbie he was talking about?

Bruce's voice trailed off again.

He and Fuchser returned to the living room.

"I have to use the bathroom," Bruce told Fuchser.

"Oh, sure, you bet," Fuchser said. Bruce went through the kitchen toward the bathroom.

Spidell came back in.

"He's in the bathroom," Fuchser told Spidell. "You want to sort of keep an eye on him?"

Neither deputy had thought to handcuff Bruce, which turned out to be a bad mistake.

23

FIGHT OR FLIGHT

Fuchser now left the house and went to talk to DeFrang. He sketched in the events and the substance of the conversation with Bruce. The detective thought it likely that Bruce had killed his wife, then put her dying or dead body in the car.

After this, Fuchser theorized, Bruce had started the car, driven it out of the yard, then down Yellow Rock Lane to Mount Pleasant Road, where he'd arranged Debbie's body to sit up in the driver's seat, put the heavy trailer hitch over the accelerator pedal, wedged the plastic water pail into the steering wheel to hold it fast, put the car in gear, and let the car roll forward down the hill.

Ellefson had estimated that the car had been going as fast as 40 or 45 mph when the cant of the road's crown had pulled the front right-side wheel into the drainage ditch. After perhaps about seventy yards, the right wheel had hit a metal culvert, which in turn caused the car to slew violently to the right, sending it into a railroad tie used as a fence post, thus triggering the airbag and catapulting Debbie across the front seat.

If this was what had happened, there was bound to be evidence of the murder either in the house or somewhere on the property. Bruce had consented to the search. Fuchser thought they should get started right away.

DeFrang wasn't quite sure that the permission-to-search route was the best way to go. He was well aware of the political stewpot that the Gene Turner situation was turning into. If the Clallam County Sheriff's Department decided that the *other* doctor who'd been in the emergency room the night Conor McInnerney died—Rowan—was likewise implicated in a murder, the community reaction was certain to be intense, especially from the embattled hospital and its politically influential staff. DeFrang wanted to do everything by the book.

That meant, in his view, getting a judicially approved search warrant, even if it meant waking up a judge in the middle of the night. DeFrang set about trying to organize the warrant, which would require Fuchser to testify over the telephone before the judge.

As DeFrang made his call, he and Fuchser could both see Rowan in the bathroom of the house. He appeared to be extremely agitated, pacing back and forth and occasionally going to the window to peer outside.

"He's looking," DeFrang said later. "He's scared. He is preparing for flight or fight, clearly, in my view. He's pacing—he knew that the gig was up. The cops are showing up, stuff is happening."

Fuchser told DeFrang what he had just said to Bruce, about the police knowing that murder had been committed, and that they were going to get to the bottom of it. That probably accounted for Bruce's agitation, both deputies thought, the first he had displayed all night.

In Washington State, as in many jurisdictions, it's permissible for police to obtain judicial approval of search warrants over the telephone or radio. In this case, it required the dispatch center to locate a judge, and then patching the deputies through. By the time Judge Kenneth Williams was roused, it was just after 5 a.m. Fuchser wanted Williams to approve a search of the entire Rowan property.

After sketching in the details of the car wreck and the

evidence found there, Fuchser described his conversation with Bruce. Following this, Fuchser began to describe evidence he'd seen at the house that convinced him that the murder had occurred there.

"Your Honor," Fuchser said, "Deputy Spidell had told me that when he first came up here, the victim's crutches were lying in the middle of the driveway. When I met the victim['s husband] at the door and then followed him in to his dining room table, those crutches were leaning against a chair that was pushed up under the table. Now I moved those crutches myself so I could sit down and I did observe blood on those crutches."

Fuchser didn't have to explain what that probably meant—that Debbie had been hurt or killed before she entered the car. There was more:

"While I was walking out to my vehicle to get the blank permission-to-search form, I shined a flashlight on the gravel in the driveway. I noticed two drag marks, and slightly to the south of those drag marks—which appeared to be heel drag marks—there was a large spot of partially coagulated blood."

While Fuchser was testifying, DeFrang continued to watch Bruce through the bathroom window.

He's going to bolt, DeFrang thought. He expected Rowan to force the window open and run away.

Fuchser turned the radio over to DeFrang. DeFrang, still watching Rowan pace, began to describe evidence that had been discovered at the car wreck—the blood-stains on the headrest of the car seat and the driver's-side door jamb, as well as the spatters on the ceiling of the car, which DeFrang thought had come from the impact of the airbag on the previously inflicted bloody head wounds.

Somehow DeFrang had learned another piece of information—Debbie's cast was not made for walking. That made it highly unlikely that she would have gone to the store without her crutches; the whole point of having the crutches was to keep Debbie's surgically repaired foot aloft.

As he was describing this, Fuchser's radio went off. It

was Spidell, calling to tell them that Bruce had just tried to kill himself.

Fuchser ran back into the house, where he found Bruce bleeding profusely from stab wounds to his torso and cuts to his neck. Spidell had grabbed Bruce and handcuffed him to a chair, where he sat, still bleeding.

What happened? Fuchser asked Spidell.

Spidell said he first noticed that Bruce was bleeding when he'd come in from the bathroom to the kitchen, mumbling something about having to feed Annika. He was carrying the child in his arms. What he'd seen first, Spidell said, were the cuts to Bruce's neck, which looked somewhat superficial. It was then that he'd noticed more blood present on Bruce's chest.

"I tried for the aorta, but I missed," Spidell said Rowan had told him.

Spidell told Fuchser that he asked Bruce why he'd stabbed himself. Bruce had responded that he did it because "voices" told him to. Annika was crying and obviously scared. The scene was spiraling out of control. Fuchser called out to DeFrang for assistance. DeFrang quickly ended his call to Judge Williams and made for the house. Inside he found a profusely bleeding Rowan.

But it was a different kind of Bruce. "It was like he was [back] in the emergency room," DeFrang said later, "only he's the patient." Gone was the passive Bruce; now present was the cool, calm emergency room doctor.

"Now the child is up and moving about, and upset, frightened, and one of the first things I do is pick her up," DeFrang recalled. "And he [Rowan] starts communicating with me, he's communicating about—he knows he's going to the doctor, he's going to the hospital. He starts *planning* for the kid. Calls his people on the telephone. Planning for the caretaking of the child."

The paramedics arrived in a few minutes, and Bruce began instructing them on how to treat him.

"He discusses his condition with the paramedics, who are arriving," DeFrang said. "He directs the cops to the phone, to the list of telephone numbers, he directs us to the knife, makes sure they're going the right way, to the right room. It was like he was controlling us, [just as] he was controlling the medical people. Asking questions, discussing his injuries. It was remarkable."

At one point, Fuchser read Bruce his Miranda rights, and asked if he wanted to talk.

"Not especially," Bruce said. He explained to Annika that he was going to have to go to the hospital, and that someone from the police would make sure that she was taken care of.

DeFrang asked Bruce why he'd stabbed himself.

"I just don't want to say right now," Bruce said, and then added something about voices in his head.

Then he told the paramedics, as he had earlier with Spidell, "I couldn't hit the aorta," as if Bruce was explaining his course of treatment to other professionals in the ER so that they would all be on the same page.

It now appeared that there had been two different Bruces at Yellow Rock Lane that night—the flat, unemotional, diffident Bruce who had calmly related the events of his wife's last night alive to Spidell, Sampson and Fuchser, and this new Bruce—still calm, but commanding, directing an emergency that he'd been trained to deal with; in effect, calling his own code.

It was, in one way, just as DeFrang had predicted: flight, this time back to the haven of his professional competence, his refuge. With the police closing in, Bruce had tried to take control of the situation—and remove himself from the immediate control of the sheriff's deputies and their psychological pressure—by plunging a knife into his chest five or six times. The deputies found the knife in Annika's room, along with spatters of blood next to her bed. Bruce had apparently inflicted the cuts to his neck while standing over his adopted daughter.

How and where had he gotten the knife? It must have happened, DeFrang and Fuchser reasoned, when Bruce had

gone to the bathroom. Sure enough, there was an assort-
ment of knives in a wooden block in the kitchen, and one
was missing.

The failure to handcuff Bruce—if not when Spidell first
suspected him, then later when Fuchser ended the first part
of his interview—was haunting. And there was an even
more chilling thought: if Bruce had killed Debbie and tried
to kill himself, had he also considered killing little Annika
while he stood over her, sawing away at his own neck?

Bruce was rushed to the emergency room at Olympic
Memorial, where his now-former colleagues tried to save
his life. Despite missing the aorta, Bruce had managed to
nick the left ventricle of his heart, and had sustained serious
internal bleeding. By the time he arrived at the hospital,
Bruce's blood pressure was dangerously low; he had passed
into unconsciousness from blood loss.

At Yellow Rock Lane, meanwhile, the sheriff's deputies
waited for the sun to come up to begin their grim search
for evidence. Two hours later, when dawn came, no one
was prepared for the gruesome discoveries that were about
to be made.

24

BLOOD

By 11 a.m. on Tuesday, March 2, the police had pretty much found what they were looking for at the house on Yellow Rock Lane: an inspection of the bedroom revealed a substantial blood spatter pattern on the carpet, walls and ceiling of the master bedroom, as well as a substantial soaking on the underside of the mattress. Bruce had apparently stripped the old bedding off, tried to mop up the blood with paper towels, and had flipped the mattress over before taking sheets and blankets from a guest bedroom to remake the bed.

Besides the master bedroom, more blood was found in Annika's room, in the bathroom, on paper towels that plugged a downstairs toilet; indeed, it appeared there wasn't a room in the entire house that didn't have some amount of blood present, large or small, in drips or spatters.

Outside the house, deputies found a small lawn cart; it too had blood-stains. A running hose ran through some wet cat litter on the driveway, which bore shoeprints; the particles of the litter led the way to a small aluminum shed in the back yard.

In the shed, the discoveries were grimmer yet. Deputies found numerous plastic garbage bags filled with bloody clothing, bloody paper towels, bloody bedding, and one taped bag that was supersaturated with blood; it looked as though Bruce had tied the bag around Debbie's head to keep the blood from her head wounds from spreading around inside the house. There was a large bedrest; it, too, was covered with blood. In a corner of the shed, in another blood-stained black plastic bag, deputies found a full-sized, single-bladed axe—clean—and a small wooden baseball bat. These looked like the murder weapons; the fact that they were found together was significant.

A pathologist, Dr. Daniel Selove, was called in to give a quick examination of Debbie's body, which was still in the car; the car itself had been removed to a deputy sheriff's nearby garage to avoid rubberneckers on Mount Pleasant Road. Both cuts on the forehead had flaps of skin that, peeled back, revealed massive incisions into the forebrain, Dr. Selove reported. The cuts seemed to match the wound patterns that could be expected from an axe. Selove guessed that Debbie had been struck three or possibly four times with the blade of the axe. In addition, Debbie's lower face, jaw and teeth had been broken, apparently in one or more blows from the baseball bat. It wasn't immediately clear which had occurred first, the axe blows or those of the midget baseball bat; but the pathology of Debbie's death seemed to indicate that the lower jaw blows could not have been fatal, which in turn suggested that the axe blows had come first, and the bat blows had been an afterthought— all of which led directly to the question of the assailant's intentions that night, and whether the lower jaw blows were intended, not to kill or injure, but to disguise the true origin of Debbie's injuries by making them seem as if they had occurred in a car wreck.

The savagery of the wounds hardly seemed anything like the gentle, soft-spoken Bruce everyone had come to know over the past eighteen months in the hospital's emergency room. The idea that mild-mannered Bruce Rowan could wreak such violent havoc on his own wife seemed, on the surface, to be absurd.

But DeFrang and others knew that sometimes things like this happened; it only proved that when it came to human behavior, you could never tell.

Over the next week, as the deputies continued to collect evidence from the house and car—eventually hundreds of items would be collected and cataloged—a theory of the crime began to take shape.

Based on Bruce's account and other indicators—such as telephone records—it appeared that around midnight or so, as Debbie lay dozing lightly in bed, her head propped up by the headrest, Bruce had exited the house, gone down to the woodpile around the side of the house, picked up the axe, and carried it back up to the bedroom, where, without warning, he had smashed its blade at least twice into Debbie's forehead, if not three or four times.

Then Bruce went to get the small baseball bat, and used that on Debbie's jaw and lower face, breaking many of her teeth in the process. One tooth and parts of others had been found in the master bedroom, along with all the blood spatters, much of it on the ceiling and walls, which indicated a frenzy of blows with the axe as well as the bat.

Following this, Bruce had gone outside, retrieved the lawn cart, and rolled it across the deck toward the master bedroom deck door, and into the bedroom. Bruce had loaded his dead or dying wife's body into the lawn cart, then wheeled the cart with its macabre cargo around the deck to the driveway.

Stopping next to Debbie's car, he'd tipped the cart forward, spilling Debbie's body onto the ground. Then he'd dragged her into the car, shoving her across the seat. He started the car, drove out of the yard, up a slight incline to Yellow Rock Lane, then down Yellow Rock Lane to Mount Pleasant Road.

At that point he'd arranged the body in an upright position and sent the car on its way.

Bruce had then returned to the house and set about cleaning up after the murder—hence all the bloody paper towels, bloody clothing in the washing machine and in the shed, the stripping of the bed. He'd probably been cleaning when Spidell and Sampson had arrived at 2:20 that morning, which was probably why he was still awake.

How had all this happened? Just what had gone on that prompted Bruce Rowan to such violence? DeFrang, Snover and Fuchser knew their best answer lay somewhere inside the mind of Bruce Rowan, but Bruce wasn't talking. He was still unconscious at Olympic Memorial Hospital from his self-inflicted wounds.

25

IN THE EYE OF THE STORM

The news of Debbie Rowan's death, and the suicide attempt of Bruce Rowan, fell on Port Angeles like a toxic, drizzling cloud, both graying out and chilling the town's senses. It was bad enough that the best-loved pediatrician on the Olympic Peninsula—the doctor to at least a third of the babies brought into the world over the past three decades—was suspected of choking the life out of one of his patients. Now the idea that a well-regarded, genial and popular young emergency room specialist like Dr. Bruce could have done such an incomprehensibly violent act upon his own wife was beyond belief.

Doctor's wife slain, read the front-page headline of Brewer's *Peninsula Daily News* on the afternoon of Tuesday, March 3. And the subhead: **Suspect allegedly faked car wreck to hide slaying, then tried to kill himself.**

If most of the town was protesting the allegations against Turner, some significant portion refused to believe what they were now told about Dr. Bruce. Friends and neighbors stepped forward in abundance to tell reporters that it didn't seem possible, that Bruce and Debbie seemed the most compatible of couples, that they were open and warm and hardly violent.

Detective Kovatch of the Port Angeles Police was stunned. The man he'd interviewed about Turner only a month earlier could never have done such a thing, he thought. "I would have voted him most likely never to hurt a fly," Kovatch said, later.

Fred DeFrang of the sheriff's department gave a short briefing. After explaining the circumstances of the discovery of Debbie's body in the car, the chief deputy told reporters that the crime scene was all wrong. "The trauma to the head did not match," he said. "There was evidence the victim died elsewhere."

After describing the evidence observed by Fuchser, Spidell and Sampson, and the circumstances that led the sheriff's department to believe that Bruce Rowan had committed the murder, DeFrang told how Bruce had stabbed himself. "These were well-placed stabs," DeFrang told the *PDN*'s Kelly. "He knew what he was doing."

If it hadn't been for the hospital's emergency room surgery on Bruce, he would have died, DeFrang said.

Despite DeFrang's dispassionate remarks, many of those who knew Bruce and Debbie from their eighteen months in Port Angeles still found it difficult to believe what they were being told. It just didn't seem possible: for them, Debbie was too animated to die, and Bruce was too placid to have killed her.

Once again, the major newspapers and television stations of the region descended on Port Angeles, intrigued not so much by the macabre nature of the killing of Debbie and the attempted suicide of Bruce, but by the fact that Rowan had been in the emergency room with Gene Turner on the night that Conor McInnerney died.

What all the reporters wanted to know was: what was the connection between Turner's act and Rowan's apparent murderous outburst?

DeFrang said he didn't know; if there was a connection, it wasn't obvious, he said.

As for hospital administrator Stegbauer, he flatly ruled out any relationship between the two events.

"There was no sign of it," Stegbauer told the *Seattle Post–Intelligencer* newspaper.

Had stress resulting from Conor's death triggered Bruce's homicidal outburst?

"These people [doctors like Rowan] are usually tops in their high school class," Stegbauer told the *Post–Intelligencer*'s reporter, Gordy Holt. "They go on to success in college and then go through the rigors we inflict on them, before we let them treat us. Dr. Rowan had survived all that."

In other words, it wasn't likely that the death of Conor McInnerney had anything to do with the subsequent murder of Debbie Rowan.

But this appears to have been Stegbauer's attempt to put the best spin on Dr. Rowan's seemingly incomprehensible act. It would soon be challenged, however, by the lawyers for Bruce Rowan. The murder of Debbie, they were about to contend, was triggered in Bruce Rowan's tortured mind by the actions of Gene Turner in the emergency room of Olympic Memorial Hospital on the night of January 12, 1998.

Within a day after Debbie's death and Bruce's hospitalization, members of both the Rowan and Fields families flew into Port Angeles. While the Rowans, represented by his parents and his brother Barry, held vigil at the hospital with the still-comatose Bruce, the Fieldses were consulting with the Clallam County Sheriff's Department, and taking care of Annika's future. Before the week was out, a motion was filed in Clallam County Superior Court to transfer legal custody of Annika to Debbie's sister Diane, who lived with her husband in Colorado.

By any definition, it was an excruciating week for both the Rowans and the Fieldses. First neighbors in Weiser, then in-laws, the horrifying fact that the son of one family had murdered the daughter of the other cast a pall over all their interactions.

For the Rowans, with a son on life support in the hospital, facing allegations that he had murdered his wife, the pain was intense: grief for Debbie was overshadowed by concern for the still-unconscious Bruce, with an undercurrent of embarrassed puzzlement: how or why could Bruce have done such a thing?

As for the Fieldses, their grief for Debbie and concern for Annika's future took primacy over their feelings for Bruce; but they were left with strange feelings of confusion. How could this gentle young man, who had been accepted into their family, have done such a thing? And what should they say to the Rowans? What should the Rowans say to them? It was madness, shot through with emotions that conflicted, rose, fell and went sideways; no one knew, really, what to say.

But as the Rowans and the Fieldses trod gingerly around one another with their separate and similar griefs, the Clallam County Sheriff's Department was still searching the Rowan house on Yellow Rock Lane. Once all the blood evidence was inventoried, along with the items from the aluminum shed, attention was paid to Bruce's home office.

It was there that Fuchser subsequently discovered two items that he believed were pertinent to the question of why Bruce had taken an axe to his wife's forehead: one was a complete set of newspaper clippings relating to the troubles of Gene Turner over the fate of Conor McInnerney; the other was a life insurance policy—the insured being one Deborah Lu Fields Rowan—in the amount of $500,000. The effective date of the policy was March 1, 1998—the very same date that Debbie Rowan had been killed by her apparently mild-mannered husband.

26

WHY?

Bruce was still under sedation at Olympic Memorial the following day, a Wednesday, when a Seattle lawyer named David Allen received a telephone call from Bruce's older brother, Barry Rowan, a resident of a Seattle suburb.

Allen was one of Seattle's most prominent criminal defense attorneys. A native of Connecticut, Allen was a graduate of Tufts University and Boston University School of Law; he'd been admitted to the bar in both Massachusetts and Washington in 1970.

Over the years, Allen, along with his partner, Richard Hansen, had handled many of the Seattle area's most controversial and highly publicized criminal cases. One such case involved a notorious series of rapes in Spokane that formed the basis of a classic book on psychopathology, *Son*, by Jack Olsen. Although Kevin Coe, the son of the managing editor of the Spokane *Spokesman–Review* newspaper, had been tried and found guilty of six predatory rapes in Spokane's upscale South Hills neighborhood, Allen and Hansen were able to gain Coe a new trial; eventually all but one of the convictions was voided after a series of appeals to higher courts.

In another controversial case, Hansen defended a man

accused of a series of rape-muggings that occurred in the vicinity of the massive county hospital complex in Seattle. After one conviction was reversed and two others ended in mistrials, the prosecutor chose not to try the case a fourth time.

In what was perhaps Allen and Hansen's most famous case, a man wrongfully convicted of rape on deliberately tainted police evidence sued the police agency and collected a seven-figure judgment.

Allen was of medium height, compactly built, and bespectacled; he had a scholarly mien that suggested reason to jurors, instead of showy trial tactics. But for all his calm demeanor, Allen was fervent for his clients' interest. To Allen, the Constitution was clear: the state had to prove the charges against a defendant *beyond a reasonable doubt*. Allen saw his job as exploring every possibility of doubt, reasonable or otherwise.

Barry Rowan sketched in the events surrounding Debbie's death and Bruce's suicide attempt. Would Allen act as Bruce's defense attorney?

Allen agreed to take the case. He made plans to go to Port Angeles the following day, and telephoned ahead for an appointment to see David Bruneau.

For Bruneau, the year that had begun badly with the Conor McInnerney controversy was turning worse. Now he had a second murder case against another popular Port Angeles doctor to consider. Bruneau had a feeling that both cases were going to come to their respective climaxes in the fall—just as he would be seeking reelection to a fifth term as Clallam County Prosecutor.

Handled badly, both cases could explode in his face. If he treated Turner or Rowan too leniently, his critics would say that, while he threw the book at the blue-collar classes, he eased off when it came to elites like doctors. On the other hand, at least half the town was screaming that the investigation of Turner was a vendetta by Bruneau against Turner's wife.

Knowing he was going to get hammered no matter what

he did, Bruneau resolved to treat the cases against the doctors the same as he would any other defendants, prominent physicians or not. If a logger had killed a living, breathing baby by covering its nose and mouth with his hand until it suffocated, he'd be in jail; if a mill worker was found in circumstances similar to those of Bruce Rowan, he'd be on the fast track to the penitentiary. The law provided no exception for members of the healing profession.

So this was a political test for Bruneau: to demonstrate that everyone was equal before the law, rich and poor alike, and to be able to explain his actions well enough to the voters to convince them that there was no vendetta, no favoritism—and therefore, that he was deserving of reelection. It would, as it turned out, be an uphill fight.

By the next day, the police were still searching the Rowan house, but the case against Bruce was starting to come together. After briefing Bruneau, DeFrang swore out an affidavit of probable cause supporting the charging of Bruce with first-degree murder.

The difference between murder in the first degree and murder in the second degree was defined by two factors: premeditation and intent. A person who kills another may be found guilty of second-degree murder if it can be proven that he or she had the intent to take the victim's life, but hadn't planned to do so. A person who does not premeditate and has no intent to kill, but does so anyway by recklessness or carelessness may be guilty of manslaughter. Murder in the first degree requires proof of both intent as well as premeditation.

In Bruce's case, intent to murder seemed obvious from the cuts inflicted on Debbie, as well as the particular choice of weapon, which required action—going down to the woodpile and retrieving the axe—indicating thought.

As for premeditation, the police pointed to three different factors: the purchase of plastic garbage bags the day of the killing; the purchase of the small wooden bat; and the previous purchase of the life insurance on Debbie.

As their case came together, both Snover and DeFrang concluded that Bruce had decided to kill Debbie several months earlier; Snover concluded that the death of Conor McInnerney simply accelerated Bruce's plan.

"I think it had something to do with the Turner case in the effect of . . . this nice world that he had taken about a year and a half developing was [now] crashing down on him," Snover said later. "Because he took the opposite side. He took the side that found fault with what Dr. Turner did. So he's becoming a pariah at the hospital. He's becoming a pariah to the supporters [of Turner], which is a vocal majority of people in town. He's all of a sudden become a part of the problem. So I think he wants to cut the ties here in Port Angeles and move on."

The fundamental problem between Bruce and Debbie, Snover believed, was that Debbie was putting down roots in the community, making friends and developing her own career separate from Bruce. It wasn't the way Bruce had seen his own life working out, Snover suggested.

"From the start, she was going to be his support in this nomadic lifestyle," Snover continued. " 'We'll be here for a while, and then we'll go do some medical good works in this poor country, and then we'll come back and earn some more money, and then we'll go off to some other third-world country.' And they had agreed that that was going to be their lifestyle, when they became a couple. And I think she changed her mind on him. I think her family will agree that she changed her life on him. Because she loved Port Angeles. She loved the people in Port Angeles."

So in the police view, Bruce's motive was becoming more clear: he literally wanted to chop Debbie out of his life and start over, with a half-million dollar stake, to boot.

That was how Bruneau explained the case to Allen on Thursday, March 5, and on the surface of it, the facts did seem daunting to Allen.

First, there was no question that Bruce had done the crime; the blood spatters all over the house proved that, along with a host of other facts, not least Bruce's suicide attempt.

Bruce's apparently frantic attempts to clean up after the killing, and his effort to throw the police off the track by staging the car wreck seemed to show clear consciousness of guilt.

But the more Allen thought about the case, the more puzzling it seemed. If Bruce really did intend to kill Debbie, couldn't he, as a doctor, have found a far less bloody and more intelligent way of doing it—some sort of drug or poison, for example, that might never be detected?

And why would a man kill his wife on the same day a half-million dollar insurance policy kicked in? Wasn't that like waving a red flag at the police? Sort of saying, look at me, look at me. And it wasn't as if Bruce needed the money; he'd been earning close to $200,000 a year as a doctor.

The whole situation seemed crazy, at least in Allen's mind. Try as he might, he could find no evidence that Bruce had been homicidally angry at Debbie any time before the night of March 1. Everyone seemed to agree that they got along well, were loving parents of Annika.

Nor did anyone describe Bruce as anything other than a gifted and committed doctor with a gentle demeanor.

It was crazy, Allen concluded; and then he thought, *Crazy is a defense.*

27

AN UNSOUND MIND?

After 10 days in the hospital, Bruce was sufficiently recovered from his self-inflicted wounds to be transferred to the Clallam County jail. He had recovered consciousness several days after Debbie's death, but still wasn't clear on exactly what had happened.

Because of his suicide attempt, Bruce was given special treatment at his new abode—the "rubber room."

This was, literally, a room with padded walls, floors and ceilings. A stainless-steel grate in one corner was the toilet, and fluorescent lights kept the room illuminated twenty-four hours a day. A closed-circuit television camera monitored his every movement. There was no television, no books, no newspapers—in fact, there was nothing in the room except a barefoot Bruce and his own inner torment.

On March 16, Bruce was arraigned for the killing of his wife; he pled not guilty. A minor squabble erupted over a search warrant that had been issued for Bruce's medical records at the University of Washington and at Olympic Hospital; DeFrang and Snover had reasoned that if Bruce had any defense at all—especially after his suicide attempt—it might lie in making an insanity plea. They wanted to be prepared to rebut this, if necessary. Allen told

Judge Kenneth Wood that at present the records were privileged, and could not be subject to a lawful search. The judge agreed and ordered the records sealed for the time being. If and when Allen entered an insanity plea for Bruce, the records might be admissible, but not before.

Bail for Bruce was set for a million dollars pending further hearings. Allen told Wood that he'd just received 361 pages of police reports on the killing, and it would take him some time to digest all the material before he could decide how to defend his client. With that, Bruce was returned to the rubber room.

The more he thought about the killing of Debbie Rowan, as he read through all the police reports, the more convinced Allen was that he could advance an insanity defense for Bruce. And as he researched the law, he discovered another interesting fact: even if the jury didn't buy the insanity defense, he might still claim that Bruce had diminished capacity on the night he killed Debbie—that somehow, Bruce's mental illness had interfered with his ability to form any criminal intent at all.

But there was a crucial difference between insanity and diminished capacity: in pleading insanity, the burden of proof was on the defense to establish that the defendant had a recognized mental disorder that affected his or her decision-making at the time of the crime.

But a person pleading diminished capacity only had to show that he had a mental condition that prevented him from forming the intent to commit a criminal act. In that case, the defense only had to produce evidence that a defendant had a mental condition that interfered with the forming of intent at the time of the crime.

Once the defense established that a mental disorder prevented the formation of intent at the time of the crime, the burden of proof was on the prosecution to show that the defendant in fact had the intent to commit the crime, not withstanding his mental condition; in other words, it was up to the prosecution to prove that the mental disorder had *not* affected the intent when the crime was committed, and to prove this beyond a reasonable doubt.

Mental defect defenses were probably the most difficult pleas in criminal law. Jurors hate them, because they remove a crime from rational, everyday experience and move it into the realm of remote, often unfathomable mental processes.

Even worse, experts in the field rarely agree about insanity or diminished capacity at trial, especially in borderline cases like Bruce's.

As a result, when insanity or diminished capacity is contested in court, juries almost invariably find the defendant sane. In fact, in Washington state there hadn't been a successful jury acquittal on an insanity defense in nearly 25 years, as far as Allen could determine.

Nevertheless, Allen prepared to use both these defenses. He soon learned of Bruce's history of chronic depression, and discovered that chronic depression, a recognized mental disorder, can indeed lead to violent, psychotic behavior.

The key question, for Allen, was whether there was sufficient evidence to establish that Bruce had a mental condition at the time of the crime that prevented him from either forming the intent to commit a crime at the time the crime was committed—diminished capacity—or which prevented him from understanding the nature and quality of his act, as well as the understanding that it was wrong—insanity.

In either case, Allen had to first establish that Bruce had a mental condition likely to affect his behavior at the time of Debbie's killing.

Well, what did Allen have to work with?

First, there was Bruce's statement that he'd done what "the voices" told him to do, when asked why he'd stabbed himself. While it didn't come directly to the issue of why he'd killed Debbie, it did indicate a possibility that Bruce had been suffering from auditory hallucinations on the night in question, which was evidence of a mental disease or defect.

Second, there was the disorganized nature of the crime: the frenzied violence, followed by the pathetic attempts to clean up and stage the "accident."

This wasn't the working of a well-educated brain, operating at capacity, Allen reasoned; there was something terribly out of joint about everything Bruce did when he killed Debbie that night.

And there was Bruce's medical history, which showed a pattern of chronic depression that went back at least to college, if not before. Bruce's twice-documented psychiatric hospitalizations were further evidence of mental disease or defect, as was his suicide attempt while in medical school.

Finally, Allen zeroed in on the weakest part of the prosecution's case: the premeditation.

If he could show there was no premeditation, then a jury was more likely to conclude that Bruce had given in to some spontaneous impulse driven by mental illness.

Was the purchase of the garbage bags really *evidence* that Bruce had planned the murder? The baseball bat? It seemed to Allen that these actions were extremely equivocal; taken separately from what happened on Yellow Rock Lane, they were meaningless, and not at all definitive of Bruce's premeditation.

Had Bruce told his best friend a month before Debbie's death that he planned to kill his wife, and how he was going to do it, as well as the details of his plan to stage the car wreck, *that* would be evidence of premeditation.

But buying plastic garbage bags? There could be a hundred explanations for that, and only one of them sinister.

As for the insurance policy, Allen believed it might easily be explained as part of Bruce and Debbie's commitment to the process of adopting a new baby.

Once the issue of predmeditation was disposed of, the case would come down to intent; if Allen was able to demonstrate that Bruce had suffered for years from a difficult form of mental illness, it was one way to explain how an otherwise gentle, caring doctor had turned into a homicidal maniac.

Allen made arrangements for psychiatric experts to interview Bruce, preparatory to an evaluation. If a consensus of experts could conclude that Bruce had a mental illness, and that the illness had him in its grip at the time of Debbie's death, he had a chance of winning an acquittal on the basis of insanity or diminished capacity.

While that would mean Bruce would be confined, at least for a while, it would spare him a cell in a penitentiary for the rest of his life.

If Allen was growing more convinced that insanity was the best route for the defense of Bruce Rowan, Bruneau was equally sure that such a defense would never work, especially not in front of a Clallam County jury.

Apart from the long track record of juries rejecting the defense in Washington State, Bruneau had only to look at the evidence to convince himself that Bruce was not nuts: his attempts to clean up after and to conceal the nature of the crime were a clear indication that Bruce knew what he had done was wrong, and that he knew exactly what he had done.

In other words, once he began to hide his crime, Bruce in essense confessed that he was sane under the legal definition of sanity.

In the meantime, however, Bruce continued to be treated by a psychiatrist retained by the jail, who prescribed a steady regimen of anti-depressants, mood stabilizers and sleeping medications, as well as the continued suicide watch. A guard told Bruce that if he had to live under the conditions Bruce had to bear, he'd go crazy himself.

As March turned into April, two psychiatrists and a psychologist retained by Allen made their way to Port Angeles to interview Bruce, accompanied by one of Allen's associates.

One psychiatrist, Dr. Alan Unis, was a member of the

faculty of the University of Washington Medical School, where Bruce had graduated six years earlier, though he hadn't known Bruce while he was at the university. Unis began by reviewing all of Bruce's medical records at the university and at Olympic Memorial Hospital; he consulted with the UW psychiatrist who had treated Bruce for his earlier depression while in medical school, only to learn that that doctor had destroyed all his records relating to Bruce. He also read all the Clallam County Sheriff's Department reports on the crime.

Sometime in mid-April, Unis came to the Clallam County jail to interview Bruce. He found a murder defendant who was clean, well-groomed, and completely coherent.

Unis had only once before testified in court about a defendant's competency or sanity—and on behalf of the prosecution. Born in Pennsylvania, the son of a police officer, Unis had a horror of the insanity defense being used to "abort justice," as he put it later.

The Bruce who greeted him in the interview room at the Clallam County jail seemed on the surface to be perfectly normal, at least under the circumstances.

Over the previous weeks, Bruce had come to understand that Debbie was dead, and that he had killed her. At first, it was difficult for him to accept; at least, the doctor part of Bruce simply couldn't believe that he had done such a thing. At the same time, Bruce was aware of a darker part of himself, that thing that had lain hidden inside him so long, that thing he'd tried to keep concealed; *that* part, Bruce somehow suspected, was perfectly capable of killing.

But was Bruce morally responsible for Debbie's death? That was a far harder question, one that Unis had to determine for himself, and eventually for the court. Moral responsibility implies awareness, and awareness implies intent, and possibly premeditation. It was possible that Bruce knew full well what he had done on the night of March 1, and was even now shamming to escape responsibility.

If, on the other hand, some part of Bruce's personality, hidden away for many years, had suddenly taken over, driving Bruce to actions that his conscious mind had no control over, then, in that case, was the rest of Bruce responsible?

This was what Unis had to decide.

The doctor began by asking Bruce about his personal history. His purpose was to look for objective evidence that some sort of mental disease or defect—one that might have affected Bruce's actions the night he killed Debbie—had existed *prior* to the events of March 1. It was perfectly possible, Unis knew, that a well-educated man like Bruce might use his history of depression to feign symptoms of mental illness; the trick was to see whether there were documentable, objective symptoms of psychiatric disturbances that pre-dated the killing of Debbie, and might account in some way for Bruce's behavior. If there were none, the chances were that Bruce was faking it.

In one sense, Unis' task wasn't much different from that of the Clallam County detectives on March 1. The idea was to induce Bruce to expound, to talk, to spread himself out far enough that Unis could detect inconsistencies. If Bruce was faking, then the more he talked, the more likely he was to trip himself up.

In all, Unis would talk to Bruce for four hours.

"I needed to find out what was going on with Dr. Rowan," Unis said later, "to see if he could fill in some of the details I'd extracted from the records."

The law in Washington State did not permit an insanity or diminished capacity plea based on "acute emotions"; that is, one wasn't crazy if one simply gave way to rage.

Prolonged, chronic depression, on the other hand, was a recognized mental disorder. Unis had to determine the severity of Bruce's depression, as well as its onset and duration.

At the end of the interview, Unis concluded that Bruce was a tortured soul, a victim of a classic case of unipolar depression.

"He's always been a walking wounded," Unis said.

"This man has never experienced a day of joy in his entire life."

While Bruce said very little during this interview about his upbringing, Unis came to believe that an essential part of Bruce's ongoing depression was a severe conflict between his empathy for others' suffering and his strong desire to avoid it, which in turn set up shame in Bruce's mind. After shaming himself, Bruce would plunge back into situations where he felt extreme empathy, was revulsed, and was in turn shamed by his revulsion, in a never-ending, continuously repeating cycle.

Becoming a doctor was therefore probably the worst thing that Bruce could have done with his life, since it only aggravated the cycle. As his mind had been trying to tell him for so long, he would undoubtedly have been happier as a commercial fisherman.

"Most of us," Unis said, "when we have conflicts in our minds, work through them by exercising a discipline over our emotions. Doctors do this all the time. They need to have empathy for their patient, but also an objectivity that prevents them from getting too emotionally involved. If they get too involved, their judgment can get clouded by their emotions.

"The problem with Bruce was that he couldn't control the sympathy he had for others' misery. As a result, he had misery himself every day of his life."

The fact that he was miserable embarrassed and shamed him; these feelings in turn drove him to construct a tight mask of superior functionality to the outside world. No one must guess that Bruce was not in complete control of his emotions, when inside things were spiraling wildly out of control.

Bruce's experience with his disabled sister profoundly affected him, Unis came to believe. "She embarrassed him," Unis said, "and he felt shame that he felt embarrassed."

Unis also came to believe that the death of Conor McInnerney had affected Bruce in a similar way. "He was horribly upset by what happened in that emergency room," Unis said. Bruce's conflicting emotions about saving the baby, his emotional conflicts about infant brain damage, his conflicts about Turner's actions, set all of these unresolvable thoughts roiling about his head, all while he struggled to maintain his outward mask.

At some point, Bruce became trapped within his own conflicts; where healthy people work conflicts through by rationalizing their thinking, a psychotic person has a breakdown in the rationalization process.

"What psychosis is, is interruption," Unis said. Like a computer programmed to calculate the value of pi, the mind runs on, purposelessly, robotically, unable to reach any ending or resolution. Often in such situations, the personality may begin to disintegrate. As disintegration proceeds, an afflicted person may begin to disassociate himself from his surroundings as a way of escaping the unresolvable conflict; it is as if one is outside of himself neutrally observing all the subsequent events.

Unis came to believe that that was what had happened to Bruce on the night that he killed Debbie.

Debbie, Unis believed, represented the key to the lock on Bruce's mind. Bruce was so miserable that he wanted to kill himself; he couldn't kill himself because it would "devastate" Debbie if he were dead. Solution: kill Debbie so Debbie couldn't be devastated, thereby freeing Bruce to take his own life.

It was, Unis said, a classic murder–suicide scenario, repeated hundreds if not thousands of times across the United States every year.

Even Bruce's actions in trying to kill himself had psychological overtones, Unis said.

"It was like a sacrificial ritual, going right for the heart, and with a dull knife."

28

BLACKBALL

While Bruce was being evaluated by psychiatrists like Dr. Unis, Bruneau was beginning to run into trouble on his other big case—the investigation of Gene Turner.

One of the main problems, Bruneau was discovering, was that there was a substantial body of scientific information on brain-death in infants, much of it contradictory. The key question in any trial, Bruneau realized from conversations with Turner's lawyers, would be whether Conor was actually brain-dead when Turner smothered him, as Turner would doubtless claim in his defense.

"We're looking through all the medical literature," Bruneau told the *PDN*'s Christina Kelly. "It amounts to a lot of research. In addition, we're looking through all the case law available on the subject."

Bruneau's careful approach to the topic, however, did nothing to dampen the degree of public support for Turner, among many of Turner's patients' parents in particular, but also among his colleagues at the hospital. The paper's continued reporting on the Turner matter—and now, with Rowan in the news, every mention of Rowan's axe-killing contained a notation that he had been in the ER the night Turner had committed *his* act—chafed some of the hospital's doctors raw.

In early April, Dr. Eric Schreiber, the immediate past chief of staff at the hospital, and a close friend of Turner, wrote to the local Rotary Club board to oppose the proposed Rotary membership of the newspaper's John Brewer. He sent a copy to Brewer.

"Individuals who join Rotary are expected to demonstrate high ethical standards in their business or profession," Schreiber wrote. "In his role as the new publisher of the *Peninsula Daily News*, I have concerns that Mr. Brewer has not yet shown the level of professionalism and ethical standards we should expect of our membership." The newspaper's coverage of the Turner case, Schreiber continued, "has not met reasonable criteria of what should be expected from a responsible and professionally run newspaper."

Schreiber now applied the Rotary Club's uppercased Four-Way Test to the newspaper's coverage of the Turner case.

"Is it the Truth?" Schreiber asked. No, he said. The newspaper made significant "factual and conceptual errors" in covering the story.

"Is it Fair to all concerned?" No again, said Schreiber; identifying Turner before he had been charged with wrongdoing was grossly unfair. "Then," he continued, "after the Rowan murder, Dr. Turner's name was mentioned more than once in articles about Bruce Rowan, even though no connection between the two cases has been established." (Schreiber was doubtless unaware of Unis' findings.) "The inclusion of Dr. Turner's name in those articles without any relevant context goes beyond being unprofessional and unfair. It is a disgrace."

Schreiber continued with the Four-Way Test:

"Will it build Good Will and Better Friendships? Heavens no," Schreiber said. "The newspaper has alienated numerous people by the way the coverage was handled. It even sparked a public protest.

"Will it be Beneficial to all concerned?" No, said Schreiber; not only was the paper's coverage of the Turner–McInnerney case detrimental to Turner, it was also bad for people like him who were on the hospital's board, who were themselves under investigation by the district attorney and the police for the alleged failure to report the matter. Worse, Schreiber said, it was bad for the hospital itself, to say nothing of its potential patients.

"The hospital has gotten calls from people with acute medical emergencies seeking out places to go other than the OMH emergency room where they 'kill people,' thus placing their own lives in jeopardy."

Schreiber complained that the newspaper had published information from the search warrants served on the hospital, which he thought was "highly irregular and perhaps even criminal." He seemed to be unaware that the documents had been unsealed by a judge.

Schreiber had other complaints as well, but most of these concerned intepretations and spin—the hospital's contention that the MQAC was a "police agency," and the like.

"In summary," Schreiber said, "the inaccurate and sensationalist coverage of the recent events by the *Peninsula Daily News* has unnecessarily damaged reputations, divided our community, misinformed the public, created unjustified fear of our health care facilities, and may have endangered a few citizens of Clallam County who avoided the emergency department at OMH when they needed it the most.

"This has occurred under the watch of John Brewer. In my opinion, Mr. Brewer oversees a substandard newspaper that engages in unethical and sensationalist practices."

Because of this, Schreiber concluded, Brewer should be kept out of the Rotary Club until the newspaper mended its ways.

Bemused, Brewer realized once again that he was no longer in New York. Imagine, threatening a blackball from the Rotary Club unless the paper wrote articles that met with the hospital's approval. It was, he thought, the essence of community journalism.

Brewer invited Schreiber to lunch. The meeting was amicable; Brewer tried to explain the paper's reponsibilities to Schreiber, while Schreiber sought to convey to Brewer the standards he thought a small-town paper should embrace. Neither convinced the other,. but they parted on friendly terms.

In the end, the Rotary board accepted Brewer's membership.

Brewer wasn't the only one who was discovering the elite closing ranks against him; so was Bruneau.

By late April, Bruneau had gotten a shock when he learned that Dr. Jackson, the Seattle neonatologist, had declined to be a witness against Dr. Turner.

This was an abrupt turnabout from his recorded statements to Detective Kovatch—that if a baby was breathing and had a heartbeat, it was "by definition" not brain-dead. Jackson said that, while he was willing to talk about medical definitions, there was no way he was willing to say that Turner had "murdered" anyone; he just didn't have enough information about what had happened in the emergency room the night Conor McInnerney died. Jackson, as Bruneau later put it, had ties to the professionals at OMH.

Having a key witness back off wasn't unheard of, but this was a severe blow to any case against Turner. Jackson had been the best witness against the doctor. Certainly Bruneau could compel Jackson to testify with a subpoena, but what kind of a witness would he make? It would be easy for Jackson to make the prosecution look bad.

Bruneau now realized that he would have to go out of state for expert witnesses; the doctors in Washington State were so intertwined with one another, it would probably be impossible to find any expert willing to testify against Turner.

Bruneau was also starting to feel the pressure of all those in the community who backed Turner. "There's no way to win here," he told the *PDN*'s Kelly. "I'm damned if I do and damned if I don't. There will be people unhappy if Dr. Turner goes on trial and people unhappy if he doesn't."

29

THE RETURN OF CONOR MCINNERNEY

By late April, after meeting with Unis and two other mental health experts, David Allen was convinced that the insanity defense was the best route for Bruce's defense.

After hearing an oral report from Unis and another psychiatrist, as well as a psychologist, Allen concluded that he had enough grist from Bruce's personality to advance an insanity defense, or, alternatively, a defense of diminished capacity.

Bruce's chronic depression, Unis told Allen, was a result of his inability to exert control over his inner self, the roiling sea of emotions so dominated by his demanding, shaming empathy. The death of Conor McInnerney had triggered a severe depression, which—after Debbie's Achilles injury, with all the pressures entailed by the role-reversal, and unexpected pressures on Bruce as a domestic caregiver—had culminated in a psychotic episode on the night of March 1.

Bruce's disjointed recollections of the evening's events was evidence of his psychotic, disassociative state at the time of the crime, Unis said.

The other mental experts substantially agreed with Unis' diagnosis. Now Allen had expert testimony to support his case, that Bruce was so afflicted by his mental condition on March 1 that he was either insane, or his capacity to form the intent to kill was severely diminished. In addition, Allen had Bruce's long, documented history of chronic depression, which formed a substantial foundation for a plea of either insanity or diminished capacity.

Now Allen began considering calling as witnesses Bruce's parents, his siblings, and a variety of friends and acquaintances to buttress Unis' findings.

Still, Allen knew that the most important witness would be Bruce himself. This would be tricky: Unis had described Bruce as cogent, rational and coherent in his interview. If Bruce came across to the jury as *too* rational, who would believe that he was insane when he killed Debbie? On the other hand, if he drooled on the stand and manifested overt signs of insanity, would he be vulnerable to vigorous cross-examination, which would be certain to show him as lying?

The objective, Allen decided, would be to expose Bruce as the chronic depressive he was, to flesh out the torture that had informed his decisions for decades, to re-create the night of the killing of Debbie in all its horrific psychic detail, while at the same time portraying Bruce as a rational, if suffering, victim of a long-hidden illness.

If the jury sympathized with Bruce, not Debbie, he would have a chance to prevent Bruce from going to prison.

The task of a defense lawyer, of course, is to present the best possible face of the defendant to the jury. Allen believed, contrary to the sheriff's department, that Bruce had never planned to kill Debbie, indeed had never intended to do it, but was instead caught up in a maelstrom of emotions welling up from three decades of unhappiness, and touched off by the smothering of Conor McInnerney. In other words, in Bruce's tortured mind, on the night of March 1, the killing of Debbie was the kindest cut of all.

But defense lawyers never put all their bets on one number; in addition to believing in the insanity argument, and the diminished capacity, Allen did further research. Even if, he decided, the jury rejected insanity or diminished capacity, the next question they would have to consider was whether Bruce had indeed committed first-degree murder, with its elements of intent as well as premeditation. Allen found that juries in earlier cases were entitled to consider "lesser included crimes," which meant, for all practical purposes, both second-degree murder (intent but no premeditation) and manslaughter (neither intent nor premeditation). If a jury rejected acquittal by insanity or diminished capacity, Allen wanted to make sure that the worst crime it would convict Bruce of was manslaughter.

As Allen reviewed the previously unsuccessful insanity pleas in Washington State, along with the facts surrounding Bruce's attempt to clean up after his killing of Debbie, he began to believe that getting Bruce off on a manslaughter conviction would in fact be the best that the Rowan family could hope for.

Near the end of April 1998, Allen filed notice with the Superior Court in Clallam County that Rowan would rely upon mental illness or defect as a defense—either outright insanity, or alternatively, diminished capacity.

Bruneau was hardly surprised, given that the physical evidence against Bruce was so overwhelming. What Bruneau did not suspect—or at least initially credit—was the idea that Rowan's defense would turn on the death of Conor McInnerney as its pivotal, triggering moment. But when this later—much later—became clear, Bruneau was hardly unhappy about it; indeed, by then, Bruneau would want the facts about Conor's death out in public in the worst way.

30

COMPASSION

While Bruce continued in his confinement in the rubber room throughout May and June and into July, leavened only by weekly visits from his family and a few friends, Bruneau turned his attention back to the problem posed by Gene Turner.

It was clear to Bruneau as the spring unfolded that he was betting against a stacked deck.

Putting Gene Turner on trial in Clallam County was the equivalent of accusing Dr. Schweitzer of war crimes; the vast majority of county residents simply didn't buy it that Turner had smothered a breathing infant to death, even if the facts were clear. The developing consensus was, if Gene Turner had done such a thing, he had to have had a good reason. Too many people trusted Turner to believe otherwise.

As June turned into July, Bruneau knew he had to make some sort of decision about the Turner–McInnerney affair. To charge, or not to charge: that was the question. Bruneau certainly didn't want to try Turner for a crime if he wasn't guilty of anything; not even the hurtful talk that Bruneau was only after Gene to get even with Norma could make him feel that way. On the other hand, Bruneau couldn't escape the gut-wrenching conclusion that what Turner had done was, well, simply *wrong.*

On July 10, Bruneau sent a letter to Turner's lawyer, Jeff Robinson, in Seattle.

"Dear Jeff," Bruneau began, "There are two consultants I have yet to hear from, but my tentative conclusions—based upon my research to date—are that Dr. Turner is criminally culpable for the death of Conor McInnerney."

There it was: Bruneau, after weighing the pros and cons of charging the most popular doctor in the history of Port Angeles with the crime of murder, had come down on the side of hailing the doctor into court. It wasn't Turner's right to decide when Conor McInnerney should die, Bruneau believed; that decision belonged to God, and God alone; or, if not God, to Marty and Michelle. When Turner had placed his hand over the nose and mouth of a helpless infant that night in the emergency room, he'd taken too much on himself; he was arrogant, Bruneau concluded.

Bruneau was willing to discuss the matter with Robinson once more before making a final decision on whether to charge Turner. If experts hired by Robinson came to a different, medically supportable conclusion about Gene Turner's actions, perhaps a different approach might be warranted.

Marty and Michelle had thought the matter over; they began to believe that Turner had indeed gone too far on the night of January 12.

Two days after Bruneau informed Robinson that he was inclined to charge Gene Turner with a crime, Marty and Michelle McInnerney filed a $1.5 million claim against the hospital, contending that Gene Turner's negligence had led to the death of Conor McInnerney, and blaming the remainder of the hospital staff for failing to stop Turner from smothering the baby.

Later, the *PDN's* Brewer observed that as the spring and summer wore on that year in Port Angeles, the climate of public opinion about the Turner-McInnerney case began to subtly change; where in the beginning, many residents had backed Turner and suspected that the McInnerneys' were in some as-yet-unknown way responsible for their baby's death, or at least after the hospital's deep pockets, by the summer opinion began to shift; or perhaps it was the weighing in of opinion from the working classes that had not been previously counted.

Slowly, at least in Brewer's eyes, the staunch support for Turner began to slip away, and ordinary people in the supermarkets and on the job began to ask the same question propounded by Bruneau, and by Marty's mother Diane Anderson: who was Turner to decide when Conor should live, and when he should die?

By July, the town seemed equally divided between those who continued to support Gene Turner and those who thought that he was wrong and should be punished, if only for the sense of equal justice. As Bruneau had feared, the sides were hardening. It was becoming clear to him that if he chose to prosecute Turner, he would alienate the town's elites, while if he failed to do so, he'd anger the working classes—particularly since he was so willing to be hardhearted when it came to locking up their sons and daughters for drug offenses rather than divert them to drug court.

On July 16, Bruneau received a written report from one of the out-of-state medical experts he'd hired to render an opinion on Turner's actions. Dr. Robert Baumann, a professor of neurology and pediatrics at the University of Kentucky in Lexington, reviewed copies of all the medical records and interviews which had so far been accumulated by the Port Angeles Police and Bruneau's office.

"You have asked me to respond to three questions," Baumann wrote. "At about 2300 hours [sic—actually, nearer to midnight], the time when Dr. Turner is reported to have held the baby's lips and nose closed, was the child brain-dead by usual medical criteria?

"The answer is no. The first criterion for brain death by the Task Force for the Determination of Brain Death in

Children is: 'coma and apnea must coexist.' The child was not apneic, that is, the child was breathing, according to the reports of most observers."

There it was, just as Jackson had said more than six months earlier: if Conor was taking breaths, "by definition" he could not be "brain-dead."

Now Baumann addressed the second question asked by Bruneau: if Conor had survived, what would his life have been like?

"It is well known," Baumann wrote, "that infants are better adapted to survive circulatory arrest than are older children and adults." But that said, he continued, the long period between the time that Conor's heart stopped beating, and his cardiac restoration by Rowan nearly 25 minutes later, probably meant that the baby had been badly damaged. "Taking all this into account," Baumann wrote, "I think that Conor, if he had survived this illness, would have suffered severe and permanent brain injury. I think it extremely unlikely that he would have ever been able to sit, walk or talk.

"Moreover, it is possible that he would never have been able to recognize his surroundings (including his mother and father), take nourishment from a nipple and bottle, or react in any way to the attention that he would have received.

"It is likely that he would die of pneumonia or some other adverse event before reaching adult life," Baumann concluded.

In other words, it was Baumann's opinion that Conor's prolonged period without breathing and heartbeat almost certainly meant he would have been completely paralyzed, and possibly even a human vegetable, a body without a brain, likely to die within a short time without ever having experienced anything close to human life as we know it.

In that case, was Turner's act more of a blessing than it was a crime? Apart from Conor, what of Marty and Michelle? What sort of hellish life would *they* have had, spending twenty-four hours a day taking care of an incontinent, probably insentient lump of human flesh? Did this mean Turner was a man of courage rather than a criminal?

Baumann continued to respond to Bruneau's questions:

"Do the events described in the records constitute the usual way of handling severely ill infants?

"No," he answered, "the described sequence of events does not represent common practice." Stopping mechanical ventilation might be acceptable, Baumann added, but once done, nothing else should happen, and the baby should be observed. "If the child ceases respiratory and cardiac function, the child is pronounced dead," Baumann wrote. "If the child continues to breathe and have a heartbeat, the child is cared for at an appropriate level, without technical intervention.

"Often in this second situation, the child dies hours or days later.

"Once a child in this situation is off the ventilator, it is not standard practice to interfere with any respiratory efforts."

According to Baumann, then, it wasn't standard practice to smother a baby to death, even as an act of mercy.

Here was the entire convoluted knot that had stuck in Port Angeles' collective gut from the beginning of the year: Turner had coldly and calmly smothered what he believed to be a brain-dead baby, out of controlled compassion; Rowan, out of a surfeit of uncontrolled compassion, stemming from his horror at Turner's act, had savagely murdered his wife and tried to take his own life in the bargain.

Any way you looked at it, people said, as they discussed it, it was arrogance—arrogance that made doctors like Turner or Rowan believe that *their* compassion was more powerful or more enlightened than anyone else's . . . that *their* tolerance for human pain was greater than that of ordinary people . . .

Ordinary people like Marty and Michelle McInnerney, for instance, who knew less of compassion than they did of grief. To say nothing of Debbie Rowan's weeping mother and father.

31

NO CHOICE

Even as Bruneau was reading Baumann's statement, a reporter for *The Los Angeles Times* dropped in on Port Angeles to see what all the commotion was about.

In **A baby's death, a town's pain**, *Times* reporter Barry Siegel summarized the events surrounding Turner's act, and the divisions that had emerged in the community.

"Would a more experienced specialist have handled things differently?" Siegel asked, rhetorically. "Why didn't Turner let nature take its course? Was perhaps the baby not going to die? Did Turner act because he thought the baby instead was going to live a wretched life not worth living?

"Even Gene Turner's closest supporters struggle for answers."

Many of Turner's biggest backers in Port Angeles tried to tell Siegel how they saw it.

"Gene is a person, a human being," said Paul Smithson, an assistant pastor at the Turners' Lutheran church in Port Angeles. "He's not above making mistakes. But what would *your* call be, after watching this baby for two hours, for four hours? It gets into gray areas. Bioethics, euthanasia, life, death. Where do you go, in those nebulous four hours? . . . It's all subjective. You have to rely on faith-based common sense."

Siegel also interviewed hospital administrator Tom Stegbauer.

"It's real hard for me to go anywhere else with it," Stegbauer told Siegel. "It was difficult for anyone to understand what really happened in the emergency room," so many months after the baby had actually died. Now, he said, it was all too easy to be judgmental.

"We're sitting here months later," Stegbauer said. "We're not looking the parents in the face, telling them their kid is dead, handing them their baby, seeing their tears, escorting them out of the ER."

The whole idea of trying to understand what had happened that night in terms of stark legal definitions was to miss the point, Stegbauer indicated.

"It's not just a clinical matter," he said. "This is *emotional*. To look at the mom and say, you lost your baby . . . to go through all that, and . . . the baby starts breathing again . . . What must have gone through Turner's mind?"

The essence of Stegbauer's defense of Gene Turner was the fundamental assertion that whatever the technical criteria, Turner knew better than anyone else that Conor McInnerney had died, even before he had been called to save him; and that the better part of kindness to Marty and Michelle was to tell them the grim truth sooner rather than later.

Such was the emotional confusion in Port Angeles by the summer of 1998, that it was difficult to visualize the truth. Had Turner smothered a baby because he wished to spare Marty and Michelle the life-long pain of taking care of a baby who would never wake up? Was he trying to prevent the county from having to absorb the enormous financial cost of caring for a brain-dead baby that might live for years, never to wake up?

Or was he trying to protect the hospital from a future lawsuit in which Marty and Michelle would be able to claim that, because of Turner and Rowan's actions, a baby that should have died was allowed to live—a so-called wrongful life lawsuit?

Indeed, some court decisions in other states had held hospitals and medical professionals financially responsible for saving the lives of people who would otherwise have died, absent "heroic" efforts to keep them alive. In some cases, parents or relatives of those patients had been wiped out, financially, from the severe extended costs of keeping a comatose child or relative marginally alive.

All of these potential motivations for Turner's actions were floating around the town by the time Siegel hit town. The factions had become so rigid that Diane Anderson, Marty's mother—who had initially sent a note of appreciation to Turner in January—was now convinced that Turner had committed malpractice by diagnosing Conor as brain-dead in the absence of results from an EEG. She was willing to express this opinion to those who asked.

"The police are doing all the footwork for us," Diane told Siegel. "Our lawyer is waiting on the prosecuting attorney. Michelle and Marty will come out of this with $20 million. Marty says he's going to own that hospital."

In the meantime, both Marty and Michelle found themselves increasingly uncomfortable in the public eye; Marty had taken a job in retail sales in Port Angeles, but had had to quit when so many people came by either to interview him, or otherwise ask why he was giving so much grief to Gene Turner.

By the end of August, Bruneau was well aware that his political predictions were about to be realized. Both the Turner case and the Rowan matter were about to erupt right in the middle of the campaign season, and it seemed quite clear that Bruneau's tenure as prosecutor was about to emerge as Issue Number One.

Bruneau had now drawn formal opposition: attorney Chris Shea, the former director of the public defender's office in Clallam County. Shea and Bruneau were long-time acquaintances: both had graduated from the same class of Spokane's Gonzaga University law school in the mid-1970s, and had battled one another throughout the 1980s as prosecutor and defender in the Clallam County courts. Already, many of the county's doctors had jumped into the election contest by donating substantial sums to Shea. Dr. Schreiber's wife, Jessica—herself a lawyer—emerged as Shea's campaign manager.

Ordinarily, Bruneau would have been confident of his ability to beat an opponent like Chris Shea. After all, *he* stood for law and order, while Shea had made his living defending those who were accused of crimes—hardly a positive résumé in a a county crammed with so many military retirees, most of them quite conservative politically. But Bruneau knew that this election would be different—largely due to Gene Turner. The investigation would inevitably emerge as a political issue in the forthcoming campaign—even as Bruneau would feel compelled to portray Shea as the hand-picked candidate of "the doctors" and the others who supported Gene Turner, no matter what good Gene had actually done over the past thirty years.

Bruneau had sacrificed effective politics to what was, in his view, a higher morality: what Turner had done was morally wrong, in Bruneau's view; and if the law stood for anything, it should stand for making *that* distinction above all else.

"We have no choice," Bruneau told Siegel. "If not the law, who? Do you leave it to the elites? Personally, I don't like God-playing. When someone starts making a decision about another person's life, that's the worst sort of overblown arrogance."

But Bruneau had the feeling he was whistling into the wind, that no one understood what he was trying to say. The only constituency he had left were the cops—and there weren't nearly enough of them to ensure his reelection in November.

Near the end of August, Bruneau received another letter from a medical expert relating to the death of Conor Mc-Innerney.

"Dear Mr. Bruneau," Dr. Paul A. Byrne, a neonatologist

from Sylvania, Ohio, wrote, "Baby Conner [sic] Mc-Innerney was living when he was admitted to the emergency department of Olympic Memorial Hospital on January 12, 1998. Dr. Eugene Turner made a false determination of death when he declared Conner to be 'brain-dead.' Dr. Turner wrongfully hastened Conner's death when he wrapped Conner in ice-cold sheets. Dr. Turner caused the death of Conner when he occluded Conner's nose and mouth."

Six days later, Bruneau charged Eugene Turner with second-degree murder in the death of Conor McInnerney. And as Bruneau considered his case, he realized that one of the most important potential witnesses might have to be a man currently residing in the Clallam County jail's rubber room: Dr. Bruce Rowan.

Of course, if Bruce really was crazy—or if he were declared crazy by a jury verdict in his trial—his value as a witness against Turner would be significantly diminished. But Fred DeFrang, for one, had no real worries on that score. Ever since his initial encounter with Bruce on the morning of March 2, DeFrang was certain that Bruce was no more crazy than he was.

"When you look at the planning and all the evidence," DeFrang said of the case against Bruce, "and the fact that there's not one person who said, 'I saw the whites of his eyes, man,' you'd have to conclude he was sane when he killed his wife. And I know what crazy looks like. Because there was no crazy on this guy's face. In twenty-seven years of law enforcement, when we see crazy, we know it. I don't need a doctor's degree to say this person is mentally ill, and in my view he was not mentally ill."

Bruneau's office retained a psychologist to give Bruce a battery of mental tests, and a psychiatrist qualified to testify about Bruce's sanity at the time of the crime, Dr. James Bremner of Olympia, Washington.

Bremner was highly respected in forensic psychiatric circles, and was well known to Unis. Late in August, he sat down with Bruce for two hours, while accompanied by David Allen. Later he would complain that Allen interrupted him so often when he tried to question Bruce that it was difficult to get unfiltered answers; Allen would complain that Bremner asked Bruce no questions about his self-inflicted wounds.

The seeds of a personality conflict between Allen and Bremner were planted, with Allen concluding that Bremner was out to hang Bruce no matter what the evidence, and Bremner concluding that Allen had actively obstructed the interview in his zeal to protect his client's interest.

In any event, Bremner soon reported back to Bruneau's office: in his opinion, while Bruce was undoubtedly depressed, there was little doubt that he was sane at the time he committed the act, just as he was sane at the present time.

3 2

NOT GUILTY

Bruneau's charge against Turner—while long anticipated—brought all the long-festering animosities of the town once more into the open. Norma Turner was upset that Bruneau put out a press release about the accusation before telling Turner himself. "You'd think after eight months it could have been [done] differently," she told the *PDN*.

Bruneau retorted that he'd told Turner's lawyer, Jeff Robinson, more than a month before that the doctor was likely to face criminal proceedings, so the charge shouldn't have come as a surprise.

And he was willing to treat Turner better than the average baby-killer: he said it wasn't necessary to actually arrest him because he wasn't a threat to the community, and there was no risk of flight. All Turner had to do, Bruneau said, was turn himself in at the jail for formal booking. An arraignment was set for September 25. Bruneau's press release announcing the charge against Turner was accompanied by a statement that neither he nor his office would make any further statements relating to Dr. Turner until the matter was dealt with in court.

Robinson immediately issued his own press release, which said that at the arraignment, "You will hear the words 'not guilty.' That will be his plea. That is his plea right now: Gene Turner didn't kill this baby."

Asked how Turner had reacted to the news, Robinson said the doctor was disappointed, but also relieved that the matter was finally coming to a head. "Now we can address it directly," Robinson said. "We can confront the charges. He's at peace with himself about what he did and why he did it."

In his press release Robinson wanted to clarify his client's position:

> On this night he used his medical skills and judgment, and tried longer and harder than many might have, to resuscitate Conor McInnerney. Now these efforts are being labeled as murder.
>
> This case is not about profound medical questions of life or death. It is about a seasoned and compassionate physician, trying to resuscitate a baby, and ending resuscitation efforts when it was clear there was no life to save.
>
> Dr. Turner is not guilty of any crime.
>
> Dr. Turner did the right thing on the night of January 12.
>
> His diagnosis of Conor McInnerney was right.
>
> His heroic efforts to save him were right. And fighting today's charge is right.
>
> And that is what we intend to do, because today's charge is wrong.

The McInnerney family fired back: "The evidence in this case is very strong that Conor was alive when he was at Olympic Memorial Hospital," said lawyer Mathew Knopp of Seattle, in his own written statement. "He was breathing on his own, he was pink, and he had a normal heart rate. It will be up to a jury to review the facts and decide the issue of responsibility."

The McInnerneys weren't happy about the charge against Turner, Knopp added, but were glad to see that baby Conor's interest in the case hadn't been forgotten.

" 'The prosecutor's decision won't bring our son back,' " Knopp quoted Michelle in his written statement. " 'Conor was fighting for his life and deserved every chance. We'd just like the hospital and Dr. Turner to accept responsibility for Conor's death.' "

That, of course, was one thing neither Turner nor the hospital could afford to do—Turner because his defense against the murder charges rested on the contention that the baby was actually, physically dead long before he saw him, and the hospital because of the multi-million-dollar payout that such an admission might cause.

The next day, Turner released his written statement about his actions on the night of January 12, his first substantive communication on the McInnerney case in months.

He'd kept quiet so far, Turner said, because he hoped that the "legal system" would objectively review the events and conclude that "we did everything that could be done to try and resuscitate the life of Conor McInnerney."

For all practical purposes, Turner indicated in his statement, Conor McInnerney had died even before he reached the hospital. "His condition met the criteria indicating death when the EMTs first examined him, when I first examined him, and hours later, when I declared him dead.

"Conor's brain was dead." His renewed breathing late on the night of January 12 was purely reflexive, Turner insisted, and was actually a sign that Conor had already expired in every physical and legal sense of the word. "In the presence of nurses I stopped these reflexive actions," Turner added. "I would never block the air passage of a living child. I only did this because I knew the baby was dead."

A few days later, Robinson permitted the *Peninsula Daily News* to interview Turner—the first time in more than eight months that the doctor had submitted to outside questioning about his actions. Both Norma and Robinson were present.

"Would you do anything differently in the Conor case

if you had to do it all over again?" Turner was asked.

"No, I would not," he said. In fact, some of the experts had suggested that he tended the baby longer than he should have, he said. "I have been accused of saying that I should have walked away after the first pronouncement of death. I could not find it in my heart to do that, so that's what engendered the last two hours of resuscitative efforts, and I would certainly do that again."

Would Turner cover Conor's nose and mouth again?

"What I did," Turner said, "was done under the circumstances at the time. I probably would not do that again, not because I don't think it's the thing to do, but because of the unbelievable amount of anxiety, angst and emotional turmoil and financial embarrassment that has come as a result of the situation."

Did Turner believe the baby was suffering at the time he smothered him?

No, Turner said; the baby was dead even before he left the McInnerney house. By the time Conor arrived at the hospital, Turner added, "there was absolutely no suffering whatsoever. The baby underwent situations that would be so painful for a person who was alive it would have been unbelievable. The baby had absolutely no reaction to pain, manipulation and so on. There was absolutely no suffering."

If the baby had shown signs of experiencing pain, that would have changed everything, Turner added, but he never did.

What about the experts cited by Bruneau when the murder charge was filed—the assertions that Conor could not have been dead if he was breathing?

None of the experts were there at the time, Turner said; they could have no way of knowing what actually happened.

Why didn't Turner simply walk away from the baby, since he was sure that Conor would die?

"There were several reasons," Turner said. "Had I done that, we would have had to have respiratory therapists there to monitor the baby; we would have had to have nurses standing by. There was a heart attack victim in the emergency room at midnight, there were other things that were tying up the ER doc and the respiratory therapists' effort. It would have been an endless—I should say, an unspecified period of time which would have tied up people who were needed for other efforts, and I felt that for the benefit of everybody concerned that it was best not to allow the situation to go on any further at this stage."

Would Turner be willing to enter a plea to a lesser offense in exchange for a lighter sentence?

"No," Turner said. "Absolutely not."

"So it's kind of all or nothing?"

"All or nothing," Turner agreed.

33

THE BLAME GAME

As September unfolded, the controversy over Turner's actions hardly abated. With letters pouring into the newspaper debating the matter, and with the campaign for the prosecuting attorney's office heating up, it was inevitable that the Turner–McInnerney case would become a campaign issue.

Shea touched it off by suggesting that Bruneau recuse himself from the case, particularly in light of the apparent bad blood that existed between him and Norma Turner; Shea said he didn't know whether Norma's previous opposition to Bruneau had colored Bruneau's decision-making in the Turner case, but even if it hadn't, the appearance of a conflict was sufficient to warrant the appointment of a special prosecutor.

"I'm surprised he didn't farm it out," Shea told reporters for the *Seattle Times*, "given the acrimonious relationship between the prosecution and Turner's wife. I'm not saying there's a vendetta, but there are always people who are going to think it's personal."

A legal ethicist from Seattle University law school appeared to agree with Shea. While a court might not find that a conflict existed, John Strait told *The Times*, "what I do know is it doesn't look good."

* * *

As the September 15 primary election neared, Bruneau
seemed unaware of just how much sentiment had turned
against him.

"Bruneau thought he was going to walk in," Brewer recalled. "Here he's been elected four times. Just before the
primary he went to Viet Nam with some of his buddies on
a tour of the old battlefields, instead of campaigning. He
didn't advertise, he didn't take one inch of advertising with
us. He was so convinced that he was going to win." Brewer
thought Bruneau bombastic as well as arrogant.

Meanwhile, letters to the editor—a traditional campaigning device in small-town politics—streamed in. Some of
the letters were so nasty and filled with innuendo that
Brewer and his staff struggled to edit them to avoid libel
claims.

"We got tons of letters," Brewer said later. "[The letters]
were very, very well read. It was followed very closely.
And we heard from every side. We heard from doctors, we
heard from every side. But mostly pro-Turner, almost solidly pro, at least initially."

A consistent thread ran through the pro-Turner letters:
what had happened at the McInnerney house on the night
Conor died?

"How can the prosecutor bring a charge of second degree murder against Turner?" one such letter read. "We
know that Conor quit breathing 'while breast feeding' at
home. Shouldn't that indicate that the investigation into
Conor's death begin at home? Instead we have an investigation of Turner and the hospital's attempts to revive
Conor. How can Dr. Turner be accused of taking a life that
had already been taken?"

Now others rushed to the McInnerneys' defense.

"I am appalled by the recent treatment of Marty and
Michelle McInnerney," another letter-writer remarked.
"They deserve our sympathy and loving support—not an-
ger and judgment.

"Who are you to say whether any person deserves to

have a baby? Is it your right to say that, just because someone does not have as much money as you, they should not be allowed to have a child to love?"

Meanwhile, a number of Turner's patients organized a car wash to benefit Turner's legal defense fund; on one Saturday afternoon, the "Turner kids" raised $950.

Bruneau just didn't see it coming; by the time the primary votes were counted, he'd been swamped by a large majority voting for Chris Shea; Shea had gotten almost two-thirds of the votes.

At that point, Bruneau knew he was going to have to get moving if he hoped to beat back Shea's upstart challenge. Apart from the adult drug court problem—Bruneau now soft-pedaled his former opposition to this—the major issue for the run-off election in November was Gene Turner, despite Bruneau's earlier pledge to have nothing more to say on the subject until it came to court. That would have to change, it was clear.

Bruneau went to the *PDN* and began advertising with a vengeance; he took out radio and television ads, and attended election forums with abandon. His message was that he was the top cop in the county, the only one tough enough to stand up for justice, the only one with the integrity to charge someone like Gene Turner. He attacked Shea as the puppet of "the doctors" and the criminal defense bar, who wanted to get rid of him because he was hard on crime. He began running ads that suggested Shea was the front for a cabal of doctors and lawyers anxious to keep things swept under the rug—and, the ads slyly asked, for what reason . . . ?

Shea, for his part, continued to suggest—in mild, thoughtful words—that "Dave" should consider asking for a special prosecutor from another county to review the case against Turner, to make sure that there was no impropriety in Bruneau's bringing the charges against the doctor.

This Bruneau adamantly refused to do. He was going to stand up for what was right, he insisted. That's what he'd been elected to do four times, and that's what he would do, no matter how loud the "elites" screamed.

Bruneau kept attempting to explain how he felt bound by the rule of law, that the evidence in the Turner case simply compelled him to take action; to do otherwise was to violate his oath of office, Bruneau said. No one seemed to be listening, or at least, too few seemed to be listening.

But Bruneau would have one more chance to convince the voters before the election.

Bruce Rowan's trial was set to begin on October 5; it would likely last right up until November, and since it was certain to receive heavy news media coverage, it might be an excellent forum to acquaint the voters with what *really* happened in the emergency room on the night of January 12—especially since Rowan was claiming that Gene Turner's actions that night had helped drive him mad.

Once David Allen presented evidence that Turner's actions had in part caused Bruce Rowan to go crazy, all the events of the night of January 12 would be fair game— Turner's words as well as his actions.

By the time people understood, through Rowan's eyes, what had happened to Conor McInnerney, they would see why Bruneau had had to charge Gene Turner with murder; and then they would vote for him—or so Bruneau believed.

TRIAL

34

SPATTERS

Bruce Rowan's trial began before Superior Court Judge George Wood on Monday, October 5. For the first time in eight months Bruce was out of the rubber room for an extended period. Better yet, he was allowed to wear real clothes instead of the ratty, smelly jail coveralls that had been his garment for almost as long as he could remember.

Eight months in the rubber room had given Bruce the time to look inside himself as he had never done before. Weekly visits from his family, who were unstinting in their love and support, along with contacts with his old colleagues in the Olympic emergency room, had calmed him, and made him feel almost human, despite the intrusive fluorescent light and the stainless-steel grille that passed for a toilet.

He knew what had happened—mostly from the accounts of others, although he still had occasional flashbacks to that dreadful night on the first of March. Now, as his trial began, Bruce had to prepare himself to hear descriptions of his conduct on the night of his wife's murder, actions that he knew would make him sound like a monster.

The case would be fairly straight-forward: first, the deputy prosecutor, Dan Clem, would call witnesses to marshall the facts of the crime before the jury—the blows from the axe, the insurance policy, Bruce's apparent attempts to cover it up with the car wreck, all of which would be offered as proof that he had killed Debbie intentionally, and with the pre-planning sufficient to support the charge of first-degree murder.

After that, Allen would come forward with his own witnesses to deny Bruce's premeditation and intent, and finally, even awareness of what had actually happened.

In the best of worlds, David Allen, as Bruce's defense lawyer, would like to have been able to induce his opponent Deputy Prosecutor Dan Clem, to stipulate to the fundamental *facts* of the case—that Bruce Rowan had indeed killed Debbie with an axe and a baseball bat, that he'd done some things afterward that were open to interpretation, but that none of this spoke to his true mental state at the time that these things had happened. With such a stipulation, Allen could avoid the most uncomfortable—and gory—details of Debbie's killing, and thereby move the focus of the trial into the area of Bruce's mental condition at the time of Debbie's death. Thus, the defense might also hope to avoid the jury's undoubted negative reaction to Bruce's violence on the night of March 1.

But Allen also knew that Clem was about as likely to do that as Allen was to win the state lottery.

If Clem wanted to convict Bruce, he needed to get every piece of evidence in, showing not only what Bruce had done, but that he *knew* what he had done—how he'd tried to hide his acts by cover-up.

That alone, Clem believed, as Bruneau had before him, would be enough to demolish Allen's preferred mental defect defense.

So getting the prosecutors to agree to a stipulated facts trial was out, Allen concluded.

The best he could do, Allen believed, was keep the worst of the dead Debbie photographs out; in that he was right, because there was no way Clem would agree to a simple stipulation which would have the effect of robbing the state's case of its best evidence.

But Allen was nothing if not flexible; from another point of view, this wasn't all bad; indeed, the facts Clem needed to present to make his case that Bruce wasn't crazy might also be useful to the defense to prove that he was; to Allen, many of Clem's facts cut both ways.

For Allen, Bruce's demon was in the details—the more people understood what Bruce had done that night, the more likely they were to believe that he *had* been under the influence of a psychotic episode.

Because, analyzed in any sort of logical manner, there was almost nothing that Bruce did that night that made any sense—at least, as Allen saw it.

The whole case was likely to turn on the expert psychiatric witnesses—Dr. Unis for Bruce's side, Dr. Bremner for the state, both Allen and Clem knew.

The two psychiatrists had diametrically different viewpoints of Bruce's mental condition at the time of the crime, as well as his culpability: while Unis believed that Bruce's chronic depression had produced a psychotic episode that rendered him incapable of forming intent, let alone premeditation, Bremner was convinced that, despite his chronic depression, Bruce knew exactly what he was doing on the night he chopped into Debbie's head with his wood axe.

As in most cases of dueling experts, the truth would have to be determined by the jury; and in that respect, both Clem and Allen knew, the key witness for either side was almost certain to be Bruce Rowan himself.

As a defense lawyer, Allen was different than most—as a general rule, his clients had no previous criminal record, that is, outside of the crimes they were charged with that had led to Allen's hiring; therefore, Allen often preferred his clients to take the witness stand in their own defense, which was rarely a strategy countenanced by defense lawyers who represented clients who had things to hide.

"I usually like to prepare my witnesses," Allen said later. By that, Allen was describing a lengthy process of asking questions of his witnesses—over and over, and over again—trying to anticipate what a prosecutor might ask, thereby assisting a witness in avoiding being caught by surprise by a clever prosecutor.

Additionally, by acting as his own prosecutor of his client, Allen usually could come to his own approximation of the truth before it was too late and he and his client were lured into some toxic logic trap.

But in Bruce's case, Allen was sure he did not want to ask too many questions ahead of time: if Bruce came across as *too* prepared, Allen guessed, no one would believe him. As a result, Allen's best guess on what Bruce might say on the witness stand had to come from the shrinks; while Allen had a general idea of what Bruce *thought* had happened— and what his experts *thought* had happened—he really had no concrete idea of what Bruce might actually say on the witness stand, once he started asking questions.

Even worse, he had only the vaguest idea as to how Bruce would perform under cross-examination by Clem. Would Clem get under his skin, and somehow drive Bruce into a posture of superciliousness, of condescension? That would be fatal to Bruce's chances. It wasn't as if Allen was dealing with a continuing psychotic; for the most part, if depressed, Bruce was consistently rational. Clem, if he prepared well, might completely demolish the insanity defense within half-an-hour, using nothing more than Bruce's own words.

Deputy Prosecutor Dan Clem was a rather controversial figure in Washington State. He'd served as the elected prosecutor in Kitsap County, to the south of Clallam County, near Bremerton, in the 1980s and 1990s; he had a reputation as a courtroom lawyer who was quite willing to do whatever it took, within the law, to win.

After several imbroglios involving defense lawyers and judges, Clem had lost his elective post in 1996; shortly thereafter he'd been hired by Bruneau; in Washington State, elected Republican prosecutors tended to look out for each other, since few had developed any sort of private practice while they were serving as prosecutors.

From Clem's point of view, by the time of Bruce's trial in October of 1998, the evidence that Bruce was guilty of first degree murder was almost overwhelming: premeditation in the plastic garbage bags, the bat, and the insurance policy; intent, in the use of the axe; consciousness of guilt, in the attempts to stage the accident and clean up the house afterward.

All of this was, to Clem, powerful evidence that Bruce was nowhere near nuts on the night that he'd killed Debbie.

After a jury was selected—that took a little over two days, what with prosecution and defense challenges—Clem set to work to prove that Bruce Rowan had killed his wife with malice aforethought, just as had been charged earlier that year by Clem's patron, David Bruneau.

The election was less than 30 days away.

As Allen had anticipated and as logic dictated, Clem began by trying to set the scene for the jurors—as picked, six women and six men, ranging in age from their mid-thirties to mid-sixties.

Being a prosecutor has much in common with being a film director, as it happens: the objective is to put witnesses on in logical sequence, allowing a juror to visualize event after consequent event, while assimilating the meaning of each event, the way an internal film might roll through the mind.

"You're telling a story," one prosecutor who was quite familiar with Dan Clem once said, years before the Rowan prosecution. "You're the narrator, the director, maybe even the principal actor. You have to create a series of scenes in the jurors' minds that tell a recognizable tale of what happened. So, you're a story-teller, and your job is to engage the audience with a believable story."

An important part of the movie was the opening statement, which stood as a sort of precis of what was to come;

like a preview of coming attractions, the purpose of the opening statement was to sketch in, for the jury, the evidence the prosecution intended to present.

For the opening, Clem deferred to Deputy Prosecutor Rick Porter. Using an oversize chart which showed the time line of events leading up to and after the murder, Porter ran briefly through the events of January, February, as well as March 1 and 2; taken together, he said, the sequence of the events showed that Bruce had planned to kill Debbie.

"It was," Porter said, "a plan that he [would] kill his wife in cold blood." The plan, Porter said, included a scheme by Bruce to put his dead wife's body in the family car, and to send it down Mount Pleasant Road in order to simulate a high-speed wreck capable of accounting for Debbie's injuries. Porter described this as a cunning scheme, by an adroit, intelligent perpetrator, who first sought to confuse the police with the "accident;" when this failed, he'd fallen back to "Plan B," in which he would claim insanity.

But when his turn came, Allen disputed Porter's description of the evidence. The events that took place on March 1 were hardly the work of some carefully plotted scheme, but instead bore all the earmarks of a man who was insane at the time of the killing, Allen insisted.

Indeed, said Allen, Bruce had made so many mistakes in carrying out his so-called plot there could be no other conclusion than that it was the result of mental illness.

"This is something that happened as a result of a psychotic episode," Allen said, after sketching in Bruce's history of chronic depression. When one considered Bruce's persistent thoughts of suicide, his history of self-medication—"something that he hid," Allen said—all of the events of March 1 and 2 came into a far more clear perspective.

Bruce's depressive cycle took a new turn for the worse in the aftermath of the death of Conor McInnerney, Allen added. Turner's treatment of baby Conor had triggered Bruce's long-suppressed conflicts about the brain damage of his older sister Peggy.

There was no doubt that Bruce had killed Debbie, Allen added; no one on the defense side was disputing that. What the jury would have to decide, based on the evidence, was whether Bruce knew what he was doing when the killing of Debbie took place; Allen suggested that there would be substantial and credible evidence that Bruce didn't know what was happening when his body had wielded the weapons that caused his wife's death, that in fact he was under the influence of a debilitating mental illness at the time.

Clem started his movie on Thursday, October 8, with his first witnesses: the babysitters who had taken care of Annika when Bruce and Debbie went to see *Titanic* on the evening of March 1; the sitters asserted that, after returning from the movie, both Debbie and Bruce had seemed utterly normal that night.

Clem next called Debbie's sister Stephanie, a resident of Olympia, Washington; Stephanie told of having telephoned the Rowan residence sometime that evening, when Bruce was on the line with a friend of Debbie's; Bruce told her that Debbie would call her back, which she did at about 11 p.m.

These accounts suggested that Bruce was normal the night of March 1, and further, that Debbie was still alive as late as 11 p.m.

Nor, according to Stephanie, did Debbie indicate there was anything wrong with either Bruce or her.

From this testimony, Clem moved the camera to Mount Pleasant Road, shortly before 1 a.m. Bradford Teel, a neighbor of the Rowans, testified that he heard the sound of a car wreck a bit after 12:30; Teel was followed by Jefferson Davis, who told about coming upon the wreck of the Subaru shortly thereafter.

From this point, Clem moved into the police evidence: the arrival of Sampson, then Spidell; the inspection of the scene by Dave Ellefson, followed by Spidell and Sampson's first visit to Bruce at the Rowan house on Yellow

Rock Lane. With that, the court recessed to the following Monday, October 12.

When the court recovened on that day, Clem kept his camera moving: soon Fuchser arrived on the scene, who described his own encounter with Bruce. This permitted the introduction of the audio evidence: Fuchser's tape recording of his encounter with Bruce that night, culminating in his attempted suicide.

"I knew a homicide had been committed," he told the jury, based upon Ellefson's analysis of the aborted car wreck. In the beginning, Fuchser added, he didn't know who was involved; but when Rowan never asked about the details of the wreck, and when his demeanor seemed so calm and matter-of-fact, with little eye contact—and after he'd seen the bloody crutches—Fuchser was convinced that Bruce was responsible.

Allen attempted to mitigate Fuchser's testimony: wasn't it true, he asked, that, after Bruce had stabbed himself later that morning, Fuchser had asked him why he'd done that?

Yes, Fuchser replied. Bruce had said that he'd been hearing voices. Allen let that one lie fallow; he would come back to it later.

After the tape of Fuchser's March 2 interview with Bruce was played for the jury, and a written transcript was entered into evidence, the prosecutors called Dr. Selove, the forensic pathologist who'd examined Debbie's wounds on the morning of March 2.

When asked what had caused those wounds, Selove was direct. "I believe a sharp instrument was used," he said. "Then a blunt instrument was used." In other words, Selove believed that the axe blows had come first, followed by the blows from the midget baseball bat. That was, Selove said, the only way he could account for the massive blood spatter in the bedroom, over 700 individual spots: after Bruce had killed Debbie with the axe, and blood was still pouring forth from the wounds, Bruce had then used the miniature baseball bat to strike her repeatedly in the face and jaw.

The small size of the bat accounted for the repeated backswings and the rapidity of blows, which in turn explained the vast number of small spots on the ceiling and walls.

As Selove described these injuries, Bruce covered his face with his hands, and appeared to be weeping silently.

The following day, Tuesday, Clem called DeFrang to the stand. He wanted the chief criminal deputy to describe his encounter with Bruce on the morning of the killing, as well as, in DeFrang's view, the observation that Bruce had been acting rationally. DeFrang, who served on the Clallam County mental health advisory board, tried to tell the jury that Bruce was hardly acting crazy, but Allen objected. DeFrang, he said, was not a qualified expert on mental disorders, and his opinion about Bruce's sanity should not be allowed in as evidence against Bruce. Judge Wood agreed with Allen, and refused to allow the jury to hear whether DeFrang considered Bruce crazy or sane on the morning that he'd first met him in the Rowan house.

This set the scene for the return of Fuchser, who described the ensuing search for evidence in the Rowan house—the weapons, the bloody bedding, the blood spatter and the blood-stained mattress—and displayed a host of photographs that amply depicted the carnage. As Fuchser testified, each of these items was introduced into evidence. As the axe was handed to the clerk, Rowan covered his face with his hands as the jury stared at him, and members of the Fields family wept.

Following Fuchser's testimony, additional witnesses were called by Clem, primarily in an attempt to depict Bruce as someone who was thinking of moving away from his wife and daughter in the months before the killing. One witness testified that Bruce had asked him about buying a custom log home, but that Debbie had squashed the idea because it was too expensive; the implication was that Bruce wanted to move out and live on his own before the murder.

But Allen blunted this inference by inducing the witness

to admit that the events he spoke of had occurred more than a year before he thought they had—at the time, Bruce and Debbie were still looking to buy a house.

Finally, near the end of the day, three documents were admitted—the life insurance policy on Debbie, the Rowan family checkbook, and the application for the new adoption.

Clem had proved almost all the elements of the killing; it would be up to Allen to prove that Bruce had a mental condition that prevented him from forming the intent to commit murder, much less premeditate it. Allen would have to develop Bruce's own psychiatric history, and almost as important, Bruce's reaction to the death of Conor Mc-Innerney as a trigger.

With less than two weeks before the election, nothing could have suited Bruneau and Clem more.

"I HAVE A
FEELING . . ."

The previous day, Clem had asked the judge to approve a field trip for the jury; Clem said it was the only way the jury could see the steepness of Mount Pleasant Road; the fact that Bruce had put the Subaru in gear with the pedal weighted down on such a steep road was evidence of the defendant's intent to cover up his crime by creating a serious car wreck, Clem argued. Allen opposed the field trip.

At first, Judge Wood demurred from a time-consuming, hard-to-organize field trip for the jury; but after Clem asserted that a videotape simply wouldn't show what he wanted the jurors to see, Wood relented.

The following day, the jurors, the judge, two bailiffs, a deputy prosecutor, a security officer, Allen, Rowan, and the jury all climbed aboard a chartered twenty-four-seat bus for the trip to Mount Pleasant Road. Allen and Rowan sat in the rear of the bus, separated from the jury by a number of rows. No one was allowed to talk; they rode in silence to the scene. Sheriff's deputies had been instructed to block off both ends of the road to prevent traffic from entering the area. Likewise, the news media was told to keep out.

At the intersection of Yellow Rock Lane and Mount Pleasant Road, the jurors alighted from the bus, along with the judge and the bailiffs. Rowan was made to remain on the bus with the security officer.

Allen later said he believed that the jury's viewing of the road actually helped Rowan's defense; besides being steep, Allen now saw, the road was also slightly crooked. It would be obvious to anyone in his right mind that the car was certain to veer off the road sooner rather than later; instead of a sane man planning to send a running, driverless but steering-wheel rigged car downhill for a great distance, the slight curve showed that Bruce had hardly conceived of a brilliant cover-up, because it had to be obvious to anyone but someone mentally disturbed that the car would almost immediately run off the road.

The jurors got back on the bus and returned to court, again in silence.

Clem was nearing the end of his case; he called one more deputy who had participated in the search of the Rowan house to tie up loose ends. He did not call Dr. Bremner, but retained him as a rebuttal witness to Allen's expert, Unis. Because Unis had made no written report on Bruce to Allen, neither Clem nor Bremner knew what Unis was going to say about Bruce. Clem wanted Unis to go first, so he could better prepare his own expert's testimony.

Next, Clem called Richard Fields, Debbie's father.

Had Fields ever observed any evidence of mental illness in Bruce? Clem asked.

No, said Fields. He'd known Bruce a long time, through many family get-togethers, and Bruce had never displayed any signs of mental disturbance.

Clem now called Diana Fields, Debbie's sister. Diana testified that the Rowans had visited her and her husband, Todd Fisher, in Boulder, Colorado, for Christmas, 1997. As the Rowans were leaving, Bruce made a remark. "I have a feeling you're going to be a parent this year," Diana said Bruce told her. A little more than two months later, with Debbie dead, Diana and Todd were granted custody of Annika.

Allen tried to short-circuit this implication—that Bruce had been planning to kill Debbie as early as Christmas— by asking whether this statement had caused her any concern. Not at the time, Diana said; she assumed that Bruce meant that Diana would have her own baby.

Nor had Debbie's friend Kathy Herbert believed there was cause for alarm. She testified that just three days before Debbie was killed, she'd seen both Bruce and Debbie, and it seemed to her that Bruce was in good spirits. Clem now showed Herbert a copy of a Christmas letter sent to friends and family members by Bruce and Debbie, a letter that contained pictures of a smiling Bruce, Debbie, Annika and Wooly. Herbert broke down and cried; so, too, did Rowan, as well as the members of the Fields and Rowan families who were in the courtroom.

Just after 3 p.m. on Wednesday, October 14, Clem rested his case. One minute later, Allen began Rowan's defense.

3 6

CONOR'S GHOST

Allen began by calling as his first witness the Olympic Memorial Hospital surgeon who had treated Bruce after he stabbed himself, Dr. Charles Bundy; he wanted to blunt the implication left by some of the previous witnesses that Bruce's self-inflicted wounds were merely superficial, and therefore indicative of a sham suicide attempt.

Not so, Bundy said; Bruce had plunged the knife deep into his chest, nicking the wall of his heart. Bruce had so much internal bleeding, Bundy said, he was surprised Bruce hadn't died on the way to the hospital.

With that, the testimony ended for the day.

Because he was pursuing a mental defect strategy, Allen knew he had to provide affirmative evidence of Bruce's mental illness; especially helpful in this regard would be testimony from people who had observed Rowan in the depths of his depression prior to the murder—if possible, years prior. That naturally meant Bruce's friends and family.

After taking testimony for most of the morning about Bruce's childhood and prior emotional background from Craig, Tensie and Paul Rowan, and a former college roommate, Allen put Bruce himself on the stand early in the afternoon of October 15.

Allen asked a few preliminary questions to put Bruce at ease, and to establish a rhythm with his client. He asked questions developing Bruce's long struggle with depression, going back to his thoughts of suicide at the age of 12, his two hospitalizations for depression, and his continuing struggle to overcome his ever-present sadness. He established that Bruce had been taking anti-depressants for years, without a doctor's supervision, writing his own prescriptions. He had Bruce authenticate his own tax returns, which showed a substantial income, an attempt by Allen to eliminate insurance fraud as a motive for Debbie's death.

Then Allen moved into the area long awaited by the prosecution.

"Bruce," said Allen, "did anything unusual or important happen during January of 1998 while you were working at the hospital?"

Yes, Bruce said. Conor McInnerney was brought into the emergency room, and he and the others had tried to save his life. He started work on the baby, even knowing that Conor hadn't breathed or had a heartbeat for nearly 25 minutes. Because the EMTs had arrived at the McInnerney house so quickly and begun CPR, he'd believed that the baby still had a chance.

Allen took Bruce through the events that had so transfixed and divided Port Angeles for the previous nine months, including Turner's first death pronouncement, and Conor's unexpected return to life.

"What did you do?"

"I asked the nurse to put all the monitors back on and give Dr. Turner a call immediately."

Bruce had reinserted all the lines into Conor's tiny body when Turner got back. The monitors were showing that Conor's oxygen level was 96 to 98 percent. "Which is normal," Bruce added.

"What did that indicate to you?"

"The child was moving oxygen. That the blood was flowing around and oxygen was attached."

"Why did you want Turner called?"

"Because he had pronounced the child dead previously, according to the nurses, and he obviously was initimately involved."

After Turner took over, Bruce had gone back out into the emergency room proper and involved himself with other patients. When he returned to Conor's room a bit later, Bruce said, he saw Turner trying to intubate the baby, and failing.

When Bruce asked Turner if he wanted him to try, Turner made his remark about needing the practice.

"I wasn't sure how to take that," Bruce said. "Whether it [was] that he felt the child was dead and he needed to practice, or that he was just in a nice manner saying, 'No, I really want to try and seat it myself.' "

The intubation efforts that had left Conor's throat bloody and swollen, and particularly Turner's seemingly casual attitude about the injuries he was inflicting, upset him, Bruce said. So did the ice-cold towel wrap. That was when he decided to call Dr. Jackson in Seattle.

Jackson told him, Bruce continued, that Turner's treatment methods sounded unusual; further, Bruce said, Jackson told him it would be impossible to know for sure whether a three-day-old infant was brain-dead, especially if the baby was breathing and the heart was beating.

After Jackson had offered to speak with Turner, Rowan went back to Conor's room to get the pediatrician.

"I went in to get Dr. Turner . . . and I met him in the doorway," Bruce said, "and asked him about speaking with a neonatologist, and he said, 'That's fine, but this case is over. This case is finished.' "

It was then that Bruce had learned from Laurie Boucher that she'd seen Turner cover Conor's nose and mouth with his hand.

"She told me that Dr. Turner had covered the baby's nose and mouth and suffocated the infant."

"How did that affect you?"

"I was devastated."

"Why were you devastated?"

"I always had a particularly hard time with infants and bad outcomes," Bruce said. "I really enjoyed doing obstetrics in residency. But I had a tremendous respect for it. Because so many doctors don't realize the long-term consequences of what they're doing.

"You know, after you deliver so many babies it's quite routine, and with my sister having had that problem, I knew what a lifetime, a short decision can make a lifetime difference for not just the baby, but the family."

After a short recess, Allen resumed:

"After January 12, how were you feeling?"

"At the time of that death and at work, it was very difficult, but once again it was toward the beginning of my shift, and I had to do it. I had to do my shift and sort of what we call compartmentalize that, try to put that aside, so I could work, and I was working the next several nights in a row, as well."

After he had some time off, the circumstances surrounding Conor's death began to affect him more severely, Bruce said.

"How would you describe your emotional state as February went out?"

"I would describe it as gradually getting worse, and that, once again I have always dealt with this in terms of function . . . and the way I considered it . . . it's like walking through water, and I feel like I have been walking through ankle-deep water, really, all my life, and when it gets harder, the water gets deeper, and the water is gradually getting deeper."

He began thinking of suicide again, Bruce said.

"How were you and Debbie getting along?"

"Very well," Bruce said. He paused.

"We . . . She knew I was having problems in mid-February or a little before that. I told her I was starting to have a hard time, so we sort of got into that mood, like we had so many times before."

"What would she do?"

"She was just so good at dealing with it. I don't think that she ever really understood what it was, what it felt like, but that didn't make a lot of difference. She just accepted it, and she let me talk or let me not say anything, and she'd hold me. And the other things would be activation. If I really needed to get out and go running, she'd see that I had time for that, and she'd schedule a lot of social events and get me active."

It wasn't lost on the jury that Bruce was describing a person who might almost have been Bruce's mother, rather than his wife. But the point was made: Bruce was dependent on Debbie.

Allen turned to the events of March 1.

"You went out to the movies?"

"Yes."

"You saw what movie?"

"Would you let me back up a little bit? Would that be all right?"

"Okay," said Allen, unsure of what was now about to emerge from his client's mouth.

"A couple of days before that, probably Saturday, Sunday, maybe Friday, I was sitting in my office and had some unusual things happen. Just doing paperwork, and I had the thoughts that kept coming into my mind, and I'd try to work on the paperwork and then the thoughts would come in and just disturbed me from my work.

"Those thoughts were, 'You've just got to kill yourself. You've just got to do this. Be done with it. Go buy a gun. Buy a gun and just . . .' and, sort of a theme, coming in, and then, as I would get distracted with Annika or something, I could focus and pull away from that and do okay."

"Did you ever go buy a gun?"

"No, I knew that with . . . Debbie and I had talked about that before and she obviously had an opinion on that."

"You went to the movies that evening?"

"Yes."

"You saw *Titanic*?"

"Yes."

"Was there a scene or something in this movie that affected you?"

"Yes there was," Bruce said. "There was an officer, toward the end of the movie, people were trying to get on lifeboats and he was trying to push them back, and some of the people wouldn't be pushed back, and he took his gun out and shot somebody and killed him, and then he appeared to be . . . the officer appeared to be in pain, distressed, I should say, distressed as a result of that, and he took the gun and he just shot himself in the head."

"What went through your mind when you saw that scene?"

"Just the relief," Bruce said. "The tremendous relief of being dead before . . . just before he even hit the ground. It was like a pheasant. You just shoot and it crumples and it's dead instantly. That was graphic for me."

Allen led again, with no objection.

"Okay, so did that thought continue in your head?"

"Yes, it did. It distracted me the rest of the evening."

Bruce now testified that after the movie, he'd returned with Debbie and talked with the babysitters for a while before going to bed.

"Did something unusual happen after that?" Allen asked.

"My recollection is, once again, it doesn't sound very reasonable, but my recollection is that Debbie said she was going to get up and go to Safeway, at some time period in there. I'm not sure what time that was."

"Did she go?"

"No, apparently not."

"What happened after that?" Allen asked, reverting to the proper form of questioning.

"After that, I was having more problems," Bruce said. "I couldn't get to sleep and the thoughts were those same sorts of thoughts. They were going through my head repeatedly, as far as suicide and you have to kill yourself, and you're a terrible person. You're a terrible father. And then I finally got out of bed."

"What happened next?"

"I went in the hallway and was walking, pacing up and down the short hallway there, into the kitchen area."

"Okay, and then?"

"And then the sound just kept . . . it just kept repeating all the things over and over and over again, and suicide is not an option, because that is what I'd tell myself when I got real bad, when I really got bad over the years, since my suicide attempt, and that was a way for me to look at other . . . try to look at other options.

"I could eat. I could try to sleep. I could go for a run. But, anything but suicide."

"So, what is happening then?" Allen asked. "Can you describe that to the jury? Were you hearing things, or—"

"Objection, Your Honor, that is leading the witness," Clem said. He knew as well as Allen that having auditory hallucinations was objective evidence of mental defect.

Judge Wood agreed. He told Allen to go back to the "What happened next?" question.

"The sounds," said Bruce. "The sounds, the repeating, got more and more pronounced, and I couldn't put it out of my head, and it got louder and louder, to the point that I just was starting to sweat and my heart was pounding and I was very shaky.

"My face felt contorted, and then, after a while, I wasn't real sure where the sound was coming from. If it was just my thoughts going through my head over and over again, still, or if it was coming from someplace else.

"I thought the sound might be going out into the world, or either that or the outside world, the sound was coming in, to me."

Clem objected to Bruce's narrative testimony. He asked the judge to order Allen to pose a question.

"At any time were the sounds telling you anything?"

Clem objected again, but this time the judge overruled the objection.

"The sounds were very similar to what I had been hearing before," Bruce said, "telling me to kill myself, over and over and over again." He had no idea how long the sounds lasted.

"What happened next?"

"When it was really not tolerable anymore . . . I can't explain why it wasn't tolerable. It just wasn't tolerable. Everything just went calm and I felt like I had just . . . was removed from the whole situation and was watching myself at that point. My face got calm and sort of flat, and I quit shaking. I wasn't sweating. I was just . . . looked like nothing was wrong, but my mind was still going."

"When you say you were watching yourself, can you describe what you mean by that?"

"It's very difficult to explain," Bruce said. "It's not as though I could say I were sitting in that chair over there and watching myself that way. It was more, much more abstract than that. I could see myself, but I was still sort of inside myself."

"Okay, what happened next?"

"I went out to the garage and got the baseball bat that we purchased that day."

"Then what happened after that?"

"I came back in and I was sitting . . . I just came into the bedroom and just as calm as could be. Just like Debbie was as peaceful as could be, and I remember her image."

"Then what happened?"

Bruce let out a howl.

"Then the bat went down really fast," he said, after he'd taken a few seconds to recover. "Really fast, and it just . . . I could just . . . the swiftness of the bat coming down and just hitting her on the forehead."

Bruce was now weeping copiously.

"Then she just groaned, and that is all she did. She didn't . . . it was just a groan."

"What's going on in your mind at this time that you're describing?"

"Nothing," Bruce said. "Just watching it. Just watching it all happen."

"What happened after that?"

. "Then I went downstairs and I got the axe out of the woodpile and I brought the axe upstairs and walked in the bedroom and I was as calm as could be. I just took it and just swung it and it just hit her. It just hit her."

"How many times?"

"Just twice."

"What reaction did you have after hitting her with the axe?"

"Nothing. I was just watching it. I didn't do anything. I didn't hear anything."

"Did you know or realize at that point in time that you were killing Debbie?"

"No, no, I would never do that. Never."

Allen wanted Bruce to say he had no idea that what he had done was wrong, but Clem objected to the way Allen phrased his question; again, he was leading his witness.

Allen tried a different tack.

"Bruce, did you indicate what was going on in your mind at the time? Let me ask you, after you swung the axe, what was Debbie's appearance?"

"There was blood everyplace."

"What was your reaction to it at the time, your mental and emotional reaction? How did you react?"

"There was no reaction," Bruce said. "There was no re-action at all. It was just . . . I have a picture of the scene. I just have a picture of the scene in my head."

"I DON'T KNOW"

"What happened after that?" Allen asked, continuing his examination of Bruce.

"I'm not sure of the time, but . . ."

"Tell me all you can recall."

"At that point I went out to the garage and got the wheelbarrow and slid her into the wheelbarrow and put her into the car."

"What did you do after that?"

"Got in the car and just drove it out to the top of the driveway there, and got out and it went down the hill."

"Why did you do that?"

"I don't know. I don't know."

"What did you do after that?"

"I came home and I was just watching this person who was working real quickly, that was watching what appeared to be myself, just working. Almost madly."

After that, the police came, Bruce said.

Did Bruce remember the taped interview with Fuchser?

"I remember the scene," he said. "I remember seeing all the police and the . . . just the various people around there."

"When you heard the tape, did that sound like your voice talking there?"

"It sounded similar to my voice, but just maybe a little different than I would ... sort of a different way than I would speak. Similar."

"After the police took the tape recording, what do you remember after that?"

"I remember going into Annika's room and then a police officer was kind of right there, and then he left and I went back out, and there was a police officer ... and I just went to the knife block and got a knife."

"What happened after that?"

"Then I went into the room and closed the door and took the knife and pulled it into my stomach."

The bathroom had a door that opened into Annika's room, Bruce explained. After stabbing himself the first time, that's where Bruce went—through the door into Annika's room.

"Why did you go into Annika's room?"

"I don't know," said Bruce. "I was watching it happen, and she was ... I took her out, and she was playing with her toys ..."

"What did you do then?"

"Then I took the knife and I had stabbed myself three times in the stomach and then took the knife and put it up on my chest, and was trying to push it in, and it wouldn't go in."

"So what did you do?"

"Then I had to pound it in, like ... kind of like a hammer."

"How did you pound it?"

"I grabbed ahold of the door frame and pulled myself into the door frame. The door jamb."

Bruce recalled that he had his back to Annika while he was trying to kill himself.

"Would you tell the jury why you would do this to yourself, in view of Annika?"

"No," Bruce said, "I don't know if ... looking back on it now, it seems like Annika was more behind me ... but there was no . . . I don't remember any consideration of anything else."

Couldn't Bruce have shut the door of the bathroom and spared Annika the sight of him trying to kill himself? Allen asked.

"Yeah, I probably could have done that. Annika probably would have been coming [in] shortly after, trying to get me."

Bruce said he didn't feel anything when he'd stabbed himself—no pain at all, he said.

"Let me ask you this," said Allen. "Why, after after hitting your wife with an axe and stabbing yourself with a knife, did you get up and get Annika cereal?"

"I don't know," Bruce said, once again.

Now Allen asked whether, while working in the emergency room, he'd ever been shown photographs of people injured in car wrecks.

Yes, Bruce said; the EMTs usually brought pictures of the wreck to help the doctor decide how to treat the victim.

So Bruce had seen a lot of injuries from car wrecks?

"Yes, definitely."

"To your knowledge, and based on your experience as an ER doctor, would those fatal injuries to Debbie be consistent with any type of automobile injury you're aware of?"

Clem objected.

"Your Honor," he said, "I have a problem with trying to qualify the doctor as an expert and trying to present him as insane at the same time."

Allen argued that the question had to do with Bruce's state of mind at the time of the killing: if Bruce was familiar with the types of injuries sustained in car wrecks, why had he chosen a wreck as the means of getting rid of Debbie's body, when obviously, if in his ordinary mind, he would have known the injuries were inconsistent with a wreck?

The judge allowed the question.

"Knowing what you knew prior to March 1, 1998, would

Debbie's injuries be consistent with an autombile accident?"

"No, not even close."

"Why did you stage the automobile accident?"

"I don't know."

Why did he make that remark about Diana Fields having children "this year"?

It was a normal remark, Bruce said, because Diana had been talking about having children for some time.

"Would you tell us whether or not that remark had anything to do with Annika?"

"No, it didn't have anything to do with Annika."

Bit by bit, Allen was trying to show the jury, both by affirmative proof and inference, that the killing of Debbie was hardly pre-planned, and not intentional.

"As a doctor . . . an emergency room doctor, what knowledge did you have of drugs that can paralyze people, or what drugs did you know about and have access to that could paralyze or incapacitate people?"

Bruce named several powerful muscle relaxants used in the emergency room for intubations. He had easy access to those substances, Bruce said.

Could he get narcotic drugs?

Yes, said Bruce; even though they had to be signed for, it might take someone some time to discover that they were missing.

"Are there drugs that you are aware of that can be used to cause people to die, without much of a trace?"

"Leading," Clem said.

"Sustained," the judge said.

"Well," asked Allen, "what do you know about drugs that can kill people?"

"There are lots of drugs that can. Many, many drugs can kill people, and I haven't looked into, or researched which ones are traceable, and which ones aren't . . ."

"Do you know of a drug or substance called potassium chloride?"

"Sure, that is a very common intravenous medicine or oral medicine."

"Would you have access to that?"

"Yes, that is very common."

"Is that something that could be traced back to you?"

"No, not easily at all. Well, I'm not sure at all. At this particular hospital . . . Some places they just have bags of it in the ER. Other places it's in a little closer control."

"And could an overdose of potassium chloride—what would an overdose of that do?"

"Given intravenously, it makes the heart fibrillate, ventricular fibrillation. Basically stops and quivers."

"What happens at that point?"

"Basically people die," said Bruce. "They need electricity to survive at that point. They need to be shocked and given other drugs to lower the potassium."

The inferences that might be drawn from Allen's questions were clear: if Bruce had really wanted to kill Debbie, it would have been easy for him to do it by giving her an injection of potassium chloride, which would have induced a heart attack. With a massive enough dose, Debbie would die. Bruce could later claim he slept through the whole thing, and no one would be the wiser.

Now Allen wanted to draw the jury's attention to Rowan's current plight, in the hope that they would find sympathy for him.

"What are the conditions you are kept under?"

"I am in a completely rubberized room that is ten feet square," Bruce said. "Ten feet on each side. Ten-feet-high ceiling. And, there's a hole in the floor in one corner with a grate, with a stainless-steel grate over it, and that is the only fixture. There are no other fixtures in there, as far as chairs or sink or anything like that."

"What is the hole for?"

"It's for urinating and defecating."

"And where do you sleep?"

"On the floor."

"What do you sleep on?"

"There is a sleeping pad."

"You say no furniture? Nothing else in there?"

"No newspapers and a pillow and some blankets, and there is . . . there are lights . . . a couple of fluorescent lights on the ceiling and a video camera that is mounted on the ceiling, pointed downward that watches all the time."

"How many hours a day are the lights off?"

"They never go off. They are always on."

"Is there a television?"

"No."

"Is there a radio?"

"No."

"How many hours a day are you in that cell?"

"Between 22 and 23."

"And how long have you been in that cell?"

"Seven months."

"Did you tell [a visitor] that this has been a, quote, 'tremendous experience so far,' unquote?"

"I probably did. It has been tremendous."

"What do you mean by that?"

"It has been tremendous in all sorts of ways. Tremendously bad sometimes, with episodes of crying and not being able to stop, and times of insight that I have never experienced before."

"What did you mean by that? Would you explain?"

"This was my first opportunity in my life to reflect. I don't know if it's an opportunity, but to not be able to do anything except look inside, and look at that black demon in there. That black demon that has been dominating my life at times, and at other times I have been able to get control of it."

"I WOULDN'T DO THAT"

After Allen's direct examination of Bruce, Clem's job required him to develop inconsistencies in the just-completed testimony. Just as Allen wanted the jury to view Bruce as completely clueless on the night he killed Debbie, Clem wanted to portray Bruce as a calculating, vengeful person who would lie repeatedly to escape the consequences of his violent act.

One way of doing that was to get under Bruce's skin.

"You were in the rubber room because your brother demanded that the jail staff have you stay in that room, isn't that true?" Clem asked, with his opening shot.

"That's not true, to my knowledge," Bruce responded.

"Pardon?"

"To my knowledge, that is not true."

"Your attorney demanded that you stay in that room, isn't that true?"

Rising to his feet, Allen objected.

"That is not true, and I object to that, and the prosecutor knows that is not true," Allen said.

"Oh no, that *is* true," said Clem.

"That is *not* true, and I object," Allen repeated.

"All right," said Judge Wood, sensing that the trial was

about to get into personal invective between Clem and Allen. "Let's stop right now."

Clem returned his attention to Bruce.

"Why are you in the rubber room, sir?"

"Because the psychiatrist who is seeing me felt like I was too suicidal to be with the general population."

"You're aware of lawsuits, aren't you?"

"Yes, I am."

"So you're aware that the jail, Clallam County, just like any other entity, does not want to lose any lawsuits. You are aware of that?"

"That is reasonable."

"So," said Clem, "if members of your family demanded that you stay in a rubber room and you had suicidal attempts in the past, the jail might listen to those demands, isn't that true?"

Allen objected; it appeared that Clem was trying to do two things with this line of questioning; first, rattle Bruce by telling him that two people he trusted—his brother and his lawyer—were responsible for his odious confinement; and second, get the authorities off the unsympathetic hook that Allen had tried to hoist them on when he'd had Bruce describe his living conditions.

Abruptly, Clem veered away, going over some of Bruce's background that had been brought out under Allen's examination. He soon came to Bruce's story about his first thoughts of suicide at the age of 12.

"Okay," Clem said, "so you felt that it would be a simple matter to simply make it look like the gun fell and went off and killed you, right?"

"Right."

"Those were not voices telling you to do that, were they?"

"No, I didn't know what that was. the majority of the problem, I didn't know what was causing me to feel that way."

"But you do recall being sad at times prior to that?"

"Oh yes."

"All right, did you ever tell your friends about your suicide thoughts when you were 12?"

"No, I wouldn't do that."

"Did you ever tell your parents?"

"No."

"Did you ever tell any of your brothers?"

"No."

"Or sisters?"

"No, I wouldn't do that."

Clem was attempting to show that there was no contemporaneous corroboration that Bruce had ever had thoughts of suicide at age 12—only Bruce's word for it.

Turning to Bruce's suicide attempt in the car when he was in medical school, Clem asked if Bruce was punishing Debbie for taking the three-day trip to California without him.

"No," said Bruce.

"You weren't trying to make her feel guilty by taking these pills?"

"Naturally not," said Bruce.

"Just answer the questions," said Clem. "You didn't die, is that correct?"

"I would assume that, just by the fact that I'm here now."

"In fact, you're a pretty intelligent guy, aren't you?"

"I didn't mean to say that," Bruce said, referring to his previous answer. "I'm sorry."

Clem picked up a copy of Bruce's college transcript.

"Okay," said Clem, "how many psychiatry courses do you think you took in medical school?"

Bruce was vague about his courses in psychology, but admitted that he'd taken several. He considered them "soft science," he added.

"Would you agree that not everybody who commits suicide is insane?"

"I don't have any way to determine that," Bruce said.

Clem brought up Dr. Jack Kevorkian and his assisted suicides.

"Do they know right from wrong when they make that choice?"

"I can't determine any of those questions when I don't know anything about the situation. I'm sorry. I'm not trying to be difficult."

"I understand," said Clem. "Do you think if a person who knows that the police are onto him might make a rational choice to try and end his life, rather than go through the heartburn [sic] of a trial and embarrassment to families, and possible imprisonment? Do you think that person might make a rational choice to end his life?"

"I don't know," Bruce said. "I guess it depends on the person."

"How about you?"

"No, I wouldn't do that."

At that point, with the hour growing late, Judge Wood ordered the trial to be recessed for the weekend. Bruce would now have three days to ponder the hard questions Clem was sure to ask him when the trial resumed on Monday.

39

WITNESS FOR ANOTHER PROSECUTION

When Bruce resumed the witness stand after the long recess, Clem zeroed in on Bruce's prior testimony that it would be possible to kill a person by an injection of a paralyzing drug. He wanted to demonstrate to the jury that Bruce was too smart to use drugs to kill Debbie, because he knew they would eventually be detected in Debbie's bloodstream.

"And that particular drug is used to paralyze people, generally patients that have to be intubated, if they're struggling?" Clem asked.

"That's one of the uses, correct," said Bruce.

"But that has to be given intravenously, correct?"

"It generally is."

"All right, so if you gave it by shot, there's an injection mark left in the patient, is that correct?"

"Depending on the size of the needle, like diabetics use a tiny needle, it's really not detectable," Bruce said.

Clem asked if the drug acted in the system for about four to five minutes, and Bruce said that it did.

"All right," Clem said, "a person dies without breathing in about four minutes—"

"That would depend on the situation, yes."

"If there is no artificial assistance, if one is paralyzed, one would die in approximately four minutes without oxygen?"

"I don't know the exact time, that sounds close."

"So you would expect this type of drug to remain—a considerable amount to remain in the blood system to be tested, would you not?"

"I don't know," said Bruce. "I don't know if that is [a drug] they test for, there are numerous paralytic agents, and I don't know which ones they screen for and which ones they don't."

"If pathologists were to find an elevated amount of this type of drug, that would be quite suspicious, wouldn't it?"

"I don't know if they screen for that in an autopsy."

"If they were looking for an unexplained death of a spouse of a doctor, don't you think they might look for drugs in urine and blood?"

"I don't know if they screen for that or not in blood," Bruce said, doggedly holding onto his position; if Clem could make the jury believe that he knew the drugs could be detected and that he might be caught, it would negate Allen's argument that Bruce had plenty of other ways to kill Debbie than with an axe.

Clem moved on.

"Do you have to apply for a license to be admitted to practice medicine in the state of Washington?"

"Yes."

"Did you do so?"

"Yes."

"Is there a question asked about your mental condition when you apply?"

"I believe there is, something along the lines of 'currently seeing a psychiatrist or—' "

"Do you remember signing such an application in the state of Washington?"

"I would have done that routinely, yes."

"Now," said Clem, "you've claimed you had a medical condition consisting of a mental or psychological condition or disorder such as emotional or mental illness since 12 years of age?"

"I didn't know I had an illness, really, until medical school, I didn't know what it was."

"All right, so by 1992, you certainly knew you had a medical condition consisting of a mental or psychiatric disorder such as an emotional or mental illness, correct?"

Bruce agreed.

Did Bruce recall reporting on his license application that he had no medical condition that would in any way impair or limit his ability to practice medicine?

"I answered it that I didn't feel like this was something that limited my medical skills," Bruce said.

Clem pointed out that the application asked if the applicant was taking any medications. Bruce had checked that one 'no' as well, again because he didn't feel that his anti-depressants impaired his medical skills.

"Now, did you apply for a license in Alaska?"

"Yes, I did."

"Did you get a license in Alaska?"

"I applied there and I answered all the questions and on that particular application they asked for specific medications I was taking, and I listed an anti-depressant, and for that reason they would not give me a, you know, license. So I applied for a temporary license."

"When did you apply for an Alaska license?"

"Approximately a year ago, roughly." A clever stroke by Clem, this: approximately a year ago would have been October or November of 1997, suggesting that Bruce wanted to leave Port Angeles and go to Alaska well before Conor McInnerney and his subsequent depression.

After taking Bruce through his drug regimen and establishing that Bruce was writing his own prescriptions, Clem turned to the area he and Bruneau wanted most to cover with Rowan.

In effect, the prosecutors were going to try to accomplish a neat trick: have Bruce testify in his own trial against

Turner, and still get Rowan convicted of Debbie's murder—
because Clem hoped to show that Bruce was perfectly sane
through his own evaluation of the baby as of January 12.
Allen had opened the door to this by claiming that Turner's
act had helped drive Bruce mad.

"I'm going to turn for a moment, Mr. Rowan, to the
January 12, 1998, incident at Olympic Memorial Hospital,"
Clem said. "You indicated that baby Conor arrived at about
the beginning of your shift, approximately. And you determined that the down-time for that child was short, so you
determined that you were going to do aggressive treatment?"

"Yes, the paramedics were there and, I believe in three
minutes, and they were undergoing CPR within five
minutes, so that was good time," Bruce said.

"All right. And you were aware that this was an infant
under seven days old?"

"Yes, he was three days old."

"And you're aware that it's next to impossible to tell
brain-death of a child of that age unless you observe the
child for several days?"

"That's what Dr. Jackson told me, from Childrens Hospital."

After a few more questions, Clem asked:

"Well, a baby at that age, it's really hard to measure
brain waves, because the brain hasn't been functioning that
long, common sense would tell you that?"

"Not necessarily," said Bruce. "In my opinion, the
baby's brain was functioning pretty naturally."

Now Clem had he wanted from Bruce: that Bruce had
been told it was difficult to detect infant brain death, along
with a bonus: that in Bruce's judgment, Conor Mc-
Innerney's brain was "functioning pretty naturally."

Now, said Clem, because of his own background—his
experience with his disabled sister Peggy—had Bruce made
any sort of judgment about Conor's "future quality of life
that baby would [have] if recovered?"

"I didn't feel I was in a position to make that judgment,

and that's how I view people coming into the ER generally—that those decisions need to be made over a period of time and not in a ten-minute or half-hour period."

Clem now guided Bruce through the rest of the events at the hospital that night, using sharp, pointed questions with Bruce's succinct responses to tell the story of Turner and Conor for the benefit of the news media and the voters.

Bruce said that as far as he could tell, once they'd gotten Conor's heartbeat started, things began to look better.

"Doctor," Clem said, "have you cared for other infants at this young age?"

"Yes."

"Have any of those other infants died when you cared for them?"

Clem was moving to undercut Bruce's claim that Turner's act had made him crazy.

"Three days of age, I don't think I ever had a baby die at three days. I've had them die at birth ... and some months later, but I don't believe a few days later, it's a very unusual time for a child to die."

"So you have had them die right at birth?"

"Right."

"That's a very sad situation, is it not?"

"It depends on the situation, I mean it almost always is, obviously."

"Did you ever hear voices when these other babies died in your care?"

"No."

Clem continued questioning Bruce about Conor McInnerney and Turner, taking Bruce through the events when the baby began to breathe on his own, and Turner had tried to reintubate him.

When Clem suggested that Conor was "breathing fine," Bruce contradicted him. He wasn't breathing fine, Bruce said, he was breathing on his own; there was a difference.

"I didn't feel it was emergent or immediately critical to get the child intubated," Bruce said, "but it was Dr.

Turner's patient at that point." When Turner rejected calling in an anaesthesiologist to help with the intubation, Bruce didn't argue, even though he would have done things differently, he said.

After a brief discussion about the ice-cold towels, which Bruce said he didn't understand, Bruce told how he'd called Jackson in Seattle for advice.

"Well, I wasn't comfortable with the care that was being provided," he said. "And I felt like Dr. Turner needed to be confronted, but I wanted to be sure that he was out of the standard of the practice."

That was why he'd called Jackson, Bruce said.

"Did you return to the room where baby Conor was?"

"Yes I did."

"Who was in there?"

"Laurie Boucher."

"How was she acting?"

"Very upset."

"Crying?"

"Yes."

"Anybody else in there?"

"Ann Duren may have been in there, and the respiratory therapist was nearby."

"What did you ask Ms. Boucher?"

"I asked, 'What happened?' "

"And she responded how?"

" 'I don't think you want to know.' "

"What did you say?"

" 'I think I should know.' "

"What did she say?"

"She told me what happened."

"What did she say?"

"She told me that Dr. Turner had suffocated the child."

"How did he do it?"

"Covered the child's nose and mouth."

"Did that upset her?"

"Appeared to me, very much."

"Did that upset you when she told you that?"

"Yes, it did."

"Did you begin to hear voices?"

"No."

Bruce went on to testify that, the following morning, he discussed what he'd been told about the baby with one of his colleagues, Dr. Daniel Yergin, a former mentor of Bruce's at the University of Washington Medical School. Yergin was now a member of the emergency room partnership that had hired Bruce. This gave Clem another opening to probe Bruce's claim of prior mental illness.

"And did you tell any of those persons, those doctors when you asked to join the partnership, that you had a mental disorder?"

"No, I didn't."

"Did you tell them you were taking medication?"

"No, I don't believe I did."

But Clem veered back to the McInnerney situation, apparently intent to milk as much from Bruce as was feasible while he was on the stand.

"When you were at home, did you get a call from anybody about what had occurred on the 12th of January?"

"Yes, I got a call from Tom Stegbauer."

"Who is he?"

"He is the CEO of the hospital."

Apparently, because of his isolation in the rubber room, Bruce was unaware that Stegbauer, under fire from the hospital board, had resigned his post two weeks earlier, on September 30—another casualty of the McInnerney–Turner affair.

Bruce testified that Stegbauer had asked him to write a confidential memorandum about the events in the ER.

"I had expressed a lot of concern about what happened and felt that we needed to do this professionally, and he said that it would be taken care of through hospital review channels," Bruce said.

"And did he say it would stay within the walls of the institution?"

"That's what he said, and I said I was uncomfortable with that."

After a few more questions, in which Clem tried to get Bruce to admit that doctors were required to notify the police in cases of suspected child abuse, Clem asked:

"You insisted to Mr. Stegbauer that the proper channels be notified, is that correct?"

"I don't know that I was that insistent," Bruce said. "I suggested it."

"Did you tell Mr. Stegbauer that you were upset?"

"No, I would think that was implied."

"Did you tell Mr. Stegbauer that it was affecting your condition?"

"I don't know what you're referring to."

"Your medical condition?"

"I'm sure I didn't."

"Did you tell your partners that the Dr. Turner incident had affected your medical condition?"

"I had discussed with Dr. Yergin how difficult the situation was."

"I would assume any time a patient dies, it's a sad event," said Clem.

"Not necessarily," Bruce said.

"Would you explain what you mean?"

"A lot of people come to the ER who are terribly ill, and they get scared, and their family gets scared, and they come to the ER, essentially at death's door, and it's not necessarily a sad occasion when they die."

"Because they have had some problems in their last days?"

"It's often a relief for everyone," Bruce said.

"Actually," said Clem, "some patients in that condition would prefer to die, is that correct?" It appeared that Clem was priming for his next question, which would be: Like *Debbie* preferred to die? But Bruce either was oblivious to Clem's trap, or too smart for it.

"I can't speak for them," he said.

"But you don't consider *them* insane, do you?" Clem asked.

40

"YOU KNEW IT WAS WRONG"

As the cross-examination moved on and Bruce testified about everyone he had discussed the McInnerney situation with, Clem achieved two objectives: he was able to develop the Turner case in fairly great detail through Rowan's description, while at the same time make the point repeatedly that, when discussing the Turner case with the police, MQAC, and virtually everyone else, Bruce had heard no voices. In other words, for all intents and purposes, he was not insane immediately after Conor's death.

But, Bruce testified, by the end of January, just as he was being interviewed by Port Angeles Police Detective Kovatch, a depression was beginning to settle in.

"It was draining, day after day," Bruce said.

Clem asked about the scene from *Titanic*, in which the officer had shot himself.

"Do you know of anybody who has tried to commit suicide after seeing that scene?" Clem asked.

"Not that I know of."

"Have you heard of people who have been charged with crimes putting forth a movie defense before?"

"No, I haven't."

"You haven't?"

"No."

"And did you tell Debbie of the impact that the suicide scene had on you?"

"I told her briefly. I remember telling her that I had a difficult time with it, and had a hard time focusing, it seems, but she was very interested in telling me what she thought about the movie."

"That she liked the romance part of it?"

"That's what it seemed like, yeah."

After a discussion of Debbie's Achilles operation, Clem returned to the events of March 1 and 2.

"Now," said Clem, "Debbie's asleep on March 1, 1998. What do you do?"

"As I previously said to Mr. Allen, I had gotten up."

"And what did you do?"

"I went out into the hallway because my mind was going around and around."

"Were you thinking of baby Conor?"

"No."

"You heard sounds, I believe you said."

"Right, it would be hard to describe."

"Was it—"

"I'll try to describe it as best as I can."

"All right, was it sound or voices?"

"It was my own internal voice, initially."

"Your internal—*your* voice?"

"Initially."

"Saying what?"

"That I was a bad father and that I had to die, and that I wanted to die and that suicide wasn't an option—about a dozen things going around and around."

"That was your voice?"

"Initially it was my internal voice."

"It was not a hallucination, your telling yourself that suicide was not an option?"

"That's one thing I would do frequently when I had problems, I would look for other options."

"Ever watch basketball?"

"Not often."

"Ever watch Karl Malone on a free-throw line?"

"No, I don't think I have."

"Ever see him talk to himself?"

"I don't think I know who he is."

"It's rather common for people to talk to themselves, isn't it?"

"Yes."

"Debbie had—Had Debbie said she wanted to go out that night?" Clem asked.

"We'd been talking about it all the previous week."

"I'm sorry," Clem said, "I mean after you had gotten home."

"That's what I remember her saying, but it doesn't seem very reasonable."

"Did she say where she wanted to go?"

"What I remember her saying shortly before that, she was—wanted to go to Safeway, but I don't know why I would remember that, she didn't even shop at Safeway."

"Her favorite store is Albertsons?"

"Right."

"She didn't like Safeway?"

"Right, right."

"So that would be an unusual comment on her part?"

"Well," Bruce said, "the whole going shopping in the middle of the night would be very—not something she would do."

"You're of the belief that she never said that, now?"

"I don't know if she did or not, all I can say is my memory and I guess I don't trust any of my memories from that."

"Eventually, did the voices tell you to go get the bat?"

"No," Bruce said, "I got—no, the voices—all they ever did was go around and around about killing myself."

"They never told you to kill Debbie, did they?"

"No, they never did."

"You knew that was wrong."

"Not at that time."

"You know it's wrong now?"

"Absolutely."

"As a doctor, you know it's wrong to kill anybody, don't you?"

"I guess killing anybody, I personally would be against it, but people kill in wars and all kinds of things."

"Well, let's exclude wars and self-defense. You know it's wrong to kill somebody?"

"I absolutely do," Bruce said.

"And on the early morning—the late night of March 1, 1998, early morning of March 2, 1998, you knew it was wrong also, didn't you?"

"March 2, 1998—I don't know anything, I didn't know anything, I was just watching something happening at that point."

"You went outside and got a weapon, correct?"

"I watched myself do that."

"You watched somebody else get the weapon?"

"Well," Bruce said, "now I know it was me, obviously now it was me, at the time or even for weeks thereafter, I wasn't sure who it was."

"Which weapon did you get first?"

"The bat."

"And what did you watch yourself do with the bat?"

"Bring it in the house."

"Where were you when you watched yourself?"

"It's hard to explain," Bruce said. "As I mentioned before, it wasn't like I was sitting in a chair over there and watching what was happening. It was—it was some place, sort of inside and being removed from it, being removed from the situation."

"Those voices were telling you to kill yourself?"

"They were."

"They were not telling you to kill Debbie?"

"They never did."

"So you brought the bat into the bedroom?"

"Yes."

"You were walking with what kind of shoes?"

"I don't know."

"Quietly?"

"I don't know."

"Did you wake her up?"

"She was sleeping soundly, just the image of her was being very peaceful."

"Where was Annika?"

"In her crib."

"Was she sleeping?"

"I don't know, I would think so."

"Did she hear anything?"

"I don't know whether she did or not."

Clem asked Bruce about the shopping trip he'd had with Annika that afternoon. Hadn't Bruce bought the baseball bat, some trash bags, some pepperoni sticks and popcorn that very afternoon before the killing?

Bruce said he had.

"Sir," said Clem, "what was the need for this bat on that afternoon?"

"No need," Bruce said, "just Annika and I needed to entertain ourselves and go out, and that was something that we'd been thinking about getting."

"Getting a bat like this?"

"Right."

"And it's only a coincidence that it was used a mere six or seven hours later to smash Debbie in the head?"

"I don't know about coincidence, it's just what happened to be used, or there was a lot of other things that could have been used."

"It was a mere coincidence that a full bag of [trash] bags, eight of them, were used in the course of this evening?"

"I'm sorry we had bought them that day."

"So," Clem continued, "is it your medical opinion with reasonable medical certainty that the bat rendered Debbie unconscious?"

"I don't have any medical opinion about that."

"Did it split her skin?"

"Yes, I think so."

"How many times did you hit her with the bat—it was you who hit her?"

"It took me a long time to understand it was me."

"Now, then you walked outside and got the axe, is that right?"

"That's generally what I remember."

"And you came up and hit her with the axe, was that you?"

"I watched it happen, I saw it happen."

"I believe on direct you said you hit her?"

"Once again, it's taken me a long time to understand that."

"Did you hit her with the blade part or the blunt part?"

"The way I have the image is the blunt part, but once again, I don't know."

Clem continued to drill Bruce on his "image." How come, if Bruce only hit Debbie once with the bat, and once or twice with the axe, there was so much blood spatter on the walls and ceilings?

Bruce said he didn't know.

"Did you try to use the bat to disguise her injuries, to make it look like a car accident, sir?"

"No."

"Why did you smack her in the mouth with the bat?"

Bruce didn't answer.

41

"SHE'S SLEEPING GOOD"

"All right," Clem continued, "do you recall when Deputy Spidell and Deputy Sampson arrived at your house?"

"Initially, the first time?"

"Correct."

"Generally, I have a picture of that."

"And you open the door and here are two officers standing in uniform, correct?"

"Right."

"Now, you knew Debbie was dead at that time, didn't you?"

"No, I really didn't. It's taken me—it's taken me months to really understand that she's dead."

"Do you recall Deputy Spidell telling you that an automobile you owned had been involved in an accident?"

"I can't remember that."

Nor could he remember much of what happened at the first visit by the deputies, Bruce said.

"Any reason you can't remember this conversation?" Clem asked.

"My mind was occupied with thoughts going around and around."

"Voices?"

"My own voice, and it wasn't when I first had this internal thought that it got louder, as I explained, until I was sweating and shaking and my heart was pounding and louder and then it came from the same thing, around and around, and at this point I didn't know if it was coming from inside my head and going out to the world or—and could even wake up Debbie and Annika."

"I'm talking about when you're talking to Deputy Spidell," Clem said.

"I'm just trying to give you a little background, it just hit a point where I just—like a switch or something came on and removed me and that's how I felt, calm and removed."

Did Bruce come back to reality because of Spidell's knock on the door? Clem asked. Was it the sight of his uniform? Did he realize he might be in trouble?

"No, I didn't realize anything there."

Bit by bit, Clem took Bruce through all the evidence, asking him what he remembered. Over and over, Bruce said that he had only the dimmest or no recollection of what had happened.

"Sir," said Clem, showing Bruce a photograph, "do you know what this is?"

"It appears to be our bedroom."

"What's that up on the edge?"

"A mattress."

"What is that red spot?"

"Looks like blood."

"What is that black thing?"

"Looks like a garbage bag."

"How did it get there between a fresh blood spot and the box spring?"

"I can't recall, I remember seeing the box spring being turned over, but I can't recall specifically."

"Tell me what you recall seeing."

"The box spring being lifted up and falling back over."

"Well, is that like levitation or what—"

Allen objected.

"Well, how did that happen?" Clem persisted.

"I watched myself do it."

"You did it?"

"Now I know that."

"And you knew it was wrong?"

"I did not know it was wrong."

"You were trying to hide evidence, weren't you, Dr. Rowan?"

"I don't know what I was doing."

Clem showed Bruce photographs of all the blood spatters on the ceiling and the wall.

"Now tell me, Dr. Rowan, how could blood of that amount, that many spots, get up there if you only hit her twice after she had commenced bleeding?"

"It may have been more times than that, I'm just telling you what I remember, there is a lot of blood."

"Would you agree that it certainly appears that whoever hit Debbie Rowan, hit her more than twice after she had started bleeding?"

"I don't know—I'm not—I don't really know how those things work, I know car accidents are different than that."

"You know car accidents cause trauma?"

"Right and they—just the pattern is usually different than it is on the ceiling there."

"And isn't that how you tried to hide the murder, to make it look like a car accident?"

"No."

"Well, you got caught, so now isn't your defense insanity?"

Allen objected. Clem tried it another way.

"Dr. Rowan, I'll try to be as clear as I can. You didn't claim to hear voices until Detective Fuchser told you words to the effect that somebody killed your wife and staged it to look like a car accident and I'm going to find out who, that's when you started hearing voices, is that right?"

Bruce said he didn't remember telling Fuchser that he'd been hearing voices; the only way he knew about it was from Fuchser's testimony that that's what he'd said.

Clem asked Bruce about taking the knife into the open doorway into Annika's room.

"And you went in there and stabbed yourself after Annika was awake?"

"She was awake, right."

"You didn't shut the door so she couldn't see you, you left it open so she could see you, correct?"

"I don't know whether the door was open or closed, at that point I was around by the mirror in the bathroom."

"Well, you said you had the knife in your chest and you were banging yourself up against the door jamb."

"That was later."

"The door was open then?"

"Right."

"And Annika was there to see it?"

"I'm not sure whether she saw it or not, she was behind there playing with her toys. I hope she didn't see me."

"Well, you wanted her to see you, didn't you?"

"No."

"You wanted the sympathy, didn't you?"

"Well, Annika wouldn't—she really wouldn't appreciate what was happening."

"So your life revolved around you, isn't that correct?"

"I'm sorry, I don't feel I can answer that."

"Well, you'd made several requests from the University of Washington Medical School, you always got your way, isn't that true?"

"No, it's not. I generally didn't have any problems, I was always the person in college and on the fishing boat saying everything's fine, I can handle it no matter what."

Clem took Bruce back through his psychiatric history, pointing out that each time he'd had problems, he was successful in getting a lot of attention from people—the university, Debbie, various doctors and nurses. Clem's questions suggested that Bruce had a pattern of making himself needy to get love and sympathy.

In fact, said Clem, the same pattern applied after the death of Conor McInnerney.

"After baby Conor died, the nurses gave you a lot of attention, did they not?"

"Well, the nurses who were working then actually took a lot of time off work, so I hadn't worked with them directly and as far as the incident, I wouldn't talk to anybody about it at the hospital because it was a confidential issue."

"Well, you commiserated with each other and gave each other moral support?"

"On the telephone, I called each of the nurses at home and we did support each other."

"And isn't it true that had Debbie died and it had been passed off as a terrible accident, you expected more sympathetic attention, didn't you?"

"I never considered it."

"Isn't that consistent, sir, [with] what you've done your entire life, that you feel put upon for whatever reason?"

"I don't know what you mean."

"You just felt inadequate?"

"I have had a lot of feelings of inadequacy for a long time, but I had a lot of confidence in other ways."

"Are you aware that studies show at least 30 percent of medical students suffer depression?"

"I'm surprised it's not higher than that," Bruce shot back.

After a short recess, Clem took Bruce through the tape-recorded statement he'd given to Fuchser on March 2, just before he'd stabbed himself.

It was Clem's objective to show that Bruce—who, by his own testimony, was no longer hearing voices at that point, but was in a flat, calm state—had consciously made up a number of lies to cover up the crime. Later, in his closing argument, Clem would be able to say that Bruce's lies—some good, others ludicrous—showed that Bruce knew what he had done was wrong. If it wasn't wrong, why lie about it?

The first lie—the big one, the mother of all the others—was Bruce's statement saying that Debbie had said she couldn't sleep, that she was getting up, and "might even go to the store." This lie implied that Bruce knew she was dead in the car, and that he needed to provide some reasonable explanation for why she would be driving.

"That was not true, was it?" Clem asked.

"Obviously not true, now, looking back on it," Bruce said.

"So why would you tell the police something that's not true?"

"I don't know, I don't know why I would do that, it would be so obvious to them it wasn't true at the time and I don't know why I would have said that."

Clem pointed out that later in the interview with Fuchser, Bruce became more specific about the imaginary trip to the store, when he added that the refrigerator was bare, and that he'd been doing the cooking, and that it hadn't been very good.

"That response," Clem said, "—doesn't it imply that you're not brokenly giving out words, you're thinking and giving out an answer?"

"It doesn't sound very organized to me, but I don't know," Bruce said.

"Well, it's not true, that's why it's not organized, isn't it?" Clem asked. "It's not true, is it?"

"Looking back at it, it's obviously not true."

"Doesn't it appear to be disorganized because it's not true, because you were lying?"

"I think if I was lying I would have thought of something much more plausible," said Bruce.

After more back-and-forth about lies, Clem asked, "Sir, do you qualify lies if they're good lies, or [is it just that] bad lies don't count?"

Hadn't Bruce told Fuchser that Debbie had probably forgotten her crutches, leaving them in the driveway? Clem asked.

"That's what it says," Bruce agreed.

"And that's not true, because Debbie Rowan was dead, correct?"

"All I can say is the same answer as before, I didn't know she was dead for a long time, before I could really understand it in my heart."

When Bruce had said that Debbie must have forgotten her crutches because she wasn't "very well organized," that was a lie, too, Clem told Bruce, "because by then she was dead."

Clem asked Bruce about his non-response to Fuchser telling him that Debbie had been murdered, when Bruce had looked down at the sleeping Annika and said, "I guess she's sleeping good tonight."

"Now, are you ignoring Charles Fuchser there, are you talking about Annika, or are you talking about Debbie in your response?"

"I don't know, I don't know which one I'm referring to," Bruce said.

"So if it's about Debbie, 'I guess she's sleeping good tonight,' I guess she was, huh?" Clem said.

42

"THERE WILL BE NO WINNERS . . ."

Once Clem was done with Bruce, it was up to the psychiatrists. First came Unis for the defense, then Bremner for the prosecution.

Bruce, Unis said, had the most severe case of chronic depression that he had ever seen. For most of his life, he had carried around an enormous amount of non-specific sadness, almost as if he had been born with a black cloud over his head.

His relationship with his older, retarded sister had affected him profoundly, and in ways that Bruce could never come to grips with. Bruce had so much empathy for those who suffered that it occasionally became overwhelming.

Bruce's symptoms of depression were classic, and longenduring: prolonged periods of lassitude and fatigue, followed by an inability to focus and concentrate. It was difficult for Bruce to get excited about almost anything. The world was so painful for Bruce that he had an almost constant sense that life wasn't worth living.

But Bruce was so ashamed of having these feelings, that he compensated by donning a mask of competency; indeed, his need to conceal his underlying angst drove him relentlessly to attempt achievements few would ever accomplish.

The death of Conor McInnerney began the last slide for Bruce; he felt that he should have done more to save the baby, while at the same time doubting himself for having tried at all. By the end of February, Bruce's constant internal dialog about his self-perceived faults and failures had become an almost excruciating torture. His one way to stop the hateful voices dialog was to shut himself off—permanently.

But, said Unis, in order to do that, the part of himself that so longed for relief had to break the emotional lock with Debbie that had prevented him from killing himself long before.

What to do? The conflict raged in Bruce's mind—just kill yourself, you're a terrible father, you're a terrible person, you should have done more to save the baby, just kill yourself and be done with it; but suicide is not an option, eat something, go running, kill yourself kill yourself kill yourself—

Until the conflict suddenly snapped Bruce into a disassociative state, in which he had no feelings at all, almost as if he was numb, a true psychotic episode. That was when he'd taken the axe and bat and taken Debbie's life.

Could Bruce be faking it? Unis was asked.

No, Unis said; because if he was faking, he would have said the voices had commanded him to kill Debbie. The evidence was strong that Bruce had entered into a disassociative state, one in which his conscious mind had no control, and his body's actions had been taken over by his subconscious, irrational mind.

And afterward, almost everything Bruce did was indicative of an eerie duality: attempting to clean up in such haphazard fashion, putting Debbie's body in the car, sending it on its way, out of his life, even though he had to know it wouldn't get very far. And the other side—"the function," as Bruce called it, which led him to put his mask of competency back on for the police when they came calling, which drove him to give soft, flat, emotionless, almost clinical answers to questions about something he barely understood was real.

Hardly, said Bremner.

"I think he was able to distinguish right from wrong," Bremner said. "He knew what he was doing."

The indications that Bruce had planned to kill Debbie for at least several weeks before the act were significant, Bremner pointed out, especially the life insurance policy. Even more significant were Bruce's attempts to conceal the nature of the crime with the car wreck, and his attempts to clean up afterward. Those acts, taken with the lies he told the police, showed a clear effort to cover up the crime; that in turn showed clearly that Bruce knew what he had done, and that it was wrong.

What about Allen's argument, that Bruce had to be nuts since he'd botched the murder so badly?

Bremner said that didn't carry much weight with him.

"It was a successful murder," Bremner said. The reason Bruce made so many mistakes was not because he was insane, but because he didn't have any experience in commiting murder.

"He hasn't had a chance to do this before," Bremner told the jury.

What about the voices going "around and around"?

That wasn't necessarily a sympton of a psychotic episode; in fact, many times people who are agitated experience a roiling internal dialog; that certainly didn't mean they were psychotic.

What about the self-inflicted wounds? Bremner said it was quite possible that Bruce had stabbed himself out of fear of arrest and the consequences of his killing. That too would indicate consciousness of guilt, Bremner said.

"Doctor," Bremner was asked at one point, "are you aware that the defendant's daughter watched him stab himself?"

"Yes, very aware," Bremner said.

"What do you make of that?"

"He was very mean or heartless," Bremner said.

* * *

Allen savagely attacked Bremner on his testimony, peppering him with questions about details of the killing and the police interviews with Bruce. Bremner seemed to indicate only a vague familiarity with what had happened at the Rowan house, at least under Allen's cross-examination, and displayed little knowledge of the nature of Bruce's self-inflicted wounds. Allen suggested that Bremner hadn't even read the police reports.

Bremner said that he had, indeed, read the reports, but that it wasn't necessary for him to know those details to make a determination on whether Bruce knew the nature of his act at the time. He believed that Bruce well knew what he was doing, primarily because of his attempts to conceal the crime.

How come Bremner, in his interview with Bruce, hadn't asked any questions about his suicide attempt? Why didn't he ask about the statements to the sheriff's deputies, about the voices, about Annika's whereabouts when he was stabbing himself?

Allen was badgering Bremner, and Bremner drew himself up and grew contemptuously reticent. At one point he asked Allen to show him one of the police reports to refresh his recollection; Allen would use that request to devastating effect in his closing argument.

Afterward—months afterward, in fact—supporters of Dr. Bremner blamed Clem for failing to prepare his critical witness sufficiently by not giving him all of the information necessary to withstand a vigorous cross-examination. But the effect before the jury, Deputies Snover and DeFrang later agreed, was that Dr. Bremner came across as "arrogant" under Allen's questioning.

When, for example, Allen suggested that Bremner had actually known nothing about Annika watching her father try to kill himself, Bremner responded, "I knew it, I just didn't want to tell you."

So there it was, two mutually contradictory opinions, each with supporting evidence. But here was where the system actually favored Bruce; where the prosecution had to prove Rowan was guilty of murder beyond a reasonable doubt, all the defense had to do is show that Bruce was insane by a preponderance of the evidence—even as little as 50.001 percent.

It was up to the lawyers now, and their respective powers of persuasion, to push the line one way or the other.

Clem began his closing argument with a digression about the legal system, and the standards of reasonable doubt. If the jury concluded that there was more, even slightly more, evidence that Bruce was *not* insane at the time of the crime—and in Clem's view there was ample evidence that he knew what he was doing, and that it was wrong—then the jury would have no choice but to convict Bruce of murder.

Clem invited the jurors to consider the facts that had been presented. Taken together, they showed that Bruce had planned to murder Debbie to cash in on the $500,000 insurance policy, thereby freeing himself to travel the world—while also escaping the "nesting" instincts of his wife.

"I want to remind you of another person in this courtroom," Clem said. "Deborah Rowan. There are bits and pieces of her here." Clem pointed out the photographs of a smiling Debbie with Annika and Wooly, of her parents and siblings, the recollections of her by her friends as being warm, caring and fun-loving, her work to establish the preschool cooperative. Those, Clem suggested, were part of the fabric of a rich life that had been cruelly, selfishly brought to an end even as she slept, by someone she had trusted.

"Don't forget Deborah Rowan," he said.

Now Clem began weaving the evidence into his argument, pointing out each of Bruce's actions that seemed logical and consistent with the acts of a man who knew he had committed a crime.

Buying a half-million-dollar insurance policy for a nonworking wife? Staging a car wreck? Trying to clean up the bloody mess? Lying to the police, repeatedly?

"Does this sound like the mind of a psychotic man?" Clem asked each time he described an action of Bruce's that seemed to contain some sense.

"The fact that he's not a *good* murderer is really not relevant," Clem said. "Why go to so much trouble to clean up and lie if he wasn't aware of his actions?"

Clem said he was convinced that the jury, when it considered what really happened in the Rowan house on the night of the murder, would conclude that Bruce had planned to kill Debbie, take the money and run.

Allen would have only one shot to push the preponderance line back to his side of the scale of justice.

"This case is a tragedy to everyone involved," he said.

"First and foremost, to the late Deborah Rowan, described by everyone as a very upbeat, happy, loving person, who died a terribly violent death at a young age in her own bedroom, one's place of safety. To her grieving family. To Annika, who has lost her mother *and* her father. To all of Debbie and Bruce's close friends, who are devastated by uncomprehension. To the Rowans, who thought so much of Debbie . . .

"To Bruce Rowan, respected doctor, loving husband, devoted father, caring son, who, *although* the suicide attempt he made was unsuccessful, effectively killed himself that evening, at least that part of himself who was the respected Dr. Rowan, and who doesn't even care to live, now.

"There will be no winners in this case, only the heartbroken, regardless of your verdict."

Nevertheless, Allen continued, he believed that he had proven that Bruce was not guilty by reason of insanity.

The state had tried to prove that Bruce was a cunning criminal, one who'd planned to murder Debbie, cash in the insurance policy and travel the world, Allen noted. But the facts showed otherwise.

Instead, Bruce had suffered a profound disruption in his

thinking on the night of March 1; a severe distortion in his perception; an inability to perceive reality and to discriminate; his cognitive processes were distorted and disorganized; he had entered a disassociative state; his emotions were flat and inappropriate; and he could feel no pain, not even when he stabbed himself repeatedly with a dull knife.

"These are the classic hallmarks of a psychotic state, according to Dr. Unis. Even Dr. Bremner agrees with that, although he disputes that Bruce had it.

"Of course," Allen said, "Dr. Bremner hadn't even read the reports, and wasn't aware of many of the most important facts of the case.

"What could be more important than being aware of these important facts—the nature of the suicide attempt, the statement about the rocks in the car, all of those things? How could he have forgotten them? Even if you'd testified hundreds of times on other cases, as he said he did, you would remember things like that. You'd expect that he'd review reports before talking to Bruce, and before testifying—he's getting paid enough."

After giving the jury his own view of the insanity law and how it should be applied—and what Bruce's past psychological history suggested about that application—Allen got down to one of his most telling arguments.

"The question that the state has been attempting, unsuccessfully, to answer is: motive. Why would Bruce kill Debbie?

"Any detective worth their salt knows there are three elements to proving any crime: motive, opportunity and means. Motive is crucial to their case, which is why they tried so hard to establish it."

The state's contention that Bruce had killed Debbie for the insurance money, Allen said, "sounds good until you scratch beneath the surface.

"Bruce didn't need money, he had plenty, he could've made that much in a few years." Allen pointed out that Bruce didn't really care about money at all, and that he had only one sport coat and a 15-year-old car, despite an annual income of nearly $200,000.

Besides, said Allen, someone would have to be crazy to kill his wife on the very day the insurance went into effect. In a situation like that, the insurance company would be all over a claimant, Allen said. And in this case, Bruce's friends and relatives all knew about the insurance.

"It would be like having a neon sign over your head saying 'suspect,' " Allen said.

If Bruce really wanted to kill Debbie for the money, he would have waited for six months or a year before doing it, Allen suggested.

Bruce simply wasn't that stupid, Allen said. The money wasn't a real motive.

Let's look at the rest of the evidence of premeditation, Allen said.

If you were planning to kill your wife with a baseball bat, why buy the miniature model? he asked. "Wouldn't you get the biggest *Louisville Slugger* you could find? Wouldn't you get the Mark McGwire model?"

Besides, Allen continued, Bruce didn't need to buy a bat at all. There were plenty of things around the house that Bruce could have used to kill Debbie—lumber, rocks, knives, construction rebar, hammers. He already had the axe, so what did he need the bat for? Bruce's use of the bat was a sign of his disordered thinking that night, Allen said, not evidence of some scheme.

All the blood in the bedroom was further evidence of Bruce's irrationality, Allen argued. "You're never going to get rid of all that blood. Doesn't take a doctor to know that. How are you going to cover it up, especially when the police find out about the insurance?"

The blood spatter showed that the killing wasn't planned, that it was a crazy, irrational act, Allen said. So much blood was impossible to get rid of, and therefore evidence of Bruce's disordered thinking.

And, if Bruce *had* planned to kill Debbie with the axe, staging the car wreck was a very poor idea—not the sort of thing an emergency room doctor would sanely consider, especially since a rational person knew that the injuries wouldn't match up to those expected in such a wreck.

"It didn't come close to fooling anyone," Allen said. In fact, he continued, staging the accident was tantamount to notifying the police. A sane man might have done it on a lonely logging road, but Bruce did it right outside his own house.

"It's just a matter of time before the police come to your door," Allen said. Staging the accident so close to home was further evidence of disordered thinking.

Bruce's lack of emotion when the police did come, Allen said, was yet another indication. "It's as if Bruce is from an alien planet," Allen said, "and doesn't know how humans react to the news of the accidental death of a spouse."

A rational, sane person, Allen added, "wouldn't suggest it was a dog who'd put rocks in the car. That's ridiculous— dogs didn't hit her in the head with rocks. It's just plain silly."

The idea, Allen continued, that Bruce would have knowingly committed the crime was absurd on its face. After all, Bruce was a doctor; he was smart enough to know that he could have paralyzed Debbie, dumped her body in the woods and claimed that she'd been kidnapped; he could have drugged her and pushed her off a pier into the water, to be found days later; he could have used potassium chloride to induce a heart attack, and, since Debbie was recovering from surgery and was somewhat overweight, no one might suspect that murder had been committed.

There were many ways a sane Bruce Rowan might have killed his wife, but the use of an axe and a baseball bat, in their own bedroom, was hardly the act of a rational man, Allen concluded.

And anyway: if Bruce wanted to be rid of Debbie, he certainly could have divorced her. It wouldn't have taken pre-planning and some wild scheme to cover up murder to be free of her. It all pointed to insanity, Allen said.

"I suggest we've more than carried our burden, not beyond a reasonable doubt, not to certainty or near certainty, but by 50 percent–plus, at least. More likely than not."

Now Allen gave his *final* final argument.

To convict Bruce of murder in the first degree, the jury had to be convinced beyond a reasonable doubt that Bruce had the premeditated intent to commit murder. But Unis had testified that Bruce was unable to form the intent, Allen reminded the jurors; therefore, how could he have premeditation?

The jury was permitted, Allen said, to consider lesser included offenses, such as second-degree murder, which only required intent.

But if the jury believed Unis, there wasn't any intent anywhere in the killing. In that case, the only justifiable verdict of guilty would be manslaughter, if the jury did not find Bruce insane.

"I ask you to make sense of this senseless crime," Allen said. "I ask you to bring closure to this senseless tragedy. I ask you to put into context Bruce's disordered thinking, his crazy, horrible actions, his inexplicable conduct, and remember, a sane Bruce Rowan would never have killed his wife.

"He meets the criteria for not guilty by reason of insanity."

Clem came to his feet for his own summation. He urged the jury to think about Bruce's lies to the police, to his attempts to hide what he had done.

"If a person lies about a little, how can you believe him about anything?" he asked.

How was one to know whether anything Bruce had said about any of this was true? Bruce was smart, he'd been to medical school, he'd taken psychology courses and made rounds in psychiatry.

Since Bruce had lied about so many things, who was to say he wasn't lying now about the voices, about the suicide impulses, about being happy with Debbie, with Annika? Who knew anything for sure?

Allen made repeated objections during Clem's final closing, contending that Clem was making improper arguments by telling the jury what "the People" demanded as justice; at one point Allen asked the judge to declare a mistrial, but was refused.

Finally Clem reached his own peroration:

"On March 1, Deborah Rowan was a living, breathing, smiling woman. On March 2, 1998, she was a piece of evidence."

In the court's gallery, members of the Fields family burst into tears.

VERDICTS

43

"DO YOU FIND THE DEFENDANT NOT GUILTY?"

Bruce's jury deliberated his fate for nearly 24 hours over three days; as the wait wore on, both Allen and Clem began to think that the jury was hung and they would have to retry the case.

All through Tuesday, October 27, the first day of deliberations, there was no sign of progress. But the following day, shortly after 11 a.m., the jury foreman sent a note to the judge: could the jury please have a tape recorder? It wanted to listen to Bruce's interview with Fuchser once more.

Judge Wood didn't want to send the jury a tape recorder; instead he ordered the jury back into open court, where the jurors were instructed to make no comment and the tape was played once more. It seemed clear that the jury wasn't interested in the words as much as they were Bruce's tone, his bearing; to Allen, that seemed like a possible good sign.

After listening to the tape, the jury retired to its room once more, to renew deliberations. Shortly before 3 p.m., they sent out another note, saying that they were at an impasse, and wanted guidance from the judge, if possible.

Neither side wanted the jury to quit deliberating, even if they were hung up; perhaps, after another day's deliberation, the impasse might be broken. The jury was told to submit any questions it had for the judge in writing. At 4:30 that afternoon, the jury went home for the third time, still without reaching a verdict.

The jury again argued all the following day, with no final result.

The day after that, Friday, October 30, two hours into their discussions, the jury sent word to the judge that they had reached a unanimous verdict.

A half hour later, the jurors filed into the courtroom; before the deliberations began, one of the original jurors, a man, had been replaced by the judge with an alternate after the judge concluded that the juror had been sleeping during part of the trial. Now Bruce's jury was composed of seven women and five men.

Had the jury reached a verdict?

"We have, Your Honor," said the foreman.

"Did the defendant kill Deborah Rowan?" asked Judge Wood.

"Yes," the foreman said.

"Do you find the defendant not guilty because of insanity existing at the time of the act charged?"

"Yes."

"Is the defendant a substantial danger to other persons unless kept under further control by the court or other persons or institutions?"

"Yes."

"Does the defendant present a substantial likelihood of committing felonious acts jeopardizing public safety or security unless kept under further control by the court or other persons or institutions?"

"Yes."

"Is it in the best interests of the defendant and others that the defendant be placed in treatment that is less restrictive than detention in a state mental hospital?"

"No."

There it was: Bruce was crazy, a danger to others and himself, and he should be locked up in a restrictive hospital setting for the forseeable future. From a doctor in charge of peoples' lives, the people had decided to take charge of his life; so said the people.

Clem and Porter were stunned by the jury's decision, as were Snover and DeFrang. So, too, was David Allen.

Bruce rose to address the jurors.

"I just wanted to say how much I appreciated your attentiveness," Bruce told them. "The most important thing for me was to get the story out accurately, and for Debbie's parents and her family to hear directly from me what happened, and for my family and friends to hear that."

It appeared that Bruce was going to burst into tears once more.

"So once again, thank you very much. I had planned to make this statement before you came back with a verdict."

Allen also thanked the jury; and as Bruce was being led away by the bailiff, and the jury filed out, he came over to Snover, DeFrang, Clem and Porter, who were still stunned.

"There's no one more shocked in this courtroom than me," Allen told them. Allen said his side had already assumed that the long deliberation signified that the jury was trying to decide between second-degree murder and manslaughter. He'd given up believing that the jury would find Bruce not guilty by reason of insanity.

Afterward, *PDN* reporter Jesse Hamilton talked to Richard Porter, who said that he and Clem didn't think they could have convinced the jury that had been impanelled that Bruce had planned the killing. That left the implication that with a different jury, Bruce might have been convicted of murder.

"They [the jury] believed he did not know right from wrong at the time." But, Porter said, "If we had it to do again tomorrow, we'd do it exactly the same way."

Hamilton reached Debbie's father, Richard Fields, in Boise. Richard, a lawyer for 35 years, was "deeply disappointed" by the verdict, Hamilton reported.

"I sat through the trial from the beginning to the end, and I can't understand why the jury, based on the evidence

I heard, could reach that verdict. This one kind of tests my
faith in the system," Richard told Hamilton.

The Rowan family was present for the verdict.

"We believe the jury returned a verdict of truth," said
Barry Rowan. "Our family has rallied behind Bruce in un-
conditional love. Our hearts have also gone out to the
Fieldses. The families were close before this happened.
There are no winners in a tragedy like this."

Four days later, the voters made someone else a loser:
they decided to throw David Bruneau out of office as Clallam County Prosecuting Attorney.

While the Rowan insanity acquittal certainly couldn't have
helped Bruneau's chances for reelection, it wasn't the main
factor. In a sense, some thought, Bruneau had simply worn
out his welcome after 16 years in office.

The *PDN's* Brewer, for one, thought Bruneau had simply made too many enemies over the years. "He was hard
on you," Brewer said. "He did this to everybody, this was
the way he was. He did this to deputy prosecutors, he did
it to the media, he did it to anybody he knew. He was hard.
If he thought you'd made a mistake, he'd just tell you you
were full of shit. Like, 'Can't you get anything right?'

"If he smelled blood, a weakness, he'd go after you. You
know, 'You can't get anything right, you can't do that, why
do you keep asking me this question for, you dumb shit?'
And people who'd never been exposed to anything like this
before would just recoil. He just made a lot of enemies. He
was 16 years there. He made one enemy a year; he made
a lot more than one a year. His can-do, his hard law enforcement attitude sort of hardened into arrogance at the
end.

"And other than the police—they weren't 100 percent
behind Bruneau, because they'd been roughed up by him,
too, but at the same time, they weren't about to say that he
should be replaced by Shea.

"A lot of the women in town say Bruneau never prosecuted domestic violence," Brewer said. "And they also

said he had no interest in white-collar crime, he only liked drug things and high-profile stuff."

Detective Sergeant Gallagher, with the Port Angeles Police, who liked Bruneau immensely, thought that times had simply changed on Bruneau, that the era of get-tough-on-crime prosecutors in Washington State that had come in with Ronald Reagan, was now passé.

"Dave Bruneau is not the most politic of men," Gallagher observed. "But the time when a prosecutor like Dave is what the people want, that's changed. Times have changed. If you look around the state, there were a lot of prosecutors like Dave who were bumped off in the election. He simply wasn't the sort of prosecutor who was compatible with the times we live in."

The Turner case hurt Bruneau, Gallagher thought, or at least the controversy over it hurt. The doctors' money, Dr. and Mrs. Schreiber, along with the controversy over whether Bruneau was bent on a vendetta against Norma Turner by charging Gene Turner didn't help, either, especially when Shea had suggested that Bruneau had a conflict of interest in prosecuting Gene.

Rowan's acquittal may have had an effect on the election in that it could have steered the few undecided in Shea's direction, but it was hardly the most significant factor; its main effect was to make Bruneau's office look inept.

How could the prosecutor lose what had seemed such an easy case on the surface? Most people in town were shocked at the Rowan verdict, because it had seemed so obvious that Bruce had to be guilty; but then, as the jurors said afterward, most people in town hadn't been in the courtroom.

A day or so after the election, Brewer sent a *PDN* reporter down to ask Bruneau for his comments about the voting.

"He said the best thing about it was that he wouldn't have to talk to the media anymore," Brewer recalled. "Particularly us." Which was particularly galling to Brewer. While he was no fan of Bruneau, he thought his paper had done a fair and even-handed job of reporting the Turner investigation; but after the election, Brewer realized that the paper had been slammed by the Turner partisans as well as by Bruneau. Which, when Brewer thought about it, convinced him that the paper had done the right thing all the way down the line.

"That was the last thing he ever said to us. Then he disappeared."

44

TO RELIEVE
OTHERS' SUFFERING

Well, Bruneau hadn't actually disappeared. With two more months to go in his term of office, he still had one last case to prepare for—Turner's.

Not that he would prosecute it. After he left office on January 5, 1999, his one-time law school colleague turned defense attorney, Chris Shea, would take over the office, as well as Bruneau's case against the doctor. And if Bruneau had conflict problems because of his long-running feud with Norma, so did Shea, but for opposite reasons: after all, his campaign had been managed by Jessica Schreiber, the lawyer wife of the former chief of staff at the hospital, and would-be Rotary blackballer of Brewer.

In addition, a great many doctors in town had contributed to Shea's campaign, in part because of the Turner case; and indeed, before the election, Bruneau had essentially claimed that a cabal of doctors wanting to thwart Turner's prosecution was trying to get Shea in to get the case against Turner thrown out.

Ten days after the votes were counted, Turner's lawyer, Jeff Robinson, filed a motion in court to have Bruneau disqualified as Turner's prosecutor. Even though Turner's trial was scheduled to begin January 25, after Bruneau would be out of office, Robinson wanted Bruneau out before then so he could conduct pre-trial negotiations with Shea, maybe even convince the prosecutor-elect to dump the case against Turner.

"David Bruneau's investigation and prosecution of this case lack the requisite appearance of fairness, neutrality and impartiality," Robinson contended in his motion. "Viewed objectively, they appear to be the culmination of a personal conflict with the Turner family resulting from their 1994 efforts to have Mr. Bruneau removed from office. Whatever appearance of propriety existed prior to the prosecutor's campaign for reelection was destroyed when Mr. Bruneau chose to campaign for reelection on the prosecution of Dr. Turner for second degree murder. He consciously chose to pit himself on one side against another side he characterized as being 'outspoken supporters' of Dr. Turner. However politically wise this decision may have been, it automatically disqualifies him and his office from prosecuting Dr. Turner in this case."

The logical person to take over the case from Bruneau, Robinson insisted, was Shea, since Shea would have to try the case when it came to trial in January. He wanted the court to appoint Shea as a special prosecutor immediately so as to give him time to prepare.

Shea didn't want the job, because he had said all along that an outside prosecutor should be brought in to review the case.

Already both of Clallam County's Superior Court judges had recused themselves from hearing the Turner case, primarily because they knew Turner quite well. A judge from another county had been called in to preside. If Robinson succeeded in having Bruneau pulled off and an outside special prosecutor was brought in, it would mean that the most notorious criminal case in the county's recent history would be decided by outsiders.

Bruneau filed a response to Robinson's motion, saying that he didn't mind if a special prosecutor was brought in, just as long as it wasn't Shea.

With Shea in agreement with this position, it was relatively easy for the outside judge, Michael E. Rickert of Skagit County, to select a special prosecutor for the Turner case. Rickert chose Snohomish County Prosecutor James Krider to act as special prosecutor. Krider, in turn, farmed the case to his chief criminal deputy, Jim Townsend.

Townsend was an experienced prosecutor; he handled a number of high-profile murder cases in Snohomish County, the suburban area immediately to the north of Seattle. Still, the Turner situation was unique; instead of a certifiably evil perpetrator, the defendant in the death of Conor McInnerney was a popular, beloved physician, renowned in the region for his caring and concern for his child patients.

As Townsend saw matters, the whole question came down to Turner's intent: regardless of whether Conor met the legal definition of being alive, if Turner *thought* he was dead, did he have any intent, as required for a charge of second-degree murder?

Well, what about manslaughter—recklessly or negligently causing the death of another? Was Turner reckless or negligent in concluding that Conor was "brain-dead" when, by legal definition, he actually wasn't? In other words, should Turner have known that Conor wasn't legally dead when he smothered him?

That was a trickier question, one that experts for both Bruneau and Robinson sharply differed on.

In addition to Drs. Baumann and Byrne, Bruneau had been in contact with a third physician, Dr. Steven Best, an Illinois neurologist. Best had told Bruneau that he believed Conor had been alive at the time of Turner's "final act," and that it was impossible for Turner to have made a determination that Conor was brain-dead. Late in December, Best reiterated his opinion to Townsend.

"A condition of 'brain death' cannot be predicted in a child who is fewer than seven days post partum," Best wrote. "And so a diagnosis of brain death should not have been made. Similarly, urgent or precipitous decisions that regard future nervous system function and viability should not be made when treating such a young and unpredictable organism as a young newborn infant. In turn, the discontinuation of resuscitation based on a notion of 'brain death' is not proper. I believe that the deviation from the expected and accepted medical practice occurred when the diagnosis of 'brain death' was made."

In other words, according to Best, Turner shouldn't have called off the bagging the first time, let alone covered Conor's mouth and nose two hours later.

"The action of occluding the airway is shocking," Best added. "I do not believe I have ever heard of the use of that procedure during medical practice."

Townsend now invited Robinson to submit the opinions of his own three experts. Robinson quickly rounded up three Seattle-area doctors who were experts in pediatrics, neonatology and neurology.

The first of these was Dr. Kenneth Feldman, a widely respected pediatrician at Children's Hospital in Seattle.

"Although Conor would not meet the formal criteria for brain death," Feldman wrote, "it is clear from the notes that Dr. Turner considered him functionally brain-dead, and this is an entirely reasonable medical conclusion. It is relatively common for dead infants to have relatively short periods of agonal respiration with or without heartbeat after death has occurred."

In this situation, Feldman continued, most doctors "would not have rendered formal care but would have waited for this activity to spontaneously cease."

The fact that Conor's oxygen level was high meant little; in fact, it could mean that because so many of Conor's cells had already died, very little of the oxygen was being used.

"I must consider it likely that the occlusion of Conor's airway by Dr. Turner was a compassionate effort to end suffering. Conor himself, however, did not perceive any pain or other feelings from the time of the initial arrest. The pain of Conor's family and all of the staff at the hospital was certainly real and evident.

"Some of this pain may have been projected onto Conor himself. This reasonably is a matter of judgement being overruled by compassionate intent and of uncomfortable appearances, but not one of criminality."

Robinson's next expert, Dr. Paula Raschko, a Seattle neonatologist, would make perhaps the most cogent argument: that Conor was, for all practical purposes, dead before he arrived in the emergency room. At a meeting with Townsend and Robinson on January 14, 1999, Raschko explained that analysis of Conor's blood gasses indicated that he had gone for as many as twenty to thirty minutes without oxygen; there was no other way to account for the blood gas readings, which showed a high level of carbon dioxide as well as a high level of acidity in the blood. Subsequently Raschko put her opinions in writing for Robinson and Townsend.

"These blood gasses indicate that Conor endured a prolonged period of time without oxygen, and are consistent with a period of 20 to 30 minutes."

The low level of bicarbonate in the blood—at first 4, then 6, when the normal range was 22—indicated to Raschko that the process of cell death and hypoxia (oxygen starvation) had been going on for some time, and was continuing to increase the acidity of the blood.

Later, when some of Conor's blood gasses crept back into normal ranges, it was Raschko's opinion that it was only the continued bagging that was overoxygenating Conor's blood, rather than an indication of any real recovery.

"The ER staff has done an effective job of ventilating Conor, but these blood gasses do not demonstrate an improvement in his condition, rather they demonstrate the continuing process of cell death and [increasing blood acidity]."

It seemed clear to her, Raschko said, that Conor had no chance of survival even before arriving in the emergency room. The level of blood acidity was so severe that massive cell death, not just in the brain, but in all the vital organs, had already taken place.

Turner, Raschko continued, should not be charged with murder; indeed, he should not be charged with any crime.

"His actions did not cause Conor's death," Raschko wrote. "What happened to the infant at home, before he arrived at the hospital, is what caused his death, and that remains the biggest question in the case."

That *was* a question: if Conor hadn't had air for 20 to 30 minutes, when had his heart actually stopped beating? The call came into the hospital at 7:40 p.m.; Marty had started CPR at the same time; the EMTs had arrived approximately four to five minutes later, and immediately took over CPR after intubating Conor and administering the first round of drugs. The CPR presumably had resulted in some blood circulation from that point forward, along with the bagging. So how could the 20 to 30 minutes without oxygen be accounted for?

This seemed to shift the focus back onto Marty and Michelle. Had they really been paying attention to the baby in the minutes just before they noticed that he'd stopped breathing? If neither had noticed that Conor was no longer respirating prior to 7:30 p.m., that might account for the extreme blood gas readings, and Raschko's conclusion that Conor had been without oxygen for 20 to 30 minutes.

The Port Angeles Police, specifically Gallagher and Kovatch, were adamant that nothing had happened at the McInnerney house prior to the call to the hospital; that indeed, until just minutes before the call, Conor had been alive, well and breast-feeding.

There was, however, a possible explanation that accounted for both time sequences: the tube that had been ineffectively placed in Conor's throat by the EMTs upon their arrival. One of Conor's lungs had collapsed; perhaps during all the bagging and heart massage at the house, Conor had not really been getting any oxygen at all, unbeknownst to the EMTs. That would account for the 20 to 30 minutes spotlighted by Raschko.

But what caused the baby to stop breathing in the first place? For that question, Robinson turned to Dr. Stephen Glass, a Seattle child neurologist. Glass said the cessation of breathing was "not well explained," which was something of an understatement.

"However," he continued in his report to Robinson, "a limited number of possibilities are available." Conor could have been suffocated "by a milk-engorged breast." But a normal baby, Glass continued, should have been able to "generate an appropriate struggle response, wiggling, moving and ultimately, at least making an effort to extricate themselves from that breast.

"No such struggling occurred," Glass concluded, because Michelle would have noticed it.

Given this, Glass said, he believed that Conor was "not neurologically normal" from birth.

"Because of an intrinsically abnormal nervous system, he was unable to arouse, move, struggle and generate an appropriate cardiac response to 'save himself.' "

There were three other possibilities that might have led to Conor's initial suffocation, Glass added: the posibility of some bacterial infection which might have altered Conor's physiological response to being suffocated; an exposure to some sort of toxin, which might have the same effect; or some sort of "in-born metabolic disease leading to underlying neurological problems, which might in turn lead to an inability to properly process oxygen."

In the absence of studies, Glass said, it would be impossible to determine which, if any, of these causes led to Conor's initial smothering.

Glass said there was one more possibility: Sudden Infant Death Syndrome, or SIDS.

While admitting that most experts believed that infants of Conor's age were inappropriate candidates for SIDS, Glass said more recent studies were indicating that such an affliction might be possible in newborns.

"Inherently, children who die of SIDS have an intrinsic,

physiologic, and anatomic abnormality in the brain, and it occurs in an area that is responsible for the integration of autonomic processes."

Given Conor's condition once he arrived at the hospital, and the unlikelihood of successful resuscitation, Glass wrote, it was appropriate to discontinue the bagging the first time just before 10 p.m. A key indicator, Glass said, was the fact that Conor's temperature was down substantially from normal, an indication that the vital part of the brain that regulated body temperature had been devastated.

In fact, Glass continued, his only criticism was that the resuscitation effort may have gone on too long. One effect of the effort may have been to hyperoxygenate the baby, which in turn may have obscured the fact that the baby was for all practical purposes severely brain-injured.

The gasping did indicate some brain-stem function, Glass conceded, but it meant very little.

"The reappearance of gasping respirations following a cessation of resuscitation such as this is exceedingly common."

In his own practice, Glass said, he had seen this phenomenon before, but he'd always told the parents that it was to be expected, and that nothing would change the prognosis of a quick death.

"This is the case for Conor," Glass wrote. "These gasping respirations do *not* indicate 'return from the dead' or some type of 'miracle' that any one of us would like to have this become. Rather these are primitive, reflexive and largely ineffective attempts that originate from the brain stem . . .

"A parallel example might be a heart of an animal such as a frog, or any number of animals, which, when removed from the body, continues to beat."

It was tragic, Glass added, that Marty and Michelle should ever have been given to understand that Conor was coming back to life; in actuality, he never had a chance.

Turner's decision to cover Conor's nose and mouth,

while not normal practice, was understandable under the circumstances, Glass said, as Turner intended only to relieve others' suffering, not to kill anyone.

So there it was: the in-state doctors argued that Turner had done nothing wrong, and should not be prosecuted; while the out-of-staters said that Turner had acted inappropriately if not criminally.

One week after receiving a copy of Glass' letter from Robinson, Townsend made his decision: the charge of second-degree murder against Gene Turner would be dismissed without prejudice.

Townsend filed an affidavit with the court requesting the dismissal based on eight separate conclusions:

1) Conor McInnerney suffered a devastating episode at his parents' home on January 12, 1998, that would have inevitably led to his death.

2) There is no evidence that this episode in the house was the result of any criminal or even negligent act by any other human being.

3) The initial declaration of death and cessation of resuscitation efforts by the defendant were proper and do not reflect any criminal intent or conduct by the defendant.

4) The original declaration of death by the defendant was supported by an extended period of no spontaneous heartbeat, respiration and pupils which remained fixed and dilated. In addition, analysis of blood gas tests demonstrated Conor McInnerney had suffered extensive and substantial internal cell death and/or injury prior to the defendant's initial declaration of death.

5) Subsequent to the defendant's initial declaration of death, Conor McInnerney resumed [sic] agonal respiration and a heartbeat, which had been induced through medication, remained.

6) At the time the defendant occluded Conor Mc-Innerney's airways [sic], the defendant had concluded Conor McInnerney was "brain-dead" and there was no chance that Conor McInnerney could survive as a result of the earlier episode which occurred at his residence.

7) The defendant's conclusion that Conor Mc-Innerney was "brain-dead" was legally incorrect since agonal respirations demonstrated lower brain stem activity.

8) Affiant believes that the defendant's occlusion of Conor McInnerney's airway was "wrongful," nontherapeutic, and a deviation from acceptable medical standards.

Taken together, Townsend continued, these findings "dictate[d] that a jury could never conclude that Turner intended to kill Conor." That would make the issue whether Turner was reckless or negligent, the difference between first- or second-degree manslaughter.

The experts, Townsend noted, were divided; the prosecution contended that Turner was reckless or at least negligent; the defense experts concluded that Turner had made a "reasonable" mistake.

What that meant to him, Townsend said, was that a jury would never be convinced beyond a reasonable doubt that Turner was guilty of anything.

There was no malice or evil in Turner's act, Townsend noted. "Based on the available evidence, it is the affiant's opinion that the interest of justice would be served by the defendant's conduct being further examined in a medical ethics context and not by further action of the criminal justice system at this time."

Thus, one year to the day after the *Peninsula Daily News* first broke the Gene Turner story, the case was headed back to the place where the hospital officials had wanted to send it all along: to the Medical Quality Assurance Commission, or "Em-Quack."

It had been a long year in Port Angeles, one filled with tragedy and pain. The struggle for justice had cost everyone dearly; the only question that remained was whether the town would ever be whole again.

OUTCOMES

Hospital administrator Stegbauer—whose initial decision to avoid the police and report directly to MQAC seemed validated by Townsend's decision—moved to Idaho and obtained a job as an administrator in another hospital.

Defeated Prosecutor David Bruneau moved to eastern Washington, where he was hired as a deputy prosecutor by another Republican prosecuting attorney.

Bruce Rowan was committed for an indefinite term at Washington's Western State Hospital, where defendants judged insane reside; Bruce asked MQAC to restore his medical license, but was rebuffed. Alan Unis continued to believe that Bruce was dangerous to himself and others, and that the worst thing he could do for himself would be to practice medicine again.

Fred DeFrang and Steve Snover remained convinced that Bruce knew exactly what he was doing when he killed Debbie; they believed the only reason the jury acquitted him of murder was because he was a doctor.

Gene Turner finally had a hearing before the medical board; doctors throughout the state testified that Turner should not lose his license, that in fact baby Conor had been dead before he even arrived at the hospital.

Terry Gallagher and Eric Kovatch were disgusted with Townsend's decision on Turner, as well as the testimony by the other doctors before the medical board, which they considered just further proof of the "thin white line."

David Allen continues to practice criminal defense law in Seattle.

HE STOLE THEIR HEARTS—THEN TOOK THEIR LIVES...

SMOOTH OPERATOR

THE TRUE STORY OF SEDUCTIVE SERIAL KILLER
GLEN ROGERS

Clifford L. Linedecker

Strikingly handsome Glen Rogers used his dangerous charms to lure women into the night—and on a cruel date with destiny. For when he got them alone, Rogers would turn from a sweet-talking Romeo into a psychopathic killer, murdering four innocent women during a six-week killing spree that would land him on the FBI's "Ten Most Wanted" list. Finally, after a twenty-mile high speed police chase, authorities caught the man now known as one of history's most notorious serial killers.

SMOOTH OPERATOR
Clifford L. Linedecker
___96400-5 $5.99 U.S./$7.99 CAN.